Not Under Bondage

Biblical Divorce for Abuse, Adultery and Desertion

Barbara Roberts

Maschil Press   2008

Published by Maschil Press
www.notunderbondage.com

Designed by Three Little Words   www.threelittlewords.com.au
Typeset in Helvetica Roman 55, 8.5pt body point /12.5pt leading
Printed by Ligare Book Printer

National Library of Australia Cataloguing-in-Publication data:

Roberts, Barbara, 1955- .
Not under bondage: biblical divorce for abuse, adultery and desertion.

Bibliography.
Includes index.
ISBN 9780980355345.

1. Divorce – Religious aspects – Christianity. 2. Divorce – Biblical teaching. 3. Family violence – Religious aspects – Christianity. 4. Remarriage – Biblical teaching. I. Title.

261.83589

ABOUT THE AUTHOR

Barbara Roberts became a Christian in 1981 but for a long time had minimal biblical teaching and lingering confusion due to her former beliefs. Unaware that Christians should avoid marrying non-Christians, she married an unbeliever in 1989 and the couple had one daughter. The marriage gradually became abusive and she occasionally took refuge in a women's shelter. In 1994 she left her husband and started attending church and Bible study. Child custody was contested but eventually awarded to Barbara, with the husband granted access.

After four years her separated husband made a profession of faith and they reconciled as a married couple. The abuse recurred and she separated for the last time in 1999, divorcing a few years after that.

In 2001 the stress in her household diminished markedly when access visits between father and daughter ceased.

She lives in Ballarat, Victoria, Australia.

||||

Teach me, LORD, the meaning of Your statutes,
and I will always keep them.
Help me understand Your instruction,
and I will obey it
and follow it with all my heart.

Psalm 119:33-34
Holman Christian Standard Bible

Key concepts of this book:

- The Bible distinguishes between "treacherous divorce" and "disciplinary divorce".

- Disciplinary divorce is permitted by the Bible. This applies in cases of abuse, adultery or desertion, where a seriously mistreated spouse divorces a seriously offending spouse.

- Treacherous divorce is condemned by the Bible. It occurs when a spouse obtains divorce for reasons other than abuse, adultery or desertion.

- If the offending partner was sexually immoral, the Bible allows the non-offending partner to remarry.

- If the offending partner abused, deserted or unjustly dismissed the other, and the offender has been judged to be "as an unbeliever", the Bible allows the mistreated partner to remarry.

About the Cover

The cover has been chosen because it conveys the experience of being subject to domestic abuse, the scriptural dilemmas of the Christian victim, and the answers to those dilemmas that this book seeks to provide.

The photograph shows an institutional corridor, such as you might find in a jail or a psychiatric hospital. Although the colours are somewhat warm, the place is hard and impersonal. The image is rotated 90° which represents the confusion a victim feels; victims often think they are going crazy.

The right side of the image shows the walls, windows and ceiling of the corridor, the left side shows the reflection in the polished floor. The fuzzy image on the left represents how disparate explanations about the Bible's teaching on divorce and remarriage have muddled many people's thinking.

The white cage-like box superimposed on the photograph could suggest the victim who feels entrapped by the perpetrator and by scriptural interpretations.

The white angular lines suggest the need to examine faulty scriptural interpretations, perhaps from unexpected angles, in order to reach the light shining from the end of the corridor, where things are clear, up is up, down is down and false guilt is banished.

Dedication

This book is dedicated to my daughter Erin, for whom I fought and won custody, by the grace of God.

Acknowledgements

I would like to thank the following theologians for their help, mentoring and feedback: John Wilson (whose encouragement and magnificent editorial help were invaluable), John Stasse, Allan Harman, Peter Barnes, William Heth, Peter Owen, Dale Noonan, Douglas Milne, David Renshaw, Stuart Bonnington, Greg Goswell, Raymond Westbrook, David Clyde Jones, Gordon Hugenberger, David Instone-Brewer, Noel Weeks, Michael Hill, Peter Bloomfield, Don Elliot and Edward Welch.

Joan Milne provided superb editorial assistance that was both insightful on the structural problems and fastidiously detailed on the minutiae. Many other people have supported and encouraged me including Mark and Linda Crabb, Fred and Sandy Cahir, Laurie Maher, Martin and Elizabeth Messemaker, Margaret J Rinck, Jason and Karen Hamilton, Dallas and Jill Alcorn, and Norman and Dorelle Shellard.

Thanks to Ross Morgan, of Three Little Words. His enthusiasm for the book has lifted me and kept me going on more than one occasion. When I found Ross — a Christian book designer whose work I loved and who lived just a few streets away — I was humbled. I had not dared to pray for such a felicitous situation.

My fellow survivors and Bible-study companions have shared their lives and struggles with me, and heard me patiently as I expressed my own. Thank-you Heather, Carole, Lisa, Maree, Sonja, Robynne, Sandra, Lisa , Jenny, Sharon, Marilyn, Jan and Rowena.

|||||

Contents

part A ▥

SETTING THE SCENE

▥ Introduction

This book explores biblical principles that can direct victims of marital abuse. It seeks to find answers from the whole of God's Word, recognizing this Word as inspired, without error and fully sufficient to guide us in all matters of life and practice. It has a special focus on divorce for marital abuse but it also discusses divorce and remarriage in cases of unjust dismissal, desertion and sexual immorality. You should find help in this book if you are:

• a victim of marital abuse;

• a divorcee for a reason other than marital abuse;

• a person who wonders whether the Bible allows divorce and remarriage and on what grounds;

• a family member, friend or counselor of a Christian divorcee;

• a pastor, chaplain or theologian who seeks to give biblical guidance on divorce and remarriage.

If you are reading this book because you are interested in God's guidance on divorce and remarriage, but are not particularly interested in the domestic abuse aspect, you may wish to skim through the first three chapters, then read more carefully from chapter four.

I am a survivor of an abusive marriage. The concept for this book emerged when my marriage of 10 years finally ended. At that time I needed a book which analyzed and explained the scriptures pertinent to marital abuse, but could not find one that went into sufficient detail. Many scriptures can be applied to domestic abuse: scriptures about suffering, repentance, forgiveness, submission and headship, separation, divorce and remarriage. This book deals only with the scriptures relating to separation, divorce and remarriage.

The subject of separation, divorce and remarriage is a minefield in Christian circles. Opinions vary as to the correct interpretation of the pertinent scriptures. Interpretation has been difficult because community appreciation of the dynamics of marital abuse only began to develop in the last decades of the twentieth century. The community, until recently, was in denial about the issue, just as victims and perpetrators often are. This affected Christians and led to scriptural interpretations that either ignored the possibility of marital abuse, or failed to recognize its peculiar dynamics.[1]

Another difficulty is that translations of the Bible have sometimes obscured what the original text actually said. For example, Malachi 2:16 has often been translated as if God is declaring "I hate divorce", whereas it probably does not say that at all. (This will be explored in chapter eight.)

A third difficulty is that we have been reading Jesus' words through our own cultural grid rather than hearing what they would have meant to his audience. We need to consider how Jesus' hearers would have understood his teachings. This approach makes it easier to make sense of many of the apparent difficulties in the various divorce texts.

THE SCRIPTURAL PLIGHT OF THE DOMESTIC ABUSE VICTIM

Being a Christian and a victim of abuse produces a spiritual dilemma. Does the Bible command a victim to stay in an appalling marriage, or does it permit separation? If it permits separation, does it permit divorce? Does it also permit remarriage? The committed Christian wants to obey God above all else, and does not dare to divorce without clear biblical permission. Yet Christians interpret the divorce scriptures in a variety of ways. Bewildered and exhausted by the conduct of the other spouse, the victim of abuse has little energy to sift through and evaluate these various interpretations.

In 1992, *Christianity Today* surveyed its readers' views on the permissibility of divorce and remarriage.[2] The results suggested layers of confusion about what the Bible permits and what it prohibits. This can be the experience of abuse victims who seek pastoral advice about divorce and remarriage.

Peter F. Rutledge in his PhD thesis said: "Research of past teachers of renown reveals what I believe to be a tragic tale of pastoral irresponsibility in their discussions on marital abuse."[3] Rev Al Miles has commented, "In many religious circles, pastors treat divorce far more harshly than they treat wife beating."[4] In a 1986 study of severely abused victims, one in three who turned to clergy said they were instructed that they could not leave the relationship or that it would be sinful to do so, and that divorce was strongly discouraged. They reported they felt trapped by their religion.[5] Attitudes among clergy seem to have somewhat improved since the 1980s, with some Christian writers and teachers bringing more balanced views.[6]

Unfortunately, some writers have had a total blind spot regarding abuse. Carl Laney (*The Divorce Myth*) is an example. This book only permits divorce when marriage is between people who are close relatives. It rejects the right of divorce, or even separation, for victims of adultery and desertion. This was the only divorce book I read during a four-year period of separation from my husband. As a victim of domestic violence, I was outside Laney's universe. I reconciled with my husband, the abuse recurred and I separated again.

Other writers appear to contradict themselves. On one hand they claim adultery is the only permissible ground for divorce, but on the other hand they say that if it is the unbeliever's violence that breaks up a marriage, then the victim is free. The victim of abuse is sorely puzzled by such an approach: how can there be only *one* permissible ground if there is another ground as well? Some writers emphasize adultery because "it strikes at the heart of marriage", yet the extreme pain of living under abuse is mentioned only in passing. Many victims find this hurtful.

It also troubles victims when commentators acknowledge violence as a legitimate ground for divorce, but do not acknowledge non-violent methods of abuse. A victim whose abuser is never physically violent, or only rarely so, feels ignored by such an approach. Abuse does not have to be physical to be destructive. *The words of his mouth were smoother than butter, but war was in his heart; his words were softer than oil, yet they were drawn swords* (Ps. 55:21).
Such unfairly weighted double messages make a survivor of domestic abuse feel hopeless, confused or angry. The victim suffers at the hand of the abuser, who professes love but shows hate, who makes inconsistent and contradictory demands from one day to the next. The victim also suffers inconsistent and contradictory advice from fellow Christians.

Many pastors face the ethical problem of how to handle the pastoral situation of an abused spouse while remaining faithful to the scriptures. Adultery is fairly commonly accepted in Christian circles as a ground for divorce, based on Matthew 19:9. Desertion is also an accepted ground based on 1 Corinthians 7:15, though it is less commonly accepted than adultery. A victim of abuse whose spouse has not committed adultery does not qualify on the ground of desertion as it is commonly understood.[7] Abusers rarely desert their partner; they want to stay in the marriage but they also want to retain a position of power, which results in continued abuse.

Some Christian advice has been more responsible, teaching that abuse victims have the right to separate, or the right to divorce. This idea is argued from the scriptures by extending general principles of Christian conduct. For example, the sixth commandment *You shall not murder* implies you should not remain in a position where you might be killed or hurt by another. Another approach is to argue that both adultery and desertion by an unbeliever violate the heart of the marriage covenant for they strike at the two key aspects of the creation ordinance of marriage: leaving and cleaving, and one flesh. Since the Bible deplores covenant breaking and grants divorce for innocent parties, we can extend this and say that any conduct that utterly repudiates the marriage covenant permits the innocent believer to divorce.[8]

These solutions establish the principle of divorce for abuse by relying on a general interpretation of the relevant scriptures. Some victims will be freed by such advice. However, many victims of abuse need more because they are troubled by texts that seem to tell them things such as:

• marriage is indissoluble, except by death;

• adultery is the only ground for divorce, with perhaps the additional ground of desertion;

• if you separate you should remain unmarried, or be reconciled to your spouse.

These ideas may help keep a victim penned into an abusive marriage, or, if she decides to divorce, they can produce guilt for years afterwards.[9] Such victims need specific verses and explanations so that they can break out of their mental and spiritual entrapment.

This book seeks to demonstrate that Paul's teaching in 1 Corinthians 7:15 can apply to victims of domestic abuse. Many have thought that this verse only applies to cases where the unbeliever walks out of the marriage, but it also applies when the unbeliever's sinful conduct so pushes away the believer that the believer flees to protect body or soul. In such cases, even though the believer *takes the final act* of separation, the separation is *caused* by the unbeliever's abusive, dishonest and manipulative conduct. Divorce is permitted in such cases; the victim is not under bondage and is free to remarry. The book explains this in detail and answers questions that some Christians have about this view.

Note to victims: The main text (chapters 1-12) is designed to be read on its own. You don't need to read any of the endnotes unless you really want to. The endnotes and appendices are aimed at scholars and pastors.

Note to language lovers: Fastidious readers may wonder why I use American spelling but employ British style for end-of-sentence punctuation. I use American spelling in deference to my largest Christian market (the USA). Also, American spelling has the virtue of simplicity without that being counteracted by any loss of meaning. I use British end punctuation because it seems more logical: end punctuation is placed either inside or outside quotation marks/brackets, depending on whether it belongs to the quoted/bracketed text or not.

▥ Chapter 1
What is abuse?

The term domestic abuse is used in this book to refer to a pattern of behavior where one adult abuses another adult and the two are (or have been) partnered intimately. An abuser abuses power in a relationship at the expense of the victim. This book mostly calls the person who has been maltreated a "victim", although sometimes it uses the term "survivor". The terms are somewhat interchangeable: all victims are survivors, even while they are still living in the abuse.

Some people may feel uncomfortable at the word victim. They are wary of encouraging a "victim mentality" — an attitude of chronically blaming others, of stagnating in self-pity and grudging resentment. This book does not use the term "victim" to promote such attitudes (nor to imply that victims/survivors take such attitudes!). Rather, it calls a spade a spade because people who have been maltreated will do well to recognize the stark, precise methods by which they have been abused if they are to become astute and vigorous survivors. (Christ said we should be as wise as serpents and harmless as doves.)

The terms victim and abuser are consistent with the Bible. The politically correct would have us label the behavior rather than the person. They say, for example, that instead of calling someone a "perpetrator" we should say "one who commits abuse" and instead of "victim" we should say "one who experiences abuse". Such politically correct expressions are unwieldy. The Bible often labels sinners by their behavior (viz. the book of Proverbs), so I have employed a similar approach.

The expression "domestic abuse" is employed in this book, rather than the alternative terms "battering", "domestic violence" or "family violence". This is because "abuse" is easier for many victims to identify with.[10] In most people's minds, the term "violence" signifies only physical violence, but domestic abuse can include emotional, social, financial and other types of mistreatment, and may not even involve physical violence.

THE GENDER QUESTION

Both men and women can be victims and perpetrators of abuse. This book seeks to support those who are victims, no matter what their gender. However, for reasons outlined below I have chosen to use "she" (or "you") for victims and "he" for perpetrators. If you are a male victim (or know male victims of abuse), you should replace these pronouns with the appropriate ones.

Research on intimate partner abuse has primarily examined physical violence. Some of these studies have also asked abut the broader spectrum of abuse (emotional, financial, social abuse, etc.). This means that relationships containing violence have been studied more thoroughly than relationships where physical violence is absent. Therefore the following four paragraphs focus on physically violent relationships. But it should be borne in mind that wherever there is a pattern of physical abuse, other forms of abuse invariably occur alongside the physical.

Much evidence exists to show that women are more frequently the victims of domestic violence and men are more frequently the perpetrators. The World Health Organization has found that "The overwhelming burden of partner violence is born by women at the hands of men. In 48 population-based surveys from around the world, between ten and sixty-nine percent of women reported being physically assaulted by an intimate male partner at some point in their lives." [11] (The rates vary from country to country.)

While some victims of domestic violence are male, the proportion of male victims appears to be small. For example, in the USA, 25% of women say they have been raped and/or physically assaulted by a current or former intimate partner or date during their lifetime; the comparable figure for men is 8%.[12] In 2001, 85% of victimizations by intimate partners were against women.[13]

While there are some genuine male victims, many instances where females attack males are marked by a long prior history of the man having abused the woman. In such cases, the woman's criminality stems from her belief that she has no other way out of the perpetrator's entrapment, with over half of the husband killings occurring in response to an immediate threat or attack by the husband.[14]

The gender differences are even more marked when comparing the seriousness of assaults. It is a biological fact that men are usually bigger and stronger than women. This means that violence by a male partner tends to be more injurious than violence by a female.[15] Men do not always need to exert this physical power: the sheer fact that they possess it, or have used it occasionally, may condition a relationship. Male perpetrators are also more likely to use dangerous weapons such as knives and guns. Furthermore, men tend to repeat their violent acts more frequently than women repeat theirs.

Most female victims report that they live in fear of their male partner. Male victims are less likely to feel intimidated and more likely to feel angry; they tend to say "I live with this crazy woman". Some studies suggest that women's violence is more likely to be an act of self-defense in a situation where the male partner is violent.[16] Where women use violence it typically resembles the violence of a cornered animal; whereas the violent act of a male is like the violence of an animal stalking its prey.[17] All such statements are generalizations, and there are exceptions — for instance, a wife who boldly uses physical violence against her husband because she knows that he is too gentlemanly ever to hit a woman.

When it comes to disclosing their victimization, males and females both feel shame. However, far more women than men seek help through the criminal justice system. Domestic violence crisis support agencies are usually only funded to assist women clients, and whether this makes male victims more invisible is hard to assess. However, most generalist counselors, psychologists and clergy encounter more female victims than male.[18] True, men often dislike counseling and are therefore less likely to seek professional support, thus causing the male victim numbers appear smaller. Nevertheless, few professionals would suggest that males and females are equally victimized in the frequency or severity of their abuse experiences.[19]

The abuse experience generally brings fewer long-term negative consequences for male victims. It appears to be easier for male victims to leave abusive situations. Compared to women victims, they are less likely to be financially dependent on their partners, or to have their freedom limited by childcare responsibilities.[20] And men rarely experience post-separation violence.[21]

ABUSE TAKES MANY FORMS

Many myths about domestic abuse are gradually being dispelled. One is that physical violence is always the major element. Another myth (which, thankfully, is less believed these days) is that violence is probably the victim's fault — that she must have provoked her partner by being verbally or emotionally abusive or insubordinate. Other myths downplay the responsibility of the perpetrator by suggesting that violence is caused by alcohol, unemployment or mental illness. Alternatively, it can be seen as two equal adults having communication difficulties and displaying lack of self-control. Initially many victims cling to these myths.

If such stereotypes and myths are inadequate or untrue, what *does* characterize domestic abuse? All of us, at times, have treated others in ungodly ways. Likewise, we have all experienced such treatment from others. Ungodly conduct takes many forms, from careless selfishness, inconsiderateness, or neglect of others, to disrespect, callousness, cruelty and criminal behavior. In this book the word abuse is used to refer to the more serious end of this spectrum. It is wrong to present the idea that we can cry "abuse" at any and every slight, but it is also wrong to suggest that we have not been abused unless we have been beaten up, received bruising or suffered broken bones. Fair-minded thinking will allow that many kinds of non-physical behavior, especially when persistent and repeated, can so undermine a person's well-being that the result is abuse.

Abuse can be emotional, social, financial, sexual, physical and spiritual. It may involve using children or legal processes as artillery of abuse. Non-physical forms of abuse can be just as (or more) damaging than physical violence. They are also harder to recognize.

Examples of these types of abuse, as perpetrated by domestic abusers, are given below. Supporters of victims may find the examples enlarge their understanding of what may go on with domestic abuse and how all pervading it can be to a person's life. Some readers may find it a little tedious to read so many examples of it. However, a person who is unsure whether he or she is suffering from abuse will find the examples very helpful.

Most abusers manifest behavior from many of the categories below; some major on certain categories more than others. Some of the behaviors might not be abuse if they are isolated incidents, just committed carelessly, as part of the occasional ups and downs of personal interaction. However, when these behaviors demonstrate a pattern of conduct designed to obtain and maintain ungodly control over another, they become serious.

Emotional Abuse
Emotional abuse is the most frequent form of relational sin. It permeates all other areas of a relationship and is at the core of the other forms of abuse listed here. It may involve put downs, criticism, cursing, yelling, ridiculing, or humiliation. The abuser may undermine the victim's sense of identity, opinions, feelings, privacy, preferred wardrobe, hairdo, or special possessions. The abuser may demonstrate an attitude of "we are married, therefore I own you".

The victim is often treated like a servant, slave, or sex object — someone with no rights and no input into decisions. Abusers may play mind games or make hurtful jokes. The abuser may lie, blame the victim for everything, enforce trivial and obsessive demands, block and divert conversations, or give the silent treatment. He may occasionally treat the victim like royalty, as a means of manipulation, or from a temporary sense of remorse for previous conduct.

Denial is a key characteristic of emotional abuse; abusers deny that the problem is located in their behavior. This can take the form of emotional blackmail: "If you complain about my actions I will outstrip your complaints and make your life miserable."

Emotional abuse can be very subtle as it works on the victim's thinking — how she will try to make sense of what she is feeling inside, and how she will bring into balance her fear, anguish and turmoil.

Using Coercion and Threats

This category comes under emotional abuse, but because coercion and threats are so powerful in maintaining control of the relationship, these strategies need special consideration. An abuser may threaten to hurt you, the children, pets, your extended family or your property if you do not do what he wants. Other tools used by some abusers are stand-over tactics, using personal size to intimidate, driving dangerously, making threats of suicide and displaying weapons.

Sometimes an abuser may threaten to report the victim to authorities or threaten to publicly expose personal information to embarrass the victim or damage her reputation. Some abusers issue vague threats such as, "Now you're in trouble". In some cases the perpetrator may hurt or kill pets, implying "It will be *you* next time". The victim may be made to betray or violate a deeply held value or belief, or act contrary to a long-held ambition. When a victim is compelled to commit or participate in illegal or sinful actions, such as committing a crime or having an abortion, she is left with an overwhelming burden of guilt and fear.

Social Abuse

When a victim is isolated from friends and family, this is social abuse. The abuser may limit access to work, study or social activities. When the victim engages in these activities the abuser may create such discomfort for the victim that the activities are voluntarily given up. The perpetrator may make demands on personal time by constantly checking up on her whereabouts, or prescribing rigid time limits for out of household tasks. Some abusers prevent their spouse from driving; some insist on accompanying her wherever she goes. The victim's phone calls may be taped or monitored, and mail may be opened. Sometimes the abuser forces the family to move house often, or ensures that the family lives in out of the way locations, so the victim and children can never make friends or develop a support network. An abuser may tell his victim lies about what women's shelters are like, to deter her from going to one.

Financial Abuse

Some perpetrators determine how the family finances are spent or managed without their spouse's consent or awareness. They may put the household on a budget that is inappropriately tight, given the amount of money coming in to the family. They may spend money frivolously on themselves, or make financial commitments which impair the growth, safety, security or goals of other members of the family. An abuser may stubbornly insist that his way of handling the budget is fine, when it is actually placing the family in financial peril. Sometimes a husband will not hand over housekeeping money unless his wife gives him sex. An abuser may demand a record of every cent spent or may make the spouse earn money when she is sick, has demanding family responsibilities, or has just had a baby. Abusers may lie about money and may coerce you to lie about money to other people. Sometimes an abuser puts all loans and household bills in the victim's name. This means that if the marriage breaks down he can walk away without any financial and legal responsibilities. Abusers can also withhold child support after separation.

Using and Harming the Children
Using or manipulating children is actually child abuse. An abuser may teach the children to dislike the other parent or disobey her legitimate authority. An abuser may make the children watch while he hits or sexually assaults their mother. An abuser may twist the truth or tell lies to the children to make them believe they are not loved by their mother. She may be made to feel guilty of bad parenting or the perpetrator may make, or carry out, threats to take the children away.

Abusers can use pregnancy to enforce their will. A woman may abuse a man by telling him she is pregnant with his child when it is not his child. Conversely, a man may accuse his wife of being pregnant to another man and punish her even though there is no evidence for his accusation.

After separation, some abusers use children like spies, making them report on the events of a partner's life. Some use visitation rights as a way to continue harassing the victim. Sometimes they use the children as conduits of abuse by filling the child with hateful thoughts towards their mother while on visitation. When the child returns he or she pours out the venom that came from the abuser's mouth. Some abusers lie about the other parent to the authorities, which causes that parent's contact with the children to be ceased, or subjected to repeated litigation. Some disregard visitation arrangements and conditions for no valid reason. An abuser may display good parenting while his visitation is supervised by professionals, then revert to abusive parenting when the visitation is unsupervised.

Sexual Abuse
To ignore when a partner says "No", to attempt to force a partner to do something that they feel morally obliged to avoid, or uncomfortable doing, is sexual abuse. This includes cases where the partner is too afraid to say no or unable to give consent. Rape is a crime within marriage.

Some abusers expect sexual willingness immediately after an incident of abuse or violence. Some indulge in suggestive behavior that they know the other person dislikes. Some men are addicted to pornography and masturbation but, as a result of it, either deprive their wives of sex or want to play out pornographic scenarios on their wife. Some women treat sex as a bartering tool to get their way in something else: "If you do this, I will reward you tonight".

An abuser who reads the Bible may insist that a wife is only allowed to refuse sex unless the husband and wife are both praying and fasting. He may claim that since Hebrews 13:4 says the marriage bed is undefiled, he is entitled to demand anal intercourse or other debasing or unnatural practices.

The Bible teaches that the sexual relationship between a married couple should be one of mutual giving: there should be reciprocal generosity, each partner rendering the affection due (owed) to the other partner. There should also be reciprocal authority, each partner having authority over their spouse's body (1 Cor. 7:3-5). Balancing these principles, we see that it is up to each partner to give pleasure, not to take it.

Sometime a victim believes that because her husband has authority over her body, she must make herself sexually available whenever her husband demands it. This is a form of prostitution and breeds disrespect in both spouses. It is also biblically unsound, because just as a husband has authority over his wife's body, the wife has authority over her husband's body. This means she can sometimes ask or tell his body not to do certain things to hers. The exercise of this provision should not be undertaken from selfishness; it means being sensitive to your partner's situation even as you are acutely aware of your own needs or lack thereof.

The fact that each spouse's body belongs to the other does not mean one spouse has the right to force the other to do anything he or she wants. The husband does not force his own body, so he should not force his wife's body. Sex should not be one person always pleasing the other and the other always pleasing themselves. Each party should aim to please the other in an atmosphere of negotiation, flexibility, and sensitivity. The Bible says the marriage bed is undefiled in order to discourage promiscuity or adultery, not to give a blanket approval for any action so long as it occurs within the marriage bed. *Marriage must be respected by all, and the marriage bed kept undefiled, because God will judge all immoral people and adulterers.* Heb. 13:4 Holman Christian Standard Bible

If pleasurable union is prevented by a genuine medical problem that cannot be cured, then the couple must work through that with prayer and care. Apart from such cases, however, constant refusal of sex, avoidance of it, or going through the motions in a resentful way is not God's plan, as that does not please one's partner. However, if there is a constant undercurrent of emotional abuse, it is hard for the victim to respond freely and joyfully to sexual advances.

Physical Abuse

This may include pushing, shoving, hitting, throwing things aggressively, choking and murder. It also includes damaging property and the neglect of basic physical and medical needs. Some abusers use objects or weapons against their victims. An abuser may block the victim's escape, abandon her in dangerous places, or lock her in or out of the house. An abuser's conduct may endanger other people's lives, such as sabotaging the car. It is common for physical abuse to begin or increase during pregnancy. The assault of a pregnant woman causes physical and emotional damage to mother and child and it can induce miscarriage or early labor.

Men who have a pattern of violent behavior against their wives do not lose their senses when they are violent. No matter how angry they seem, they are generally *in control of themselves* because this gives them simultaneous control of the woman.[22]

Spiritual Abuse

An abuser may redefine, twist and invert the meaning of biblical passages to justify abusive treatment. The biblical model teaches that a husband should lead his wife and family in a God-glorifying direction, and a wife should respect her husband. This model does not teach that a husband may coerce, intimidate or oppressively dominate his wife, or that wives should submit endlessly to such behavior from husbands. But an abuser often maintains that scripture ordains a chain of command which gives him authoritarian power over his wife and children, regardless of how much he may sin. He may use courses in Christian living to justify treating his wife like a naughty pupil.[23]

He may claim that women are not created in the image of God. He may say that since Eve was deceived, no woman should trust her own thinking — she should let her husband think for her. He may claim that, as his suitable helper, her only role is to meet his needs and make him look good before his fellow Christians. He may intimidate her into not disclosing the abuse by saying she must be silent in church. He may claim that anyone who tries to aid the victim to leave him will face God's wrath, since *what God has joined together, let not man separate*. He may blame her for the fact that he has never gone into ministry.

He may rape her (during the courtship or the marriage), then say that since she was in the city and did not cry out for help, she ought to be stoned to death. This is a cruel misrepresentation of Deuteronomy 22:23-27 which condemns a betrothed woman who *willingly* has sex with a man other than her fiancé, but says if a betrothed woman is *forced* into intercourse by such a man, she is innocent. (In contrast to the abuser's twisting of this scripture, true Christianity will assert that just as a betrothed victim of rape is not condemned, so we must not condemn a wife who is raped by her husband.)

He may justify his abuse by saying that he is disciplining her out of love, just as God disciplines those he loves. He may claim she deserves punishment because *if we claim to be without sin we deceive ourselves and the truth is not in us*. He may say she should be comforted by his punishment because Psalm 23:4 says *your rod and your staff they comfort me*. He may label her as proud and arrogant if she resists him and unforgiving if she is reluctant to grant forgiveness. He may justify his violence because Jesus overturned the tables of the moneylenders.[24] He may believe the power-lust he feeds on is the power of the Holy Spirit.

Some abusers stop their spouse from going to church, reading the Bible, or teaching the children about the Bible. Some command the victim to read nothing but the Bible and to attend every church service. Some say things like, "God told me you're not to drive the car any more".

When a victim tells the abuser (or bystanders) that her husband has behaved badly, she may be accused of "being judgmental". Christians are familiar with the scripture *judge not, that ye be not judged*. Many people think it prohibits mentioning anything negative about another person's behavior, that "being judgmental" is a heinous sin, almost the height of unchristian behavior (coming not far below adultery in the "wickedness" stakes). To unfairly accuse someone of "being judgmental" is an extremely common type of spiritual abuse, often used by manipulative abusers who want to deflect criticism from themselves, and also used by misguided Christian bystanders who do not understand the scriptures properly. We will address this subject more in chapter two where we discuss the biblical teaching on rebuking, making complaint, and verbal self-defense.

THE DYNAMIC CYCLE OF ABUSE

Most abusers do not practice their abusive behaviors all the time. There may be periods in which their behavior is fairly normal and they show love and affection for their spouse and family. Most victims will testify that their abuse was *continual* (recurring) but not *continuous* (uninterrupted).

Many, but not all, victims have been able to identify a pattern, a cycle in these changes. Everything goes well for a time, then gradually the selfishness and put-downs increase until there is a big episode of abuse, after which the abuser may be very sorry and "repentant", treating the victim with exaggerated kindness. But nothing is resolved in this aftermath. The abuser is simply trying to gain forgiveness without having to take responsibility for his bad behavior. This is the buy back period — the abuser tries to regain the victim's affection and loyalty, while never really addressing his own terrible behavior. Then gradually the tension builds … until the same sort of thing happens again. A cycle can occur every few minutes, days, weeks or months.

The victim's outlook and emotions go up and down with this cycle. When she is being treated well, she is happy and hopeful: it seems like this is the man she married. During the tension-building phase she may blame herself that things are not right. "If I only change *this* or *that* he will settle down again." In the explosion she is traumatized and bewildered. She may blame herself even more, or realize it is his fault and withdraw her affections from him, hence the need for buy back.

HOW PERPETRATORS AND VICTIMS PRESENT TO OTHERS

Caution needs to be exercised when identifying the victim, for when a victim separates from the relationship the abuser often portrays him/herself as the victim. This blame-shifting attracts sympathy and attention from bystanders who may misread and even believe the opposite of the true situation.

The perpetrator often presents to the public as a model, mild-mannered citizen — he seems like a good husband. Yet in reality the marriage is characterized by his selfishness, manipulation and irresponsibility. He lies, minimizes and twists the truth. If the victim declares the relationship over, the abuser often wants the relationship to continue and will say so insistently and persistently. He may appear to be deeply sincere and heartbroken. He will often make a show of conversion or recommitment to Christ and/or to counseling when his wife separates. But for all this outward display, he will downplay and minimize his responsibility for the situation and subtly make it look like his wife is at fault.

In such circumstances, it may seem to outsiders that the wife wears the trousers. What outsiders do not realize is that the wife's prominence in decision-making is a result of her husband mismanaging his headship.[25] She has to make unilateral decisions in the face of his negligent attitudes in order to keep the family functioning.

Although the victim will often appear calm, there may be a log jam of trauma below her calm exterior, so she may not present the problem clearly to outsiders. This is not surprising, given that victims often hide the problem even from themselves. They have spent all their energy walking on eggshells and trying to "fix" the relationship. The abuse problem can be masked by labels of mental illness, the perpetrator's addictions, work or financial difficulties.

Most victims tolerate and become worn down by serious abuse before recognizing that abuse is the problem. Many excuse their spouse's bad conduct and overlook its damaging effects for a very long time. Typically, they choose to suffer in silence. This denial (non-recognition of the existence of abuse) is a way of coping. Typically, abusers project blame onto the other spouse: "I only did that because of the way you are behaving." This makes the victim go into obsessive self-examination and self-recrimination: "It must be my fault; if I change this or that, it won't happen again." Such a victim has constant anxiety as to whether any of her own behaviors may have been abusive or ungodly, and is fundamentally unsure whether what she is suffering can be called domestic abuse.

While still in the marriage, most victims of abuse do not identify with the label "victim of domestic violence" or "battered wife". (That can't be me! My marriage isn't that bad!) They are more likely to recognize the word "abuse" than the word "violence" as describing their marriage. Even so, recognizing abuse in a marriage is usually a hard, long process. The Reverend Al Miles has served as a hospital chaplain for 18 years and in that time hundreds of women have disclosed violence inflicted by intimate partners. Almost none of these victims identified themselves as battered women.[26]

When a victim is starting to come out of denial and wants to discuss or disclose her predicament to others, the reactions of friends and associates vary. Disclosing abuse can be risky and dangerous. Some people minimize the seriousness of the situation and imagine they can patch it up with a few words of advice or prayer. Others take the abuser's side and blame the victim. Fellow Christians may question her faith, her Christian walk, or the standard of her forgiveness. Since many perpetrators claim they've been treated unfairly, some genuine victims are frightened of making the same claim because they don't want to be characterized as false accusers. Bystanders who *do* believe the victim often think she must be stupid to have put up with the abuse and ask judgmentally, "Why didn't you leave?" Other bystanders feel so uncomfortable they don't know what to say, and this makes the victim feel ignored, shunned or judged.

It is not surprising that victims are reluctant to report domestic abuse. If they have previously disclosed and received insensitive or dismissive feedback, this may deter them from trying again. In Australia, only 20% of incidents are reported to police or other services.[27] (This figure would be much lower in many Third World countries.)

To admit to being a victim is a humiliating experience. A victim often feels she is at the bottom of society — an undesirable outcast, a welfare statistic, a failed wife and perhaps even a failed mother. The shame can persist for months or even years afterwards. A victim may be terrified of revisiting her abuse memories because they bring up such raw pain and anger that she judges herself to be unforgiving and therefore un-Christian. In addition, the prospect of discussing competing scriptural interpretations of separation and divorce with her church may seem overwhelming. She fears that if she attempts such things, it will only increase her shame, pain and humiliation.

When it comes to the practicalities of ending the marriage, the victim may dread facing an unknown future, having to support herself financially and having to cope with the children's distress at the marriage breakup. Above all, her fear of the abuser's retribution can be very real, based on her past experience of his behavior.

▥ Chapter 2
Biblical action steps

When we are ill-treated by others, there are several biblical principles that show us how to respond. Some of these principles are forgiveness, longsuffering, turning the other cheek and loving our enemies. Sermons and books often address these familiar topics while neglecting others which are equally important. These principles include the initial actions of rebuke of the offender, followed by complaint to authorities and where necessary separation. These actions may follow one another relatively quickly.

PRINCIPLES TO FOLLOW WHEN SOMEONE OFFENDS US

Rebuking the offender
The Bible urges us not to be a partaker of another's sin (Eph. 5:6, 7; 1 Tim. 5:22). The psalmist taught, *You who love the LORD, hate evil!* (Ps. 97:10a) — this means challenging wrong beliefs and practices. Jesus did this with parables (Matt. 21:28-45), questions (Matt. 22:41-46) and direct criticisms (Matt. 23; 22:18; Luke 13:15).

To rebuke is to tell the truth about sin. Truthfulness is the first piece of Christian armor we should put on (Eph. 6:14). Paul said we should love without hypocrisy (Rom. 12:9). Moses said *You shall not hate your brother in your heart. You shall surely rebuke your neighbor, and not bear sin because of him* (Lev. 19:17). When Tamar was raped by her half-brother Amnon, she rebuked him both before and after the event (2 Sam. 13:12-13; 13:16). Jesus taught us a set of four steps which we should follow when we rebuke a brother or sister (Matt. 18:15-17; cf. Luke 17:3). Paul taught that if a pastor received an accusation against an elder with two or three witnesses to verify it, the elder should be rebuked before the whole congregation (1 Tim. 5:19, 20).

Making complaint (breaking the silence)
It is not sinful to pour out our complaint to those who should hear. Job says *Therefore I will not restrain my mouth; I will speak in the anguish of my spirit; I will complain in the bitterness of my soul* (Job 7:11). Furthermore, we should expose wicked conduct by reporting it to those in authority, as David reported Saul's murderous behavior to Samuel (1 Sam. 19:18a). We must not lie when we make our complaints — that would be slander. Nor should we complain to all and sundry — that would be unwise. But we may tell the truth if we are wise in choosing whom we tell. If we choose to tell the truth there should also be some purpose in doing so.

This may include applying for a protection order from the secular courts, or reporting a crime to the police. It is not wrong to appeal to the state if we need protection. We ought not to interpret 1 Corinthians 6:1 as forbidding us to seek protection from the secular justice system when danger is near. God's appointed governments (i.e. courts) are there to help us live quiet and peaceable lives (1 Tim. 2:2). Secular courts have the power of the sword to punish and restrain evildoers (Rom. 13:1-4), whereas the Bible does not give the New Testament church power to enforce a protection order through arrest, conviction and penalty.

When falsely accused, it is not wrong to defend yourself
The principle of self-defense appears in many places in the Bible. Judah's daughter-in-law Tamar stood up to Judah and rebuked him (Gen. 38). Jesus defended his own ministry at times (Matt. 9:4-6; 15:3-9). When Paul and Silas were illegally beaten and imprisoned, they identified their legal rights before the authorities; they would not collude in keeping the persecutors' sins hidden (Acts 16:36-40). Paul later appealed to Caesar (Acts 25:8, 10-11). He appealed for just treatment, because as a Roman citizen under Roman law he had the right to do so (Acts 22:25). He defended himself when Festus called him "mad" (Acts 26:24-26). Note that wherever Paul identified his rights it was not from arrogance or self-aggrandizement but in order to continue preaching the gospel.

In chapters 1-4 of First Corinthians, Paul defended himself against accusations being leveled at him by divisive elements within the Corinthian church. In Second Corinthians, especially chapters 10 and 11, Paul boldly defended himself against the false apostles' denigration of him. He pleaded with the Corinthian church; he argued against the unfair and illogical claims that his detractors were making; he set forth his blameless record of conduct. He did not succumb to their denigration with depressed resignation. He did not put on an air of martyrdom and say, "It must be the will of God for my reputation to be slandered, so I'll do nothing about it."

You do not have to give in to false pleas
Paul said *Let each of us please his neighbor for his good, leading to edification* (Rom. 15:2). In other words, our pleasing people should build them up in godliness. To please an abuser by allowing him to go on abusing is not building him up in godliness. It only enables him to sin for longer.

You do not have to cave in or back down just because the other person makes belated demonstrations of "reformation". A good illustration of this occured after the twelve spies returned from exploring Canaan, when the Israelites were in the wilderness (Num. 13 and 14). God had sent twelve spies to explore Canaan and made a conditional promise that he would give the Israelites victory over its inhabitants (13:2; 14:8). The majority of the people didn't believe God; they complained in faithless self-pity and began to form other plans. By this stage they had rebelled ten times. So God withdrew his favor (14:23) and replaced it with a chastisement tailored to the faithless fears of the rebels (14:29-37). The ringleaders of the rebellion were killed instantly. Then the remaining rebels presumptuously set about obeying God's initial command. God did not for a moment think that this belated change of heart showed true repentance. He warned them, but they proceeded to do it their own way and so were smitten by the Amalekites.

God was not hoodwinked by the belated obedience of the rebels. The faithless Israelites had already shown their true colors. God separated himself from them; he set boundaries. He did not listen to their sudden reformation, but stayed firm in his resolve.

THE PRINCIPLE OF SEPARATION

The Bible teaches a principle of separation. We are not yet considering whether this principle applies specifically to marriage, just establishing that there is a general principle of separation.

Paul instructed the young pastor, Timothy, to avoid wicked unbelievers and pseudo-believers. These instructions can be found in 2 Timothy 3:1-5. Words in square brackets are from the King James Version; they are added because they help illuminate certain meanings.

> But know this, that in the last days perilous times will come: for men will be lovers of themselves, lovers of money, boasters, proud, blasphemers, disobedient to parents, unthankful, unholy, unloving [without natural affection], unforgiving [trucebreakers], slanderers [false accusers], without self-control, brutal, despisers of [those that are] good, traitors, headstrong, haughty, lovers of pleasure rather than lovers of God, having a form of godliness but denying its power. And from such people turn away!

Paul tells Timothy to turn away from people who are *without natural affection*. This term means "without love for family members". *Having a form of godliness* describes someone whose public persona is moral and pious. Most people think, "He is such a nice person!" *Despisers of those that are good* describes people who seem to hate the goodness in others precisely because it pricks their own consciences. We find an example of this in the account of Amnon's rape and hatred of Tamar in 2 Samuel 13. When Tamar spoke up and rebuked Amnon for his wickedness, he hated her all the more for her righteousness.

There are other verses that instruct separation: *Have no fellowship with the unfruitful works of darkness, but rather expose them* (Eph. 5:11). *Cast out the scoffer and contention will leave; yes, strife and reproach will cease* (Prov. 22:10). *Make no friendship with an angry man, and with a furious man do not go, lest you learn his ways and set a snare for your soul* (Prov. 22:24- 25). *Go from the presence of a foolish man, when you do not perceive in him the lips of knowledge* (Prov. 14:7). *Do not eat the bread of a miser, nor desire his delicacies* (Prov. 23:6-7); see also Proverbs 24:1-2 and Romans 16:17-18.

Fleeing from persecution

Separation sometimes means fleeing from persecution. David fled from murderous Saul (1 Sam. 19:11, 12) and from mutinous Absalom (2 Sam. 15:13-17). Rahab hid the two spies, then told them to flee from Jericho (Josh. 2:4-6). When the northern kingdom of Israel went into idolatry, the priests, Levites and true followers of God fled to Jerusalem (2 Chron. 11:13-14). Elijah fled from Jezebel when she sought his life (1 Kings 19:2-3).

Numerous examples of fleeing from persecution can be found in the New Testament too. Joseph and Mary fled to Egypt and hid the young Jesus until Herod died (Matt. 2:13-14). Jesus left the land of Judah and went to Galilee when he heard that John the Baptist had been cast into prison (Matt. 4:12). When the Jews sought to destroy Jesus or the crowds sought to coerce him he often changed location (John 6:15, 8:59; 10:39; Matt. 12:14-15). He taught his disciples that if they were persecuted while spreading the gospel they should flee to another city (Matt. 10:23). The believers obeyed this when Saul's persecution took hold at Jerusalem (Acts 8:3,4). After Paul's conversion he had to apply the same principle when others sought his life (Acts 9:23-25; 2 Cor. 11:33; Acts 14:4-6, 19,20; 17:5-10; 19:30-31). When his life was threatened from extremist Jews he sought protection from the civil authorities and acted with secrecy to protect himself (Acts 23:10-24). We clearly should not put ourselves in dangerous situations if we can flee with integrity.[28]

God can sovereignly deliver
God delivers us from violent men (Ps. 18:48, 72:12-14, 141:4; Jer. 22:3) and sets free those who have been imprisoned (Luke 4:18 citing Isa. 61:1; Isa. 42:6-7). The apostles were set free from prison by God (Acts 5:19). Later, when Peter was imprisoned on his own, the Lord brought him out (Acts 12:17). Paul and Silas were freed from prison because God sent an earthquake (Acts 16:26). This does not mean God will always deliver — sometimes the believer is not saved from persecution (for example, James in Acts 12:2) — but we may take encouragement from the fact that sometimes God does close the mouths of the lions or providentially rescue his people.

In gospel proclamation, separation from the unrepentant is sometimes advisable
Jesus left Nazareth because its unbelief was so great (Mark 6:5-6). He taught his followers to do the same when people stubbornly would not receive the gospel message (Matt. 10:14; Luke 9:5; 10:11). He said we should not cast our pearls before swine (Matt. 7:6). Likewise, when Paul found opposition to the gospel amongst the Jews, he declared he would go instead to others who might believe (Acts 18:6). In Ephesus he separated the disciples from those in the synagogue who rejected the gospel (Acts 19:9).

Sometimes we should separate even from those who confess Christ
One place where the Bible directs us to separate from a brother is 2 Thessalonians 3:6, 11-12, 14-15. *But we command you brethren, in the name of our Lord Jesus Christ, that you withdraw from every brother who walks disorderly and not according to the tradition which he received from us. ... For we hear that there are some who walk among you in a disorderly manner, not working at all, but are busybodies. Now those who are such we command and exhort through our Lord Jesus Christ that they work in quietness and eat their own bread. ... And if anyone does not obey our word in this epistle, note that person and do not keep company with him, that he may be ashamed. Yet do not count him as an enemy, but admonish him as a brother.* Here we are told to withdraw companionable fellowship from an erring believer who has sinned in lifestyle, but not to withdraw to the point of treating him as an unbeliever.

However, when believers persist in certain kinds of wickedness we should separate from them even more and no longer class them as brothers. In 1 Corinthians 5, a professing believer had been sleeping with his father's wife. Paul instructed the church at Corinth: *When you are gathered together, along with my spirit, with the power of our Lord Jesus Christ, deliver such a one to Satan for the destruction of the flesh, that his spirit may be saved in the day of the Lord Jesus. ... put away from yourselves that wicked person* (1 Cor. 5:4-5, 13b). Paul's instruction was to excommunicate this man, that is, remove him from church membership.

Expanding on this theme, Paul wrote: *But now I have written to you not to keep company with anyone named a brother, who is a fornicator, or covetous, or an idolater, or a reviler, or a drunkard, or an extortioner — not even to eat with such a person* (verse 11). This says there are six sins for which professing believers should be put under discipline: fornication (sexual sin); covetousness (greed, grasping materialism), idolatry (worshiping something in place of

God), reviling (verbal abuse, slander), drunkenness, and extortion (taking something by force, using violence or the threat of violence). Most Christians are well aware of the seriousness of fornication but unfortunately they often treat the other five sins less seriously.

This verse commands us "not to eat with" such people. What does this prohibition mean? Many believe it means exclusion from the Lord's Supper.[29] But is that all it means? The term "eat with" (*sunesthio*) means not merely to eat, but to take food in company with. In all the other places where it occurs in the New Testament, it refers to sociable fellowship while sharing ordinary meals, not merely the Lord's Supper (see Acts 11:3 and Gal. 2:11-13 where Peter ate with Gentiles; also Acts 10:41 and Luke 15:2[30]). We have already seen that 2 Thessalonians tells us to withdraw companionable fellowship from a brother who sins in a *lesser* way than that which is described in 1 Corinthians 5:11. Therefore, when 1 Corinthians 5:11 says not even to eat with them, it must prohibit not only sharing the Lord's Supper but also keeping company and associating intimately with such people.[31]

While rebuke and discipline are painful, especially when those delivering it are people we have been close to (*faithful are the wounds of a friend,* Prov. 27:6a), their aim is always restorative. Putting a person under discipline gives him the opportunity to face the full consequences of his choices in the hope that this may bring him to repentance. Thus, Paul tells us to *deliver such a one to Satan for the destruction of the flesh, that his spirit may be saved in the day of the Lord Jesus* (1 Cor. 5:5). Thomas Schreiner has observed that: "Associating with or even eating with a person under discipline is banned, for such fellowship would communicate that nothing serious has happened. Relating to the person as usual would display a lack of love, betraying apathy about the person's salvation."[32] If a so-called Christian persists in heinous sins and is allowed to remain in intimate fellowship with believers, his conscience will probably harden further as he basks in the false satisfaction of passing as a Christian.

The fact that Jesus ate with sinners does not contradict this. Jesus ate with unconverted sinners (to evangelize them) and with repentant and forgiven sinners (to deepen the bonds of loving fellowship). But towards those who hypocritically professed to be following God, Jesus was strongly critical. Judas is a special case, permitted by God for the fulfillment of prophecy.

STEPS IN THE BIBLICAL DISCIPLINE PROCESS

In Matthew 18:15-17, Jesus gives us a step by step process for bringing discipline to a sinning Christian. The goal of the process is to bring the sinner to repentance. In step one, the offended individual privately rebukes the one by whom they feel offended. If the matter is unresolved, step two is taking one or two people with you to confront the person again. If there is no repentance, step three is bringing the offender before the church (which may mean the body of elders). If their formal rebuke brings no repentance, step four is to treat the offender "as an unbeliever".

It is not "playing God" for a church to declare that someone should be treated as an unbeliever. Although only God sees the heart and knows who are truly his own, the church is called to make functional judgments according to a person's conduct, as Paul makes clear in 1 Corinthians 5:11.

If there is repentance during any of these steps, further steps of discipline become unnecessary and biblical nurture and restorative discipleship should take over. At all times the sincerity of a person's repentance should be determined by their emotional and verbal response to rebuke and their subsequent conduct.

Repentance ought to bear fruit in reformed conduct and changed attitudes (Matt. 3:8; James 2:17; Luke 3:8; Acts 26:20). However, we must remember that such fruit takes time to develop. *Take heed to yourselves. If your brother sins against you, rebuke him; and if he repents, forgive him. And if he sins against you seven times in a day, and seven times in a day returns to you saying, "I repent," you shall forgive him* (Luke 17:3-4). No edible fruit grows in a day and neither does the fruit of the Spirit. The parable of the unforgiving servant urges us to be patient with offenders (Matt. 18:29).

HOW LEGITIMATE IS IT TO APPLY THESE PRINCIPLES TO DOMESTIC ABUSE?

For a victim of abuse it may be something of a revelation to consider these principles. When she reads 2 Timothy 3:1-5, almost every word in Paul's list applies to her spouse. *Despisers of those that are good* (KJV) is particularly reminiscent of the abuser's mentality. Some reforming abusers have even confessed that "She wound up being beaten for doing exactly what I wanted her to do."[33] Indeed several of the six items in 1 Corinthians 5:11 fit also. But she will probably hesitate to jump to the conclusion that this means she should leave her abusive husband. After all, she may still love him, or at least feel a wifely obligation to treat him kindly, overlook his faults and stay loyal to her marriage vows. After all, 1 Peter 3:1 says wives should submit to their husbands even if they do not obey the word (i.e. the word of Christ).

Since church and marriage are two distinct institutions, verses on conduct within the church do not necessarily shed light on conduct within a marriage. These principles of justice, integrity and separative discipline apply in the public and ecclesiastical realm. We must further examine scripture to find whether they apply within the home. What does God expect us to hold as more fundamental: societal relationships or self-protection? Gospel witness or separation from the unrepentant? Long-suffering, or rebuke and self-defense?

These are all very difficult questions and contribute to the bewilderment of the victim. She feels completely tied up in knots: what does the Bible really say, what parts of it apply to *her*? If she thinks of one scripture, she can immediately think of another scripture that seems to negate it.

In the next two chapters we will examine the teaching in 1 Corinthians 7 which tells us how the principle of separation applies to marriage.

HOW THE CHURCH CAN ASSIST

Helping perpetrators

It is possible for abusers to truly reform and a few, it seems, do. It is currently believed that the best method of treatment for abusive men is participation in a men's behavior-change group run by trained facilitators, especially when this is combined with firm sanctions imposed by outside authorities against the man's bad behavior. Some men, after participating in such a group for some time, have reformed to the degree that they were appointed to facilitate groups themselves. Their testimonies reveal that in the early stages of their own treatment they were in profound denial, did not think they really had a problem and "talked the talk" of reform without "walking the walk". Dropout rates are high in all such groups and graduation from a group is no guarantee that the man has actually changed.

Sometimes when pastors or fellow Christians are told about such severe marital problems they offer to pray for the abuser and victim. To many victims this offer will seem hollow, unless it is followed by action. Churches need to support the victim and make the abuser accountable. I have not yet heard of an abuser who reformed just through prayer alone.

Some Christian leaders are wary of sending people to secular groups. This caution is understandable. It would certainly be best if the Christian community itself ran behavior-change groups for abusers. However, where professionally facilitated Christian groups are unavailable, it is better to use a secular group than none at all. A secular group may not address spiritual issues, but it will focus on attitude and behavior change. Such change is essential to reformation, as God told Cain when Cain was angry towards Abel (Gen. 4:6-7). In addition, discreet inquiries may reveal that a group is actually led by Christian facilitators who are employed in a secular organization.

Clergy can make a difference by referring a male abuser to a perpetrator program. Batterers who have been referred by clergy are more likely to complete the program than those without clergy referral, and this holds true for court-mandated as well as non court-mandated batterers.[34]

Helping victims
Not all victims leave abusive relationships. Sometimes a victim will stay in an abusive relationship even when her Christian supporters believe that she should separate for safety's sake. Often the victim will go back to an abuser many times, despite the doubts of others about the abuser's genuine repentance.

Supporters can do some things to help such a victim assess the reality of her situation: listen with concern but without judgment, help her to think about her predicament, show you care for her safety and explain the biblical principles covered in this book. The abuse has eroded her sense of value and autonomy; she needs to redevelop it and can only do this if she is encouraged and allowed to make biblical choices at her own pace. A victim needs to know that her supporters will be available, providing nurture and guidance, whether she stays in the relationship, or whether she leaves.

A female victim is at greatest danger around the time of separation. The risk of being murdered by her husband goes up by about 50% when she leaves him.[35] Post-separation abuse often continues for months (years in the most serious cases). The practical life issues the victim faces are usually very complex. Finances, safety, parenting, property and other issues are often intertwined.

The pastor cannot necessarily assist with all of these areas, but the wider church community can help if they are motivated and equipped. Secular organizations can provide advice and literature to help equip a congregation in many of the practical details. However, the role of remedying the victim's spiritual misunderstandings rests primarily with the church. Often victims are not ready to look at the scriptural issues until months or years after separation when life has become more settled. Other victims need answers to the scriptural aspects first, before they dare take action on the practicalities.

part B ⦀

DIVORCE AND REMARRIAGE

⬛ Chapter 3
Does the apostle Paul permit divorce for an abused spouse?

1 Corinthians 7:10-16 *10 Now to the married I command, yet not I but the Lord: A wife is not to depart from her husband. 11But even if she does depart, let her remain unmarried or be reconciled to her husband. And a husband is not to divorce his wife.*

12But to the rest I, not the Lord, say: If any brother has a wife who does not believe, and she is willing to live with him, let him not divorce her. 13And a woman who has a husband who does not believe, if he is willing to live with her, let her not divorce him. 14For the unbelieving husband is sanctified by the wife, and the unbelieving wife is sanctified by the husband; otherwise your children would be unclean, but now they are holy. 15But if the unbeliever departs, let him depart; a brother or a sister is not under bondage in such cases. But God has called us to peace. 16For how do you know, O wife, whether you will save your husband? Or how do you know, O husband, whether you will save your wife?

Paul's teaching about divorce in 1 Corinthians 7 divides into two sections. The victim of abuse will probably think the second section (verses 12-16) has nothing to do with her situation because the abuser, generally speaking, does not voluntarily depart from the marriage. She is far more likely to take to heart the instruction in the first section (verses 10-11) not to leave her husband.

Since it seems that 1 Corinthians 7 does not give specific teaching about divorce for domestic abuse, some Christians fall back on the general principles of self-protection and covenant fidelity to justify divorce in such cases. Others believe that because there is no apparent mention of abuse, divorce must not be allowed. The victim of abuse tends to be in the latter group because many victims are better at understanding the letter of God's Word than they are at interpreting general principles from scripture.

It is important to note that both sections of this divorce passage are commands and in both Paul speaks with apostolic authority, under the inspiration of the Holy Spirit.[36] Verses 10 and 11 echo what Jesus had taught. Verses 12-16 deal with a subject not touched on by Jesus. This subject — divorce where a believer was married to an unbeliever — is, despite surface appearances, the key text for divorce in domestic abuse. We will deal with verses 12-16, especially verse 15, in this chapter. The next chapter deals with verses 10 and 11.

WHAT WAS THE PROBLEM, OR PROBLEMS, IN CORINTH?

It is possible that the Corinthians had written to Paul asking about sexual asceticism (abstaining from sex because it seemed unspiritual). The apostle ruled in chapter 7 against sexual asceticism, while at the same time he promoted celibacy (without demanding it) for those who were not married. It has been suggested that married couples in Corinth, particularly the wives, were separating in order to abstain from sex, and we should not understand verses 10-16 as general teachings on divorce, since Paul was only dealing with the question of divorce for asceticism.

However, it is by no means certain that the Corinthians were struggling with only one issue (sexual asceticism). They could well have asked an assortment of questions about singleness, marriage, divorce, remarriage, betrothal, and changing one's status after conversion. Or they may have recounted a number of different situations in the congregation involving intimate relationships, and asked Paul how they should handle each case. Even if they only asked about sexual asceticism, we have no grounds to assume that Paul's teaching in chapter seven pertains only to that topic. He could well have taken the opportunity to deliver broader teachings on marriage and divorce.

WHAT IF I WAS THE ONE WHO LEFT THE MARRIAGE?

It is often thought that verse 15 teaches the desertion principle, that is, divorce is permitted if an unbelieving spouse departs. When Paul wrote these words, he may have been thinking about a simple case where an unbeliever deserted a believing spouse. However, there is nothing to indicate explicitly that Paul was thinking only of simple desertion when he wrote the passage. Verse 15 begins *But if the unbeliever departs, let him depart...* The Greek word translated as "depart" ("leave", or "separate" in other English versions) is *chorizo* which means "to place space between", that is, to separate through the use of space. In the first century, *chorizo* was one of the standard terms for divorce. The same word occurs in Matthew 19:6 and Mark 10:9 where Jesus is discussing divorce with the Pharisees: *What God has joined together, let not man separate.*[37] The King James Version says *...let not man put asunder.*

In domestic abuse, the victim frequently feels a great deal of guilt, self-blame and over-responsibility for the conduct of the abuser. This web of emotions causes the victim to stay in the relationship, often for a long time. However, by any objective assessment, an ongoing domestic abuser is effectively pushing away his spouse and dividing the marriage. The fact that many victims eventually leave abusive relationships testifies to this pushing away. Abusers may plead for the marriage to continue or beg for it to be resumed, but their overall conduct conveys the exact opposite. The spouse who has disobeyed God by dishonoring the partner and causing separation is, in fact, the spouse who bears guilt for the separation.

Verse 15 applies to more than desertion by an unbeliever. The key question is not "Who walked out?" but "What (or who) caused the separation?" Would it be sensible to say that David was the sinful rebellious one when he left Saul's court? No, he left because of abuse. David left, but Saul was the cause of his leaving.

In verse 15, the word *chorizo* occurs twice: *if the unbeliever separates (chorizo), let him separate (chorizo).*[38] The unbeliever is doing the separating, not the believer; the believer is commanded to let it be done. This tells the believing spouse (and the church) to allow the marriage to be over, because the unbeliever has already destroyed the covenant.[39] The New Jerusalem Bible says, *If the unbeliever causes separation, let the separation take place.* As Jay Adams notes, "it is the one instance in which divorce is required".[40]

It could even be argued that verse 15 should read, *If the unbeliever causes separation, let there be divorce.* This translates the first *chorizo* as "separate" and the second *chorizo* as "divorce". It would convey that Paul saw the separating conduct of the unbeliever as resulting in legal divorce. This rendering does not twist the meaning of *chorizo,* because *chorizo* means both "separate" and "divorce".

Constructive Desertion

Before no-fault divorce came into vogue, there was a ground for divorce under English law called "constructive desertion".[41] Constructive desertion was deemed to have occurred if one spouse so ill-treated the other that the victim was justified in leaving the abusing spouse, having been driven to do so. The act of desertion was understood as having been caused by the abuser.[42] The concept of constructive desertion was recognized by theologians in the sixteenth and seventeenth century (see appendix 2). Since *chorizo* means "separate" as well as "depart", 1 Corinthians 7:15 can cover constructive desertion.

In the Greco-Roman law of Corinth, divorce occurred simply when one or both parties ceased to regard the other as spouse. Legal procedures were not necessary unless there were difficulties with dowry or the legitimacy of a child. Paul wrote in this legal context. However, divorce in our culture means more than separation, it demands a legal procedure. Our context requires that if the unbeliever does not initiate this procedure, the believer can initiate the legal process in order to regularize the *de facto* divorce.

It may seem strange that divorce might be *required*, especially when Jesus spoke strongly against divorce. However, when Paul began this section at verse 12 he indicated that his words were adding to and therefore different from Jesus' words. So when Paul said "let there be separation" in verse 15, he presumably intended a deliberate contrast with Jesus' command, *What God has joined together let not man separate.*[43] Paul was saying: "If an unbeliever's conduct has separated what God joined together, let it be so."

This tells the believing spouse not to live in hope interminably. It protects a victim of abuse from prolonged subjection to the extortion of an abusive spouse. It says, "Don't make yourself into a doormat." It also prevents an abandoned spouse from living in perpetual limbo while waiting for the deserting spouse to come back.

Treacherous divorce and disciplinary divorce

In a culture where formal procedures and divorce papers are necessary, it is helpful to think about divorce under two headings: treacherous divorce and disciplinary divorce.[44] Treacherous divorce is when a spouse takes out a divorce without biblical grounds. The partner being dismissed is innocent because he or she has not caused the divorce and is being discarded for little or no reason.

Disciplinary divorce occurs when divorce is used as a disciplinary tool. Just as we may withdraw social privileges from a rebellious teenager, we may formally withdraw the privileges of the marriage relationship from a covenant-breaking spouse. This situation arises when a spouse has willfully repudiated the marriage covenant by adultery, abandonment, abuse or harmful neglect, but has not commenced the legal process of divorce. The injured party may take out a disciplinary divorce in order to be freed from the sinning spouse. In cases where the marriage broke down because of a husband's abuse, the declaration of divorce, which is a public and formal decree that the marriage has ended, may help to counteract the perpetrator's wishful thinking that somehow he might be able to get his wife to reconcile. (An abuser often wishes for reconciliation with his wife years after the marriage breakdown. After all, she came back to him so many times before.)

When divorce is used as a disciplinary method, the grounds are stated, are verified as biblical, and the one being disciplined is judged the guilty party. Disciplinary divorce could also be called justified divorce.

1 Corinthians 7:15 covers all kinds of disciplinary divorce. Adultery, desertion (abandonment) and constructive desertion (abuse, harmful neglect) are all occasions for disciplinary divorce. 1 Corinthians 7:15 also covers treacherous divorce where an unbeliever divorces a believer without good reason.

"Willing to live with"
To confirm that this passage can apply to domestic abuse, let's look at verses 12 and 13. *But to the rest I, not the Lord, say: If any brother has a wife who does not believe, and she is willing to live with him, let him not divorce her. And a woman who has a husband who does not believe, if he is willing to live with her, let her not divorce him.* The term "willing" is the Greek word *syneudokeo*. It means: to join in approval with, approve of, sympathize with, applaud, be pleased together with, be like minded with, agree, consent, or be willing.[45]

Most English translations have translated verse 13 with expressions like "if the unbeliever is willing / agrees / consents to live with her, let her not divorce him". This conveys the idea of the unbeliever's mental assent to living with a Christian spouse, without necessarily conveying that the unbeliever feels approval and sympathetic delight in the object of his choice. Since an abuser usually wants to continue the marriage, such translations inadvertently give the idea that in cases of abuse, divorce is prohibited.

However, the abuser desires a marriage in which he maintains his power. The words *willing to live with his wife* cannot mean "is willing to live with her because of opportunities to sin against her". That would be nonsense and imply Paul approved of sin. *Willing to live with* must mean "pleased to live as a spouse ought to live" — showing goodwill towards the marriage.

Reading verse 13, the bewildered victim thinks, "My husband says he wants to go on living with me, so I have to keep the marriage going." This conclusion seems to be confirmed because so many commentators say verse 15 only applies to desertion. Indeed, verse 15 has commonly been called the "desertion principle" and been illustrated as follows: "If a wife becomes converted, the husband may want to have nothing to do with this new Christian who is so unlike the woman he married. If the unbeliever wants nothing more to do with the marriage, divorce is not wrong."

While this interpretation is valid for some marriage situations, it is rarely valid for the victim of abuse. Hearing it she feels invisible, because it fails to recognize her plight. Abusers do not usually decide to leave the relationship simply because their partner has converted to Christ. The differences between an abuser's values and the converted spouse's values are greatly overshadowed by the already existing power imbalance between them. The core definition of abuse is that the abuser does not value the victim's ideas — *her opinions don't count.* Indeed, the conversion of the victim during the marriage may simply provide the abuser with additional techniques of abuse. He can now quote scripture to coerce and denigrate her. He is also provided with a ready-made network of Christian bystanders to use as allies, whom he commonly uses to guilt-trip his wife into reconciliation.

The illustration is also limited because there is more than one reason why a Christian may become married to a non-Christian.

• Some believers marry spouses who appear to be Christians, only to find out later that they were sadly mistaken.

• Sometimes both spouses come (apparently) to faith after they are married, but one partner's faith then withers under pressure, like the seed which was sown on rocky ground (Matthew 13:20-21), with reversion to former selfish behavior.

• Some Christians marry unbelievers *after* their conversion. Yes, the Bible commands believers not to marry unbelievers (2 Cor. 6:14; 1 Cor. 7:39), but a new convert sometimes marries before learning these instructions.[46]

• Sometimes a Christian marries an unbeliever while backslidden, only to recommit to the Christian life later on.[47]

Let us come back to *syneudokeo.* The concept of *being pleased* and *approvingly consenting* to live in the marriage must carry the idea of respecting and honoring the believing spouse and the marriage relationship. Paul seems to mean: "The unbelieving husband does not have faith, but he may approve of his wife and her godly values. If this is so, let her not divorce him." The persistent perpetrator of abuse is not like this.[48] He is happy to live with his wife, but only because it gives him power over her. Instead of the approval of *syneudokeo* he shows the opposite: an evil thinking towards his wife. So the command of verse 13 *let her not divorce him* is not applicable.

DOES THIS LET DIVORCE HAPPEN TOO EASILY?

Many Christians are afraid of "opening the floodgates" of excuses for divorce. However, allowing divorce for constructive desertion is not the same as allowing divorce simply for "mutual incompatibility". Nor does it imply that a Christian spouse can separate in reaction to a transient incident or a light offense. Even in heavy offenses and repeated abuse, efforts should be made by the believer to bring the abuser to repentance. All efforts to urge a perpetrator to repent should be done with humility and a readiness to forgive.

However, it is important to be aware that most victims of abuse have already made many efforts in this direction before they seek help from a pastor or other professional. Indeed, the victim has usually borne too much for too long and the pattern of abuse has become deeply entrenched. A review of the secular research literature on domestic abuse revealed that:

> In general domestic violence victims had incredibly high levels of commitment to their relationships and nobody left after a few incidents of violence and abuse. Women usually took some responsibility for the violence against them at the beginning of their relationships; however, over time most recognized that it was "not their fault".

Despite this insight, some women continued to live in relationships where there was violence because of their commitment to the relationship and/or to the institution of marriage.[49]

Religious victims have even higher levels of commitment to their marriages than non-religious victims. One study found that the average length of marriage for religious victims was 11.4 years compared to 8.6 years for non-religious victims. In the case of religious victims, the abuse had continued for an average of 9.4 years, whereas for non-religious victims the figure was 7.4 years. Religiosity of the victims bore no relationship to the severity of the abuse.[50]

Some claim that separation or divorce should only be allowed if the abuse is life threatening. Hebrews 12:4 is sometimes used to support this argument: *You have not yet resisted to bloodshed, striving against sin.* There are difficulties with this approach. The Hebrews scripture is about persecution relating to Christian commitment, yet most domestic abuse occurs irrespective of Christian commitment. Furthermore, when the abuse threatens life, it may be too late to escape.

To tell victims they can't leave unless their life is threatened is to condemn them to a defeatist depression with no end in sight. The victim dreads the abuse and yet is encouraged to hope for a life-threatening situation — because only then is divorce permissible. This attitude is callous to victims. It also places a premium on physical violence and minimizes the "living death" effects of emotional abuse.

THE TERM "DESERTION PRINCIPLE" IS NOT HELPFUL

Since abusers rarely leave the relationship voluntarily, it would be better to call verse 15 "the abuse, desertion, or unjust dismissal principle". When it is simply labeled "the desertion principle", most abuse victims believe they have to remain in their appalling marriages because their spouse has not deserted.

I know a woman who fled from her abusive husband on several occasions but always came back because she believed it was a sin to desert her husband. Her husband eventually left because he wanted to hide from the police who were about to catch up with him over unpaid fines. Only then did she feel free to let the marriage be over. She believed that she had no right to separate what God had joined together, but if her husband (or God's providence) brought about the separation, she could be free.

Another woman's husband indulged in adultery as well as abuse. From time to time he would abandon his wife to pursue his adulterous relationship. Whenever he returned, expecting reconciliation, she felt obliged to let him back because, by her understanding of the term, he was no longer a deserter. She did not understand that she need not let him back (and should not have let him back) unless he was willing to live in the relationship agreeably and forego the abuse as well as the adultery.

Many victims of domestic abuse have read 1 Corinthians 7:15 with grief and despair. Believing it only applies to desertion, they have found no permission for them to divorce. Believing they would be labeled as the deserter if they left the awful marriage, they have felt terrible guilt. Believing the problem of domestic abuse is not mentioned in scripture, they have felt disregarded by the Bible and the church. Yet this is the very verse that does apply to them.

WHEN THE ABUSER PROFESSES TO BE A CHRISTIAN

Let us imagine that a victim leaves her husband because of his abuse. The husband is a professing Christian and the wife has already sought his repentance using steps one and two of Matthew 18:15-17, to no avail. She now asks the church to formally proceed with step three. The church leaders find that the husband professes willingness to reconcile but is unwilling to do the things they require him to do in order to ensure the reconciliation is safe for the wife.

It is important to be wise in discerning counterfeit repentance because some abusers are good at feigning repentance. Words do not offer a sufficient guide to whether repentance is genuine or not. There should be evidence that the offender feels grief and hatred for his sin, not just grief at being found out, or fear of loss of privileges. He should be willing to make proper reparation to anyone injured by his conduct. This would include being willing to tell the truth to persons he has lied to. It would also include paying reasonable child support if the children are not living with the perpetrator (1 Tim. 5:8; Isa. 58:7). Should a behavior-change group be available, the abuser should we willing to attend and not drop out half way through. He should be prepared to make himself accountable to the pastor, other married men in the fellowship, and/or a counselor experienced in domestic abuse who seeks the victim's viewpoint and is not bound by such tight confidentiality that he cannot report essentials back to the pastor.

If the disciplinary process proceeds through to step four, the elders should rule that the offender is to be treated as an unbeliever and the wife is to be treated as a victim of constructive desertion under 1 Corinthians 7:15.[51]

NOT UNDER BONDAGE

The term *under bondage* in verse 15 is the Greek word *dedoulotai*, from the word *douloō* which means to make one subservient to another's interests, to cause to be like a slave.[52] Therefore verse 15b says a brother or sister is not subservient to an unbelieving spouse in such cases.

This actually strengthens the interpretation discussed so far. If the unbelieving spouse causes separation, the believing spouse is not bound to maintain a non-existent marriage.[53] The believer need not remain slavishly loyal to an absent person, which would be like living in limbo forever. The believer need not be in bondage to her own good intentions.[54] She need not remain with an unbelieving, domineering partner who brings her into captivity by combining soul-destroying abuse with occasional kindness.

This does not necessarily imply the victim *has* to leave such a partner. Abigail did not leave Nabal; however, she did not allow his sin to put the entire household in jeopardy (1 Sam. 25) and once he had sobered up she told him how she had protected their household. I believe it is impossible to tell a victim that she ought to leave or stay at any particular juncture — the decision when or whether to leave must be left to each victim. All we can do is lay out the biblical principles that permit separation and help the victim assess the discernible risk factors, leaving the ultimate choice to her.

We will come back to *not under bondage* in the next chapter, to consider whether it means "free to remarry".

God has called us to peace

God has called us to true peace in which godliness may increase (see Romans 14:19). He has not called us to the false peace of adaptive submission to a wicked spouse. As Michael Hill has observed: "The biblical notion of peace or *shalom* means more than just the cessation of hostility. It is a state of affairs where everyone delights in God and in their neighbor and in creation. It refers to a set of right relationships." [55]

The inveterate abuser is not really prepared to work for such peace. Instead, he tries to act as if love and intimacy can still exist despite his terrible behavior. Although he may plead, "I'll change! It will never happen again!" or "I'll get counseling", these are often tactics to draw the victim back into his false version of peace, the one where he is comfortable because he can go on denying his problem.

SHOULD THE VICTIM STAY TO LEAD THE ABUSER TO THE LORD?

> Verse 16 says, *For how do you know, O wife, whether you will save your husband?* And verse 14 says, *For the unbelieving husband is sanctified by the wife, and the unbelieving wife is sanctified by the husband; otherwise your children would be unclean, but now they are holy.*

Most people take this to mean that a believing wife should stay in the marriage because her witness may lead her husband to the Lord. Certainly this applies to verse 13 where the husband approvingly consents to live with her as a spouse ought to live. In that situation the marriage will be peaceful and the witness of the believing wife may well lead to the husband's conversion. Such an unbelieving partner is sanctified because he is exposed to the external blessing and influence of God as he conforms outwardly to God's standard for marriage. Indeed, some unbelieving husbands are won to Christ by the submissive and godly conduct of their wives (1 Peter 3:1-6).

However, the question "How do you know whether you will save your husband?" can embrace both optimism and pessimism.[56] John MacArthur calls verse 16 "God's caution against marital evangelism".[57] You have no warrant to assume that your witness will convert your spouse. It may be that he will not be converted. Or the Lord may not use you but may use other means to save your husband. If you have faithfully witnessed to your husband but he is unwilling to live approvingly with you and his conduct causes separation, you should not condemn yourself saying that your witness to your ex-spouse was apparently fruitless.

▥ Chapter 4
May I remarry if I have suffered divorce?

1 Corinthians 7 ¹⁰Now to the married I command, yet not I but the Lord: A wife is not to depart from her husband. ¹¹But even if she does depart, let her remain unmarried or be reconciled to her husband. And a husband is not to divorce his wife.

Verses 10 and 11 relate to a situation where both spouses are professing Christians. Paul does not indicate this at the start when he says *Now to the married I command...* It only becomes apparent when he says *"to the rest..."* in verse 12 where "the rest" obviously means believers married to unbelievers.[58] This indicates that the ones being addressed in verses 10 and 11 were Christians married to Christians.

A victim of domestic abuse may think verses 10 and 11 apply to her predicament more than verses 12-16. This is so even if she is married to an unbeliever. Unless she understands the concept of constructive desertion, she may not apply verse 15 to herself. On the other hand, verses 10 and 11 seem directed at her, for she has probably contemplated leaving her husband or has actually left.

The confused victim may hear a clear prohibition in *"a wife is not to depart from her husband,"* and feel guilty for separating or desiring separation. She may skip quickly through *"but even if she does depart"* without giving thought to whose perversity might have caused the departure. She may come to *"let her remain unmarried or be reconciled to her husband"* and feel herself being nailed into the coffin.

In all these commands, it can sound as if the woman is responsible for everything. She must not depart. If she departs she must remain unmarried, or be reconciled to her husband. Her husband does nothing here. Yes, there is a command that he must not divorce her, but that is not her concern, nor her experience. The victim, well-trained by the abuser to blame herself and to take accountability for every problem, thinks "All the guilt for separating and all the responsibility for reconciliation are on my shoulders."

Because divorce is frowned upon in some Christian circles, many victims hear the words *"be reconciled to her husband"* as a command. However, Paul recognizes that some cases will not end in reconciliation. Reconciliation may occur if both spouses are true Christians, because sin should be repented of and the fruit of the Spirit will, in time, grow. But Paul does not command reconciliation; he only rules out a new marriage to a third party because that would prevent reconciliation of the first couple.

WHY THE SPECIAL COMMENT ABOUT A WIFE DEPARTING?

In verse 11 Paul says *"but if a wife does depart…"*, giving pastoral recognition to the possibility of a wife separating. He takes pains to enunciate the rest of his divorce pronouncement for both sexes, but he does not take pains to invert 1 Corinthians 7:11a. He does not say: "but if the husband does divorce his wife, let him remain unmarried or be reconciled to his wife".

The careful gender equity balance in the rest of Paul's teaching would suggest that verse 11a applies to men as well as women. Why does he add a special clause about the wife in verse 11, without adding a similar clause for the husband? We can only make educated guesses.

It is possible that Paul added the special clause for women because women in gentile society commonly took the initiative in divorce, so women in Corinth (more than men) needed to be cautioned against treacherous divorce.[59] Another possibility is that Paul added the clause because he recognized the likelihood of wives being abused. If, through sin, a marriage is not working, a woman is more likely than a man to be intimidated or in danger, so her need for safety might drive her to escape.

DO VERSES 10 AND 11 PERMIT SEPARATION, BUT NOT DIVORCE?

Many well-meaning Christians would permit or advise a victim of physical abuse to separate from her husband as a temporary expedient. Allowing a victim to temporarily flee for safety's sake is better than telling her to stay submissively in the abusive situtation, but it can be a mixed blessing. The victim may hear such temporary permission as "After he calms down it will be all right again and you can go home." Temporary separation needs to be followed up with counseling to help the victim come out of denial and to focus on safety planning for the long term. Permitting only short-term separation has the effect of minimizing the abuse and disregarding the entrenched nature of the problem. It presupposes that a separation will somehow "fix" the abuser.

People often teach this because the translations in our present Bibles promote the somewhat inaccurate idea that separation is tolerable but divorce is forbidden. The misunderstanding has arisen because we read that wives should not depart (*chorizo*) and husbands should not divorce (*aphiemi*), which suggests a distinction is being highlighted. This distinction appears to be confirmed because Paul seems to tolerate separation, stipulating only that if wives do depart, they refrain from marrying new husbands. However, *chorizo* and *aphiemi* are probably not significantly different in this passage since both can mean legal divorce.[60] Furthermore, the distinction we make today between separated spouses and divorced spouses was not perceived in the Greco-Roman culture of Paul's time. Under Greco-Roman law, full and legal divorce took place merely by one party separating with intent to end the marriage.[61] (This explains why it is legitimate to translate *chorizo* as either "to separate", "to depart" or "to divorce".)

It would be more helpful if contemporary English translations used the word "divorce" in both verse 10 and verse 11 — "A wife is not to *divorce* her husband, but if she does *divorce* she must remain unmarried or be reconciled to her husband. And a husband is not to *divorce* his wife".[62]

The inaccurate idea that separation is tolerable but divorce is reprehensible has meant many churches turning a blind eye if a spouse separates, but stigmatizing the person who takes steps to formalize the separation with divorce papers. This has led to many victims of domestic abuse separating but never divorcing, resulting in estranged spouses being legally and therefore psychologically tied to each other for years. This can give rise to "point scoring" between the estranged spouses about who will stay "righteous" by not filing for divorce. There can also be problems with inheritance if one spouse dies.

The concept that "separation is okay but divorce is not" is also challenged by verse 11 where the woman being discussed is told to remain *unmarried*.[63] The word used is *agamos*. The prefix *a-* means "not" and the word *gamos* means "married", thus *agamos* means "not married to anyone". It is a general word covering those who have never married along with widows and divorcees (the "de-married").[64] Indeed, the word "widow" (*chera*) has some overlap with the word *agamos,* for while *chera* often meant "a woman whose husband had died", it could also mean "lacking a husband" and was sometimes used for a divorced woman.[65] The *agamos* Christians in verses 8 and 9 are not in a current marriage and are permitted to marry. The *agamos* Christians in verse 11 are not in a current marriage and they are permitted to marry but only by reuniting with their former spouses.[66]

REMAINING UNMARRIED GIVES OPPORTUNITY FOR THE DISCIPLINE PROCESS

With a persistently abusive professing believer, the "no remarriage" rule of verse 11 must apply initially. During this time, the two people should "remain in the church's fellowship and come under its nurture and discipline".[67]

The discipline process should follow the steps of Matthew 18. Here, Jesus described how far to go to attain repentance and reconciliation, delineating the steps along the way and the point where a dead end is reached. Romans 12:18 implies that with some people it is not possible to live at peace: *If it is possible, as much as depends on you, live peaceably with all men.* For abusive marriages, resolution may eventually be achieved by the abuser's repentance, which can, with due caution and guidance, lead to reconciliation of the relationship. Alternatively, the church may rule that the abuser should be treated "as an unbeliever", bringing verse 15 of 1 Corinthians 7 into play.[68]

IF THE ABUSER IS DECLARED "AS AN UNBELIEVER", REMARRIAGE IS PERMITTED

In verse 11, Paul explicitly prohibited a new marriage in the case of two believers who had separated or divorced. It was necessary for Paul to be very explicit, because the assumption of Jewish and Greco-Roman law was that divorce freed the parties for remarriage.[69] The essential words in a Jewish divorce certificate were "Behold, you are free to marry any man".[70] In Greco-Roman law, divorce certificates were not necessary; the presumption was that remarriage was both permitted and expected after divorce. Indeed, Roman law offered financial incentives for Roman citizens to remarry after divorce.[71]

Paul announced in verse 12 that he was now beginning a different teaching — for cases where only one spouse is a believer. Since he had so carefully flagged verse 12 as the beginning of a different teaching, we cannot assume that the remarriage prohibition of verse 11 carries over to verse 15. Indeed, if Paul had intended to prohibit remarriage for the case in verse 15 he would again have had to do so explicitly.[72] But he did not prohibit remarriage; instead, he gave a totally contrasting rule: *the brother or sister is not under bondage in such cases.* These words recall the exact language used in ancient divorce documents, "you are free to marry any man". In this context, the words "not under bondage" clearly imply "not obliged to remain unmarried as the woman in verse 11 was obliged to remain unmarried".[73]

We have already seen that Paul describes the divorcee in verse 11 as unmarried (*agamos*). The innocent divorcee in verse 15 could also be described as *agamos*. Paul's general instruction to *agamos* Christians was that those who were so gifted should practice sexual abstinence, yet the gift of abstinence is not given to all. *For I wish that all men were even as I myself* [unmarried]. *But each one has his own gift from God, one in this manner and another in that. But I say to the unmarried* [agamos] *and to the widows: It is good for them if they remain even as I am, but if they cannot exercise self-control, let them marry* (verses 7-9a).

God's grace can enable a divorced Christian to live the single life, but it is unscriptural to say that celibacy is required of all divorced Christians. Paul recognized that the gift of celibacy is not possessed by all *agamos* persons (a group comprising the never-married, the divorced and the widowed). It is unlikely that he would have thought that every divorcee should exercise self-control for abstinence by remaining unmarried until death.[74]

There is also an ethical argument for liberty to remarry. If "not under bondage" does not mean "free to remarry", the result is a moral anomaly. Hundreds of years ago, John Owen, one of the great Puritan writers, wrote about this moral anomaly: [75] Owen was speaking about divorce for adultery, but there is no reason why his remarks cannot be applied to other kinds of disciplinary divorce.

> If the innocent party upon a divorce be not set at liberty [to marry again], then,
> — (1) He is deprived of his right by the sin of another; which is against the law of nature; — and so every wicked woman hath it in her power to deprive her husband of his natural right. (2) The divorce in case of adultery, pointed by our Savior to the innocent person to make use, is, as all confess, for his liberty, advantage and relief. But on supposition that he may not marry, it would prove a snare and a yoke unto him; for if hereon he hath not the gift of continency, he is exposed to sin and judgment.

The term "not under bondage" also suggests emancipation. In some Roman marriages, the wife was legally "under the power" of her husband. If that were the case, divorce was conceived as *emancipatio* — emancipation from the legal authority of her husband.[76] In addition, the term would have reminded Paul's readers of a slave being emancipated. To set a slave free required certain procedures and the writing of an emancipation certificate. These procedures and the wording on the certificate were similar to the procedures and wording in Jewish divorce.[77] The Corinthian congregation (which contained both Jews and slaves[78]) would have understood these analogies. To them, it would have confirmed that Paul was referring to the right of this divorcee to remarry.

Some may object that because the word "under bondage" (*dedoulotai*) is not used in the literature of the time in relation to marriage or divorce, we have no warrant to think it refers to divorce here. They argue that when Paul spoke of being "bound" in Romans 7:2 and 1 Corinthians 7:39, he used a different word — *deo*. However, there is no reason to assume that Paul employed only one word when referring to the marriage bond.[79] True, *dedoulotai* was commonly used in the first century in reference to slavery, but other Bible teaching on marriage also used language taken from the realm of slavery. Paul used *eleutheros* ("freedom from slavery" cf. 1 Cor. 7:21) when discussing marriage in Corinthians 7:39 and Romans 7:3. The slave wife, whose father sold her as a maidservant but whose master then elevated her to wifely status, was granted freedom if her husband mistreated her (Exodus 21:7 — 11).[80]

We may put it this way: the believer in verse 11 is obligated to maintain sexual fidelity to her estranged husband by either remaining unmarried or being reconciled. The believer in verse 15 is not obligated to maintain sexual fidelity to the former spouse and therefore is free to remarry.[81]

Using the process of church discipline

In cases where both spouses profess Christianity, the process of biblical discipline according to Matthew 18 is important in deciding whether a given spouse is acting as an unbeliever. If a church is asked to assess a matter of marital abuse, the principle of natural justice requires that the church leaders notify the alleged offender that they intend to make a decision about the matter of divorce. This allows the person a chance to give the other side of the story. Witnesses may also be called, such as people from a church to which the couple formerly belonged. Interviews may be conducted privately, so long as the main parties are kept reasonably informed about the progress of the investigation. If the alleged offender does not take the opportunity to put his viewpoint, a finding may be made based on the evidence available.

What to do if the church does not do its part

Sadly, it is sometimes hard to get a just hearing; many churches are not interested in truly biblical teaching. Sometimes churches use the principle of discipline in a grace-less way: by breaching confidentiality, demonstrating fleshly bias, or viewing restoration of the marriage as more important than restoring individuals. Sometimes they heap guilt upon the wrong person(s) or even cast them out because they have not investigated the matter in sufficient depth. Christian leaders are at times unable to accept the reality of the sin and the devastation it is causing and so they cannot bring the help that is needed.

If you believe your church has failed to employ Matthew 18:16 and 17 properly, you have a few options. The best option would be to ask a higher body in your denomination to review the matter. If this is not possible (some churches do not have an appeals process beyond the local church), you can appeal to a "sister church" that your local church respects. Or you can leave your church and find one that handles pastoral care more biblically, then ask them to make a ruling on your case.

Presenting a case

If your abuser is a professing Christian, the biblical precept is that you should not decide the matter for yourself without reference to a church court. Knowing your own heart is not enough: we are all capable of deceiving ourselves and justifying things to suit ourselves (Jer. 17:9). The Westminster Confession wisely counsels that the persons concerned in divorce be "not left to their own choices and preferences in their own case".[82]

If you are a victim, it is best to present the allegations of abuse as plainly as you can. You could use Ephesians 5:25-29 as a starting point. Contrast your spouse's behavior with the standard set by scripture. When describing your spouse's behavior, describe injuries and conduct specifically. Most victims are very vague when describing abuse. This makes it hard for bystanders to believe or sympathize with them. Sometimes this is because they actually haven't *taken in* what has been done to them. It is hard to mentally digest the fact that a person hates you or has deliberately endangered your life, so the abuse is left in some "unprocessed" place in the mind.

What should church leaders do about this problem? They should be aware that they may not be hearing the entire story from the person who is seeking help. They can ask questions to lead the person to be more specific e.g. "What exactly do you mean when you say, 'He lost his temper'? What did he do?" The victim must be helped to realize that it is not sufficient to say "He lost it" if the reality is "He called me a vile name, threw a plate at me and pushed me against the kitchen bench, then he disconnected the phone so I couldn't ring the police."

Friends or church leaders who suspect abuse may be occurring should try to link the victim to a domestic violence support service, or to another survivor who has come out of denial and can talk about what happened to her. This may spark recognition and identification in the person who is still in denial. It helps to recognize that it generally takes a long time for all the veils of denial to lift and that each victim needs to progress at her own pace.

The prospect of church disciplinary procedures may seem rather daunting to the victim. However, the end result is worth the effort. A fair hearing and a just determination will bring reassurance and security to the victim. With that peace of mind she can move on with her life.

WHAT ABOUT THE PRINCIPLE "REMAIN IN THE STATE IN WHICH YOU WERE CALLED"?

1 Corinthians 7:20 says *Let each one remain in the same calling in which he was called.* This teaches that we should not strive to change our life situation if that situation makes no difference to our ability to obey the Lord. Some life situations, like being circumcised or uncircumcised, slave or free, have no material bearing on our ability to follow the Lord (verses 18-22). If we are concerned merely to change such outward things, we have missed the point, viz. *keeping the commandments of God is what matters* (verse 19).

However, we do not have to stay rigidly in the state we happened to be in when our conversion took place. In matters that have no bearing on our ability to keep the commandments, we may change our status should the opportunity arise. For example, a young single person may enter into marriage for the first time. A widow who has converted to Christ may marry a fellow believer. Slaves, if granted their freedom, may embrace this opportunity (1 Cor. 7:21).

In matters where we would compromise the commandments of God by maintaining our current status, we ought to change that status. A converted prostitute must say, "I cannot continue being a prostitute." A victim of an abusive marriage may say: "Since my unbelieving spouse is thinking evil of me, not good, since he shows such an entrenched unwillingness to live as a spouse ought, which is separating this marriage relationship, verse 15 commands me to let him separate it. I should obey that scripture and allow my marital status to change; I am not under bondage and may live in peace."

Some time after employing disciplinary divorce, the divorcee can say, "My church leaders verified that I had biblical grounds for divorce, so remarriage is permitted. I know the married state can be distracting and have earnestly tested whether I have the gift of celibacy in doing kingdom work (verses 7-9). However, I desire more intimate companionship and know that God does not "put a leash" that prohibits my remarriage (verse 35); it is not a sin to marry (verses 9, 28) so long as I marry a Christian (verse 39)."

part C ▥

CLEARING AWAY MISCONCEPTIONS

Chapter 5
Fighting the giants

Once a victim of domestic abuse learns that 1 Corinthians 7:15 permits divorce for abuse, she is only at the beginning of solving her scriptural plight. Holding on to this verse yet still traumatized because of the abuse, she feels (rightly or wrongly) like a tiny David against an army of Philistine giants. It takes courage to even stand and look at these formidable opponents (and she hates to think of them as such, because they are her fellow Christians expressing these views). Each giant is shouting something different and they seem to be opposing her in a more or less unified fashion — at least, they all shout very loudly, so she assumes they are angry *at her*. Each one seems convinced that he is right. The clamor of their voices reaches her loud and clear:

- "Marriage is indissoluble while the other partner lives."

- "Divorced people are still married in the eyes of God."

- "Divorce is only permitted if there is adultery."

- "Divorce is only permitted if the parties are close relatives."

- "Remarriage causes defilement."

- "All remarriage is forbidden."

- "Remarriage is only permitted if the other partner has died."

- "Remarriage is adultery."

- "Remarriage is only permitted if there has been adultery."

- "God hates divorce."

This may sound confrontational, but that is often how it comes across to the victim. Her dilemma is not helped by the Christian who puts a hand on her shoulder and gently reminds her of Jesus' saying, *If you love me, you will keep my commandments.* With an effort, she tears her mind away from the paralysis of guilt which so often overwhelms her when she hears that statement. She looks more closely at the giants and realizes, "They are not just angry at me, *they are angry with each other.*" The giants are far from united. Something must be wrong with at least some of their views if they do not agree. With this hopeful clue, the task of the victim, and the task of the rest of this book, is to tackle each of these giants one by one. We will discover that although they seem to have giant voices, they are, in reality, more like midgets than giants.

In the rest of this chapter we will (1) disprove the idea that only death can dissolve marriage; (2) discuss whether Christ's faithfulness to his bride should be applied to all cases of divorce; (3) demonstrate the absurdity of the doctrine of the indissolubility of marriage; and (4) show that the "husband of one wife" texts do not prohibit remarriage after divorce.

IS DEATH THE ONLY THING THAT DISSOLVES MARRIAGE?

> Romans 7:1-4 *¹Or do you not know, brethren (for I speak to those who know the law), that the law has dominion over a man as long as he lives? ²For the woman who has a husband is bound by the law to her husband as long as he lives. But if the husband dies, she is released from the law of her husband. ³So then if, while her husband lives, she marries another man, she will be called an adulteress; but if her husband dies she is free from that law, so that she is no adulteress though she has married another man. ⁴Therefore my brethren, you also have become dead to the law through the body of Christ, that you may be married to another, even to him who was raised from the dead, that we should bear fruit to God.*

Some claim this text teaches that only death dissolves the marriage bond. They say that marriage is indissoluble except by the death of one of the parties. There are four reasons why marital indissolubility is not in view in Romans 7.

Firstly, Paul is not giving a full teaching on the subject of marriage, divorce and remarriage in Romans 7. He is merely using an element of the law of marriage to illustrate his main point, which is the place the Mosaic Law occupies in the new covenant era. A basic rule of biblical interpretation is that doctrine should not be based solely on analogy and illustration. Incidental passages should yield to passages giving explicit and detailed teaching on that particular doctrine.[83]

Secondly, the text does not imply the husband's death is the *only* way a woman can be freed from the marriage bond. Paul knew that both Mosaic and Greco-Roman divorce freed a woman from her husband and permitted her to remarry, but to mention divorce here would not have illustrated his point. His purpose was to explain the relevance of *death* in freeing one from Law, for it is by Christ's substitutionary death that the church has become dead to the Mosaic Law and freed to marry Christ (verse 4).[84]

Thirdly, nowhere in Mosaic or Greco-Roman Law is remarriage after divorce normally regarded as adultery.[85] There were only two circumstances where marriage after divorce was prohibited. A Jewish priest could not marry a divorced woman, whether her husband had died or not (Lev. 21:7, 13-15).[86] A man could not marry the woman he had divorced if she was widowed or divorced from a subsequent marriage (Deut. 24:1-4). There was no law against other divorcees remarrying.

Fourthly, the wording of Romans 7:2 actually specifies what is being talked about. The woman in verse 2 *has a husband*. The Greek word is *hypandros* which literally means "under a man". She is currently married; if she was divorced the man would no longer be her husband. Although verse 3 seems to refer to the possibility of her marrying another man (*if, while her husband lives, she marries another man...*) the word "marries" is not the normal Greek word for marriage, but a totally different word meaning "becomes". The phrase literally means she "becomes" another man's.[87] Some modern translations say "goes off with" another man, or "gives herself to" another man, or "lives with" another man.[88] The idea is that a currently married woman joins with another man, which is why she is called an adulteress. The "indissoluble" view has understood verse 3 in the following manner: "If a *divorced* woman marries another man while her ex-husband lives, she will be called an adulteress; but if her ex-husband dies she is free from that law, so that she is no adulteress though she has married another man." This interpretation takes unwarranted liberties with the text.

1 Corinthians 7:39 *A wife is bound by law as long as her husband lives; but if her husband dies, she is at liberty to be married to whom she wishes, only in the Lord.*

We can probably apply the same logic to this passage as we applied to Romans 7. The text says a wife is bound as long as her husband (not her former husband) lives. It tells us that if her husband (not her ex-husband) dies, she is at liberty to remarry. The passage is speaking about a woman in a current marriage and what is permitted when that marriage ends with the death of the husband. In this verse Paul cannot mean the marriage bond can *only* be dissolved through death for that would contradict Jesus' teaching that the marriage bond may be dissolved because of adultery. It would also contradict Paul's other teaching in 1 Corinthians 7.

Many believe that in verse 39 Paul was summing up his marriage teaching with a generalization. They understand him to be saying that under normal circumstances marriage is lifelong but if one spouse dies the other may remarry, so long as he or she chooses a believer. This interpretation would mean that Paul is simply not mentioning contingencies and special situations, such as when disciplinary divorce ends a marriage.

Others believe that Paul may have been signaling the end of Levirate marriage. In other words, he may have been saying that a widow no longer had to marry her dead husband's brother in order to produce a son for the dead man, as had been the law under Moses. She could now marry a partner of her own choice, so long as he was a believer.[89]

Another possibility is that Paul was referring specifically to "betrothal widows", betrothed women whose intended husbands had perished in the "present distress", before the marriage could take place. This sees the betrothed persons theme running from verse 25 right to the end of the chapter.[90]

CHRIST IS EVER FAITHFUL TO HIS BRIDE — SHOULDN'T WE BE THE SAME?

In Ephesians 5, Paul says the husband/wife relationship is analogous to Christ and his bride, the church. In the Old Testament there are references to God apparently divorcing his wife Israel, but then taking her back despite her sins. Some people apply this by saying: "Christ is ever faithful to his bride, the church, even though the church sins. A spouse should remain similarly faithful to his or her mate. Someone who has been abandoned, betrayed or divorced by their spouse should imitate this high call to faithfulness, and therefore never remarry."

This argument has to be called into question. In Ephesians 5, Paul was using the relationship of Christ and his bride to illustrate and enlarge upon male headship and female submission; he was not addressing divorce and remarriage at all. If Christ's faithfulness to his bride was an applicable illustration for the question of divorce and remarriage, why did Paul not employ it in 1 Corinthians 7 — the place where he most thoroughly discusses and instructs about divorce and remarriage?

Some people may feel personally called to remain faithful to an errant spouse. That is between God and them. But it is not right to make this an injunction that all should follow. Nor is it wise to present it as an ideal; when this is done, a Christian who has a sensitive conscience, but does not follow this 'ideal faithfulness', feels like a second-class Christian.

ONE FLESH: MUTUAL COMMITMENT — OR INDISSOLUBLE UNION?

Genesis 2:24 says, *Therefore a man shall leave his father and mother and be joined to his wife, and they shall become one flesh*. This verse is often called the creation ordinance of marriage. It is speaking about a stage when neither sin nor death had entered the world, so naturally it makes no mention of the fact that marriage can end in death or divorce.[91]

The word "join" is a Hebrew word meaning "be glued firmly", suggesting a strong bond. However, the bond of marriage is moral, not metaphysical.[92] A moral bond is not inseparable: it can be withdrawn or untied.[93] A mutual and unconditional commitment to the good of the other is the foundation of marriage. In the case of abuse, one partner has withdrawn his commitment to the good of the other. Hence if he does not change his behavior, he is to be treated as though he has deserted the marriage.[94]

Jesus quotes the creation ordinance and adds a solemn prohibition: *What God has joined together let not man separate* (Matt. 19:5-6; Mark 10:7-9). He does this not to condemn all divorce or to declare all remarriage invalid, but to rebuke those Pharisees who claimed that according to Deuteronomy 24 men were entitled to divorce for any matter. Jesus should be understood to be saying: "The *one flesh* principle is God's intention for marriage; if you Pharisees had properly recognized this text you would not have distorted Deuteronomy 24:1 so badly."[95]

Paul also quotes the creation ordinance in Ephesians 5:31-2 and refers to a *great mystery*. The word *mystery* is the Greek word *mysterion* meaning information knowable only by revelation from God. Paul immediately explains that the revelation of which he speaks is the union of Christ and the church. This union, which also unites Jew and Gentile, had been hidden in God since the beginning of the ages but is now revealed in the church age (Eph. 3:3-10; 1 Cor. 2:7-8; Col. 1:26-27). In contrast, the marriage union was revealed since the days of Eden.[96]

While the husband-wife union is analogous to the Christ-church union, an analogy must not be pressed too far. Although a husband should love his wife sacrificially, he is not the savior of his wife.[97] Although Christ and his church are one in Spirit, an ordinary husband and wife bond does not create a mystical, single, indissoluble entity in the heavenlies.

In addition, Paul uses the "one flesh" text to say that having sexual relations with a prostitute makes the two individuals "one body" (1 Cor. 6:16). No one would suggest that a relationship with a prostitute should be permanent, or that an unmarried person who went with a prostitute could never marry someone else.[98]

The indissolubility argument gives rise to absurdities

Imagine a woman who grew up in a non-Christian home where her father was manic-depressive and her mother was timid and ineffective. In her late teens she fell pregnant to her boyfriend and they got married — it seemed a good escape from her family life. The husband became a gambler and drug addict, showing little regard for the children's welfare and becoming increasingly violent towards her. He compelled her to cooperate with him in crimes to support his addictions. After ten years, pregnant with a third child, she managed to leave him. She then became converted and joined a local church. A few years later she was courted by Christian man. The church said her she couldn't remarry because her first marriage still existed in the eyes of God. The woman might ponder her predicament: "If I had not married Jim, but only *cohabited* with him, I would have been free to marry this man who is courting me. But since I married Jim, they say my relationship with him is indissoluble. Is this the law of Christ, or the law of the Pharisees?"[99]

The Bible never says divorced persons are "still married in the eyes of God". If divorced persons were "still married" then they would be under obligation to grant all the privileges of marriage to each other, including maintaining regular sexual intercourse and living together despite their divorce.[100]

The teaching of indissolubility compels "being alone" if a first marriage has failed, whereas God said it is not good for man to be alone (Gen. 2:20). It prohibits remarriage and thus tends to place people in sexual temptation for long periods, whereas Paul advised against lengthy abstinence because of the likelihood of temptation (1 Cor. 7:5) and recommended remarriage to those "de-married" who did not have the gift of abstinence (verse 9).[101]

Those who teach indissolubility usually tolerate a divorcee's remarriage after the event, saying, "If you have already remarried, you should maintain that current marriage as God's will for your life." This is pastoral wisdom for individual cases, but it creates a double standard. According to this double minded approach to indissolubility, divorcees who *have already* remarried can stay in their new marriages (burdened, perhaps, with a sense of sin, but nevertheless having the comfort of a marriage companion), but divorcees who are *not* remarried must stay alone forever. This is unjust: it lays a veil of false guilt on many who have biblical justification for their divorce and remarriage, and it makes some divorcees into eunuchs without biblical justification.

Even worse are the few churches that have avoided this double standard by preaching that a remarried divorcee should leave the second spouse because the second marriage is continuous adultery. Such teaching has been known to turn people off Christianity for life. The New Testament never tells us that a divorced and remarried believer should leave the second spouse and return to the first spouse, not does it say children from the second marriage are illegitimate.[102]

The total indissolubility argument is manifestly absurd. Consider the following proposition. "God's design for marriage is that it be a lifelong commitment. Therefore, even if one of the parties persistently and grievously hurts the other party so the covenant is broken beyond repair, the marriage still exists in the sight of God." This argument is as nonsensical as to say: "God's design for Adam and Eve was for them to live eternally in the Garden of Eden, in unfettered communion with him and without shame. Even though Adam and Eve broke God's law and rebelled against him, they still live in the Garden in God's sight." This is absurd. God recognized the reality that Adam and Eve had sinned. He gave legal remedies for that sin: Jesus' death upon the cross (the spiritual remedy) and the sword of the state to punish and restrain sinners (the temporal remedy).[103] God recognizes reality when a sinning spouse has utterly broken the covenant of marriage. He permits a legal remedy for the betrayal of the covenant — that remedy is divorce with full freedom to remarry.[104]

There is a grim similarity between the doctrine that a marriage is indissoluble and the words of an abuser. The abuser sets different rules for the victim than for himself. He denies historical realities about events in the relationship. He makes out that his behavior is consistent with his words. The indissolubility position says that the law about marriage is different from all other biblical law, it denies the historical reality that the marriage is shattered, and it makes out that its teaching is consistent with the Word.

THE HUSBAND OF ONE WIFE

Paul wrote that church leaders should be *the husband of one wife* (1 Tim. 3:2, 12; Titus 1:6). Some interpret these passages to mean that remarried divorcees are not allowed to hold leadership positions. They use this interpretation to support the idea that remarriage after divorce is sin.

However, *husband of one wife* probably means a church leader should have exemplary sexual morality.[105] It may be similar to our phrase "he only has eyes for one woman". If he is married he should not show sexual interest in a woman other than his wife. He should not keep a concubine as well as a wife — an acceptable practice in Greek culture. He should not resort to slaves or prostitutes for sexual pleasure, as was common in Greek and Roman cultures.[106] If he is single he should not have a casual or self-indulgent approach to the opposite sex.

All the other interpretations of this phrase are implausible. It cannot mean church leaders must not have two successive marriages as this would exclude remarried widowers as well as remarried divorcees.[107] It cannot mean remarried divorcees should all be excluded from leadership, as that would imply a double standard. All remarried divorcees would be prohibited from church leadership, even if they bore no guilt for the divorce or had repented of their sin; yet men who repented of pre-marital sex, theft, alcoholism, witchcraft or murder might (with other criteria being present) be eligible for church leadership.[108]

The parallel phrase *wife of one man* (1 Tim. 5:9) is given as the characteristic of a godly widow who would be entitled to the church's financial support. This phrase cannot mean "currently married" because in 5:9 it is used of widows. Nor can it mean "not remarried after her husband had died" for Paul encouraged younger widows to remarry only five verses later.

Neither can these phrases be about having more than one spouse at a time. Such an interpretation would make nonsense of 1 Timothy 5:9 because it wasn't legal for women to have more than one husband at a time. Gentile men could not legally have more than one wife at once and Jews living in Asia conformed to this practice. Thus Paul would not have been writing to the Asian-based Timothy warning him against polygamy.[109]

SUMMARY

Marriage is not dissolved only by death. The marriage bond is intended to be enduring, but it is not utterly inseparable since grave sins can bring about the dissolution of that bond. The injunction that a church leader should be "the husband of one wife" has nothing to do with remarriage after divorce.

When a victim of abuse finds herself hurt by the misunderstandings of fellow Christians, let her take courage. There are sound arguments against false interpretations. The well-intentioned hand resting on her shoulder with a guilt-inducing message, or the Philistine giant denouncing all divorce and remarriage, are not the iron fist of God that locks her into marriage with an abusive spouse. They are the voices of mistaken Christians whose interpretations of the Bible need to be called into question.

▥ Chapter 6
Is there any hope from the Old Testament?

The Ten Commandments contain many principles relevant to the marriage relationship. For example, to not tell lies means relating truthfully to one's marriage partner; to not murder implies non-violence; to not commit adultery implies sexual loyalty; to honor parents implies that spouses who share the upbringing of children should honor each other in their roles as parents to those children; to not steal implies not squandering assets that are supposed to support your family, nor taking away a person's sense of identity. If every spouse followed the spirit of these commandments there would scarcely be need for divorce.

The Mosaic Law did not explicitly prohibit divorce except in two unusual cases. These two prohibitions have little relevance to domestic abuse so we will not address them here. (They are dealt with briefly in appendix 5.)

Under the Mosaic Law the death penalty was applied to certain crimes such as murder, kidnapping, adultery, rape, incest, homosexuality and witchcraft. This meant that a person might become de-married because their spouse underwent execution after having been found guilty of a capital crime. Apart from this "divorce by execution", the Mosaic Law specifically prescribed divorce for two circumstances: when a husband neglected his purchased wife, and when a husband disliked a wife who had formerly been a prisoner of war. We will discuss these two cases because they have significance for abusive marriages.

DIVORCE FOR NEGLECT OR DEPRIVATION BY A HUSBAND

> Exodus 21:7-11 *⁷ And if a man sells his daughter to be a maidservant ... ⁸ If she does not please her master, who has betrothed her to himself, then he shall let her be redeemed. He shall have no right to sell her to a foreign people, since he has dealt deceitfully with her. ... ¹⁰ If he takes another wife, he shall not diminish her food, her clothing, and her marriage rights. ¹¹ And if he does not do these three for her, then she shall go out free, without paying money.*

Preachers and authors rarely discuss this passage[110] and many victims of domestic abuse have never noticed it. If a victim reads it she probably doesn't connect it with divorce because the words "go out free" do not readily connote "divorce". The abuse victim who has puzzled over this passage may perhaps have thought: "God gives slave-wives in polygamous marriages the right to basic necessities, yet he doesn't mention anything about a full wife in a monogamous marriage. It doesn't seem fair!"

The narrative describes how a woman might be sold by her father as a servant on the understanding that the man who purchased her would marry her. A purchased wife in this position had certain rights. If she did not please her master he had to let her be redeemed: someone in her family could repay the purchase price to the master. The master was not allowed to sell her to foreigners since he had dealt deceitfully with her. The deceit was surely the fact that he had said he would treat her as a wife and then backed down from this commitment. If the husband later took a second wife and deprived the first wife of food, clothing or sexual relations,[111] the law said *she shall go out free, without paying money*, that is, she should be freed from the marriage bond without having to be redeemed by her relatives.

The civil laws in the Old Testament were designed for the ancient nation of Israel, and no nation lives like that today. In the Western world, no man sells his daughter to be a slave-wife, and no man may have two wives. For us, this law does not condone bigamy or the selling of daughters, but it does illustrate an abiding principle that is relevant for today. If a purchased wife was entitled to divorce when her husband deprived her of things essential to her peace, permanence or security, surely a free wife would be entitled to them. If a wife in a polygamous marriage was entitled to them, surely a wife in a monogamous marriage would be.[112] If a husband abuses his wife so that her peace, permanence and security are endangered, she is likewise entitled to a divorce.

This law was designed to prevent injustice to wives and was given alongside other laws dealing with justice for servants, widows, orphans, the poor, sojourners, interpersonal violence, and animal control. This package of laws was given after the Israelites had received the Ten Commandments and before the tabernacle was built. Clearly God saw all these laws as fundamental necessities for the new Israelite nation.

IF A MAN DISLIKED HIS CAPTURED WIFE, HE MUST SET HER FREE AND NOT MISTREAT HER

> Deuteronomy 21:10-14 *[10] When you go out to war against your enemies, and the LORD your God delivers them into your hand, and you take them captive, [11] and you see among the captives a beautiful woman, and desire her and would take her for your wife, [12] then you shall bring her home to your house, and she shall shave her head and trim her nails. [13] She shall put off the clothes of her captivity, remain in your house, and mourn her father and her mother a full month; after that you may go in to her and be her husband, and she shall be your wife. [14] And it shall be, if you have no delight in her, then you shall set her free, but you certainly shall not sell her for money; you shall not treat her brutally, because you have humbled her.*

The abuse victim's response to this passage will probably be similar to her thoughts on the Exodus passage above; she will probably not realize it deals with divorce. She may be dismayed at the thought of a prisoner of war being compelled to become a wife to the conquering party. She may think, "Well it's all very well for that woman to not be treated brutally, but what about me?"

The passage says that when an Israelite soldier wished to marry a prisoner of war from another nation, he had to grant the woman respect by allowing her a month of mourning; after this he could make her his wife. If he had no delight in her he must set her free, not sell her for money. The phrase "set her free" is the Hebrew word *salah* which means divorce. Because the man had humbled her, he must not treat her brutally.

The focus of the passage is the right of the captured wife to fair treatment.[113] It does not bestow male privilege, granting the man liberty to divorce his captured wife merely because she didn't please him. On the contrary, it commands him to release her rather than take advantage of her for his personal gain. Normally a prisoner of war was made into a slave, but this prisoner had been made a wife. Her status as wife afforded her dignity. If he no longer wanted her as wife he could not convert her into a slave, and he was forbidden to mistreat her.

It is not right to limit the application of this law only to captured wives. Whatever applies to someone of the least status in society must necessarily apply to all those of greater status. This principle explains why a superficial reading of the Mosaic Law makes no mention of the rights of an ordinary wife. When I first scoured the Old Testament for guidance about marital abuse it seemed to me that God gave more rights to slaves and prisoners of war than he did to wives! However, the Old Testament teaching on marital relations clearly applies by inference to the case of an abused wife.

In this text the NKJV simply says "set her free", but the Hebrew carries the sense of setting her free if she so desires and letting her go wherever she wishes to go.[114] This is surely a comfort to the abused woman who has been totally preoccupied with trying to please or placate the abuser.

DIDN'T MOSES PROHIBIT REMARRIAGE AFTER DIVORCE?

The Mosaic Law prohibited remarriage after divorce in only two circumstances. Leviticus 21:7-14 states that a priest could not marry a divorced woman. Deuteronomy 24:1-4 said a man could not remarry the woman he had divorced if she had been married to someone else in the intervening period. Deuteronomy 24 has been a highly disputed text in both Jewish and Christian circles and it relates to Jesus' divorce teaching in the New Testament, so we will deal with it at some length.

> Deuteronomy 24:1-4 *¹When a man takes a wife and marries her, and it happens that she finds no favor in his eyes because he has found some uncleanness in her, and he writes her a certificate of divorce, puts it in her hand, and sends her out of his house, ²when she has departed from his house, and goes and becomes another man's wife, ³if the latter husband detests her and writes her a certificate of divorce, puts it in her hand, and sends her out of his house, or if the latter husband dies who took her to be his wife, ⁴then her former husband who divorced her must not take her back to be his wife after she has been defiled; for that is an abomination before the LORD, and you shall not bring sin on the land which the LORD your God is giving you as an inheritance.*

The victim of abuse often feels shamed and disgraced by this passage. The word *defiled* stings like a branding iron. She tends to think that the text says remarriage after divorce makes a woman polluted, vile, filthy and abhorrent. The words *he has found some uncleanness in her* sound like an echo of her own husband's fault-finding. The woman in the text seems to be unable to please her husband, just like a victim of abuse. The main point the victim hears from the text is that if she becomes divorced and remarried, she will become even more detestable, not only to her husband but to the community at large.

In fact, the text is much more a warning and restriction to husbands than a degradation of wives. Let us first observe that verses 1-3 contain no commandment or regulation, they merely narrate a hypothetical situation. They indicate that in the Israelite community some men were divorcing their wives because they found *no favor* in their eyes, *found some uncleanness* in them, or even *detested* them. Only in the fourth verse is there a regulation: the first husband cannot remarry the woman should her second marriage terminate.[115]

Divorce was effected by the husband writing a divorce certificate and giving it to his wife. This practice served many purposes. It removed the man's power to annul the woman's vows. He was no longer responsible for her vows, she was responsible for them herself (Numbers 30).[116] It declared to the woman "you are free to marry any man". It removed ambiguity about the two parties' marital status, preventing a charge of adultery being made by the former husband should the woman enter a new marriage. It helped provide certainty about the real parentage of any child.[117] It helped prevent impulsive divorce and stopped a husband from casually abandoning his wife but reclaiming her later. The divorce certificate, when accompanied by appropriate repayment of dowry, set the husband free from further obligation to provide for his ex-wife.

Is "some uncleanness" a ground for justified divorce?
Many assume that verse one indicates a biblical ground for divorce. Reading the words "she finds no favor in his eyes because he has found some uncleanness in her", these people deduce that the expression "some uncleanness" refers to a genuine offense on the part of the wife, such that her husband had grounds to divorce her. They maintain that divorce was only permitted (or only took place) when the wife had committed serious misconduct.

This line of thinking has led to speculation about what the misconduct could have been. Looking at the Hebrew of the phrase "some uncleanness" (*erwat dabar*) is not particularly helpful. *Dabar* means "matter" or "thing". *Erwat* literally means "nakedness" but it can also mean lack of protection, disgrace, blemish, or dishonor for authority.[118] In Deuteronomy 23:12-14 the phrase *erwat dabar* refers to unburied excrement around the Israelite camp. While excrement is not unrelated to the private parts, this text clearly has no sexual connotation — it suggests a more general concept of anything unclean / unseemly / disgusting / objectionable. Therefore, although *erwat dabar* could be literally translated "nakedness of a thing", it does not necessarily mean sexual sin in Deuteronomy 24. Despite this, certain people read "some uncleanness" as the wife's adultery. Others say it could not be adultery because the penalty for adultery was execution, so it must mean some other kind of serious offense by the wife.

However, all this misses the main point which is this: verse one does not necessarily set out grounds for legitimate divorce at all.[119] It doesn't say "When a man takes a wife and marries her, and it happens that she finds no favor in his eyes because he has found some uncleanness in her, he <u>is permitted</u> to write her a certificate of divorce…" The words "because he has found some uncleanness in her" may not even indicate a legitimate reason why "she finds no favor in his eyes". The words "he has found some uncleanness in her" could simply be a restatement of the idea of "finding no favor". The Old Testament often states an idea two different ways for emphasis, to paint a picture, or because it was the way people said it. Moreover, no one suggests that when Moses wrote about the second husband "detesting" the woman (verse 3) he was indicating justified divorce! The expressions "found some uncleanness" and "detests" tell us nothing about what Moses considered to be legitimate grounds for divorce.

All that can be said about these expressions is that they are part of the preliminary narrative which sets the scene for the commandment in verse four. It could be called "pre-law narrative". Verse one simply describes how some Israelite husbands were behaving — taking objection to their wives and deciding to divorce them. Possibly Israelite men used the term *erwat dabar* quite commonly, across a wide range of situations.

For instance, a callous husband might have taken objection to his wife when he wanted to get rid of her for a trivial reason, perhaps because she no longer appealed to him.[120] A man might have used the phrase *erwat dabar* to insinuate that his wife had committed a grave offense, when in reality he was dumping her out of his own selfishness. Then again, a benevolent husband might have used the non-explicit *erwat dabar* to save face for his sinful wife. If Joseph had gone ahead and divorced Mary, he might have used such wording to minimize her public embarrassment.

Then again, an aggrieved husband might have taken objection to his wife when she had committed some serious offense. Serious offenses might have included: seductive, pre-adulterous conduct; squandering the family fortune; persistently humiliating the husband before family and friends; or slandering his name. Adultery by the wife that could not be proven by two eyewitnesses and so could not receive the death penalty (cf. Deut. 17:6; 19:15) might also have led to divorce. If a husband suspected his wife of adultery but lacked necessary witnesses, he could test his suspicions by bringing her before a priest for the Ordeal of Bitter Water (Numbers 5:11ff.). If a wife baulked at the ordeal, she might not be executed but she would probably have been divorced.[121] If a wife underwent the ordeal and it pointed to her guilt, the vindicated husband would likely divorce his wife; while Numbers 5 does not mention divorce as an outcome, it does not rule it out. We can assume divorce was allowed after the Ordeal of Bitter Water because when Moses wanted to prohibit divorce he did so explicitly (Deut. 22:19, 28-9).[122]

Erwat dabar is a non-specific term. Blenkinsopp says "the term was probably chosen precisely because it was vague, ill-defined, and non-restrictive".[123] Perhaps Moses used the term *erwat dabar* because it was a common expression of the Israelites. Or perhaps he used it because he wanted to show he was talking about a husband who chose to divorce his wife, but did not want to go into the reason(s) why a husband might choose to do this (let alone whether such reasons were justified in God's sight). The husband's reasons for divorce were really not significant to Moses' rule in verse four. The prohibition in verse four applied irrespective of *what* the husband had found objectionable about his wife.

Jesus said Deuteronomy 24 was given because of men's hardness of heart.
The teaching of Jesus indicates that men in Moses' time were sometimes employing divorce without justification for trivial or treacherous reasons. Jesus taught that Moses gave Deuteronomy 24 in the context of men hardheartedly divorcing their wives. *Moses, because of the hardness of your hearts, permitted you to divorce your wives* (Matt. 19:8).

Jesus made this comment because some Pharisees posed him a question about the interpretation of *erwat dabar*. All rabbinic schools in Jesus' day presumed (I would say wrongly) that Deuteronomy 24:1 designated legitimate grounds for divorce. Agreeing on this wrong presumption, the rabbis proceeded to argue over what the legitimate grounds were. (We will look more at the rabbinic views in chapter 9.) Rather than taking sides in the Pharisees' debate,

Jesus tackled their belief that *erwat dabar* must designate legitimate grounds. He did this using a two-pronged argument:

• Firstly he pointed them back to the "one flesh" principle from Genesis. Jesus did not bring up the Genesis texts in order to turn the discussion to the topic of monogamy (although his exegesis of Genesis does imply that monogamy is the norm). He brought up Genesis to show that the Pharisees had wrongly interpreted Deuteronomy 24. If they had given the Genesis texts their due weight, they would not have twisted Deuteronomy 24:1 into a ground for divorce.

• Secondly he explained that "hardness of heart" was the reason Moses gave the passage in Deuteronomy 24. Jesus said *Moses, because of the hardness of your hearts, permitted you to divorce your wives* [emphasis added]. The people with hard hearts were those divorcing their wives, which means the callous individuals in question must have been male. If we read this verse literally, without presupposition or bias, we find it was principally *male* hardness of heart that led to Moses' ruling against the initial couple's remarriage. This is an important point because some commentators mistakenly say that Moses permitted divorce because *women* were hard-heartedly committing sexual sin. Often they argue backwards from the situation in the first century, where some rabbis believed *erwat dabar* meant nothing but adultery, and, since Jesus also allowed divorce for sexual immorality (Matt. 19:9), those rabbis must have been right. However, *erwat dabar* cannot simply equate with adultery committed by a wife because the Mosaic penalty for proven adultery was capital punishment. Jesus does not implicate women as the primary sinners. He does not say, "Moses, because of the hardness of *their* hearts, permitted you to divorce your wives." Nor does he implicate Israelites in general by saying, "Moses, because of your hardness of heart, permitted those divorces." As it stands, Jesus' sentence specifically implicates hardhearted husbands.[124]

Yes, Moses "permitted" the Israelites to divorce their wives, but it does not follow that either "despising a wife" or "finding some uncleanness in her" are permissible grounds for divorce. We looked earlier in this chapter at the divorce passages in Exodus 21 and Deuteronomy 21. These were prescribed and affirmed in order to protect wives from serious abuse or neglect. In contrast, many of the divorces described (but not prescribed) in Deuteronomy 24:1 were merely tolerated by Moses. We know God is long-suffering towards sin, but he is neither the author nor approver of sin.[125] Therefore we know Moses would not have approved of treacherous divorce or indulged those who wished to engage in it. Clearly Moses suffered[126] (or reluctantly tolerated) males divorcing their wives, and he issued the regulation in verse four to prevent a terrible consequence that ensued when men hard-heartedly engaged in divorce.

Why is the woman described as "defiled" in verse four?
If an abused woman remarries after having been divorced, is she thereby contaminated? Verse four states the prohibition: *Her former husband who divorced her must not take her back to be his wife after she has been defiled.* Many commentators have assumed that because the second marriage seems to give rise to the defilement, the second marriage must be sinful and therefore all second marriages (after divorce) are sinful. This assumption intimidates victims of abuse (and other divorcees). It sounds plausible but there is a problem, because when the woman's second marriage is first mentioned it is not said to be wrong, defiled or illegal in any way. It is treated as normal and is neither explicitly condoned nor condemned.

Normally it was not considered adulterous for a divorced woman to enter a second marriage. It was her right and entitlement, considering the first husband had legally divorced her. The second marriage was valid in itself.[127] It did not defile the woman to herself, to her second husband, nor even to a third husband. She was only defiled to her first husband. The second marriage made her permanently "off limits" to the first husband as a future marriage partner.[128]

We could paraphrase Moses' words to mean: If you get rid of your wife, having declared her objectionable, and she marries someone else, you will never be able to have her back. You have declared her unclean (to you); she has acted accordingly and married another, so you must abide by your declaration.[129] McConville suggests verse four should be translated as "Then her first husband, who divorced her, may not take her back as his wife, after she has been declared defiled," [emphasis added]. He adds, "The first husband, in particular, has forfeited his right to marry her because he shamed her, driving her as a result into a second marriage." [130]

The prohibition would have restrained some people from divorce and remarriage.

Moses described the undesirable practice of hardhearted divorce in order to discourage sin by regulating the process and consequences of divorce.[131] The prohibition in verse four restrained an impulsive man from dismissing his wife, for he might regret it later — she might marry another man before he realized his mistake. It restrained an abusive man from using the divorce process as a tool in his arsenal of abuse tactics. It restrained a man from dishonoring his wife by pronouncing her "objectionable" for a trivial or selfish reason. And it prevented a man (and perhaps his ex-wife too) from engineering a breakdown in the second marriage such that it led to divorce, or even perhaps plotting the second husband's death in order to effect remarriage of the first couple.

It also restrained a divorced woman from entering rashly into another marriage. While she remained unmarried, the possibility (but not the obligation) lay open for renewing the marriage with the first husband. If the husband had been at fault, he might rethink and come to his senses. If the wife had been at fault, the discipline of divorce might bring her to repentance. One way or the other, it might become possible and desirable to renew the first marriage. The law, by inclining the woman not to enter precipitately into another marriage, would increase the likelihood that the first marriage could be salvaged.

However, if there were no signs of the man's repentance, or if the wife considered herself glad to be free of her ex-husband, she might look for another husband. By deciding to marry someone else and entering in to a new sexual relationship, she effectively affirmed the finality of the first divorce. By entering into the new marriage she ratified the first divorce and ruled out any possibility of reconciliation with her first husband.

Why is renewal of the first marriage prohibited?

The reason for the prohibition is this: if the man remarries his dismissed wife after she had been married to a subsequent husband, he effectively turns her into a prostitute and himself into a pimp.[132] These are strong words, so let me explain! He must have dismissed her for trivial reasons, as proved by the fact that he later wanted to remarry her. He had abdicated his responsibility of protection to his wife (which was part of his role to lead her in a God-glorifying direction) and placed her in a position where she became the husband of another man. A husband who for selfish purposes makes his wife sexually available to another man is similar to a pimping husband who sells his wife's sexual services to another man.[133] A woman who seals the fact that her first husband is no longer her husband by marrying someone else, but then renews intimacy with her first husband, is similar to a prostitute or an adulteress. The first husband, as head of the original marriage, would bear primary responsibility for hypocritically debasing the institutions of marriage and divorce so that they resembled pimping and adultery.[134]

The Deuteronomic regulation constrained each sex to treat both divorce and remarriage as solemn events, to be entered into with much seriousness, for a new marriage by the woman would forever cut off any possibility of restoring the first marriage. It made men think twice about divorcing their wives and made divorced women think twice about marrying someone else. Sprinkle comments, "From this passage it is tempting to say: What God has put asunder, let no man join together."[135] Once a divorced woman had embarked on a new covenant with a different husband, the solemnity of this "new start" was never to be undermined or treated lightly, even if her "new start" failed through her second husband's death or divorce. Her first husband could not treat it lightly and neither could she. They were each to take responsibility for the fact that their former marriage was truly over and would remain so for ever.

THE KEY TEACHINGS OF THE MOSAIC LAW

The Law encouraged fidelity, loyalty and respect between husband and wife. However, apart from a couple of minor exceptions, the Mosaic Law on divorce did not explicitly prohibit men engaging in divorce when they disliked their wives. If the husband initiated divorce this was tolerated, but if the ex-wife married someone else and that marriage terminated, the first couple could never reconcile. When a husband's dislike led (or might lead) to wife abuse rather than male-initiated divorce, the law commanded the man to divorce.

So we see that Deuteronomy 24:1-4 taught the following:

• normally, a second remarriage after a divorce was not subject to penalty (it was therefore quite different from adultery, which was penalized);

• a man who divorced his wife claiming to have found some fault in her was forbidden to remarry her after she had been married to a second husband;

• a woman's remarriage after such a divorce sealed the end of the first marriage forever.

It is ironic, and very sad, that some Christians have interpreted almost the complete opposite — that remarriage after divorce is always and in every respect equal to adultery, and that a second marriage following a divorce does *not* confirm that the first marriage has indeed ended.

▥ Chapter 7
But I want to be faithful to my marriage vows!

Some Christians claim the marriage covenant may never be broken because God never breaks his covenant. They say there is a difference between covenants and contracts: that covenants are unconditional because they are fulfilled through grace alone, whereas contracts stipulate terms and conditions. They say Christians should not have a "contract mentality" which focuses on terms and conditions, because that is how the world behaves.

Victims of marital abuse often apply this viewpoint to themselves, believing they must stay unconditionally committed to the marriage no matter how badly their spouse sins. The belief that marriage covenants ought to be unconditional intimidates a victim of abuse from examining her spouse's behavior. If she is "tempted" to think critically about his conduct, she censors her thoughts: "I must not think of this marriage as a contract; I must not have a mental balance sheet about my husband's contribution to this marriage." She may suppress all thoughts of irritation or annoyance because she doesn't want to think critically of others. This kind of thinking turns her into a doormat because it precludes the problem-solving stance characteristic of healthy relationships.

It is misleading to say a covenant has nothing in common with a contract when discussing the biblical world-view. Although English has the two words "contract" and "covenant", the original languages of the Bible use "covenant" for both concepts.[136] We may continue to cultivate the view that covenant is "the solemn engagement of one person to another … the giving over of oneself in the commitment of troth … the promise of unreserved fidelity, of whole-souled commitment".[137] We should enter a marriage fully intent on it being permanent. We should do our best to contribute to its longevity. However, we must not exclude any implication of terms and conditions from our understanding of the marital covenant. The marriage covenant is not entirely unconditional.

The reason for this is that God's covenant is somewhat different from human covenants. God's covenant with his people is unconditional and unilateral, being fulfilled entirely through the electing grace of God, who cannot sin. However, all human covenants are conditional and bilateral, being agreements between two parties who are sinners. Since marriage promises are mutual, it follows that the blessings and security of marriage are dependent upon each party fulfilling his or her promises. Penalties may need to be invoked if the promises are not honored.

Even God's covenantal dealings with his people are sometimes expressed in condition-like terms, such as the Mosaic covenant which promised blessings for obedience and curses for disobedience. When Israel repeatedly broke the covenant, God said: *And I took my staff,*

Beauty, and cut it in two, that I might break the covenant which I had made with all the peoples (Zech. 11:10). God repeatedly used the images of separation and divorce when complaining about Israel's unfaithfulness to the covenant, for example, in Jeremiah chapters 2 and 3.

In the same spirit, God occasionally made specific promises to a person or group but he did not fulfill them when that person or group behaved sinfully. One example is when the spies returned with a bad report (Num. 14; cf. Exod. 33:1-2); another is how God dealt with the house of Eli (1 Sam. 2:27-36). The common theme is that if one party persistently breaks the covenant, the sinned against party is permitted to state that the covenant is dead. A "covenantal death certificate" may then be issued on the basis of the sin that has already occurred. In the case of marriage, the document signifying the death of a marriage covenant is a divorce certificate.

Some Christians cite the covenant between Israel and the Gibeonites to argue that divorce is not permissible. The story goes like this: God told Israel to make no covenant with the tribes from Canaan. The Gibeonite tribe manipulated Israel into making a covenant with them by pretending they didn't come from Canaan (Josh. 9). Although this covenant was ill advised, God expected Israel to actively honor it by making war against the Gibeonites' enemies (Josh. 10). Later, when Saul broke the Gibeonite covenant, God chastised Israel (2 Sam. 21:1-9). This story had been used to claim that all divorce is sinful. However, the story only shows it is wrong to break a covenant *without good grounds*. In the Gibeonite story, the Gibeonites behaved well once the covenant had been made; Israel had no grounds to abandon the covenant. God chastised Israel not for breaking the Gibeonite covenant as such, but for breaking it without cause.

IF I BREAK MY VOWS, WON'T I BE GUILTY?

Many victims stay in abusive marriage because they would feel terribly guilty if they broke their vows. The Bible does treat vows seriously. However, the Old Testament has special rules about women's vows, which, like other Old Testament laws, illustrate an abiding principle.

Numbers chapter 30 describes different rules for women's vows depending on whether the woman is a young woman in her father's house, a married woman, divorced or widowed. The rule for married women is as follows. If a married woman makes (or has previously made) a vow and her husband hears it and makes no response to her on the day that he hears it, then her vow shall stand, she is bound to keep it (verses 6-7, 10-11). However, the husband can annul his wife's vow: *... if her husband overrules her on the day that he hears it, he shall make void her vow, ... and the LORD will forgive her* (verse 8, 12). If the husband does assent to his wife's vow but later annuls it, he will be guilty: *... if her husband makes no response whatever to her from day to day, then he confirms all her vows or all the agreements that bind her. ... But if he does make them void after he has heard them, then he shall bear her guilt* (verses 14-15).

Once a husband has confirmed his wife's vows, he clearly has a responsibility to ensure she keeps them. In a sense, *her* vows become *his*.[138] Following this principle, it is impossible for a vow to be used to bring about family disunity, or to permit insubordination alongside godly leadership in the home.[139]

We can derive from Numbers 30 an application to abusive marriages. A wife's marriage vows were certainly witnessed by her husband — when the couple underwent the marriage ceremony. The fact that he holds his peace about them from day to day shows that he confirms these vows. Yet vows are subject to God's law: a person may not use a vow to sidestep the law of God (Mark 7:6-13). If at some stage a husband's conduct becomes so bad that his wife is constrained to break her marriage vows and file for divorce by the principles of 1 Corinthians 7:15, Exodus 21:10-11 and Deuteronomy 21:14, then Numbers 30 indicates *the husband shall bear her iniquity*. The penalty for breaking her marriage vows will fall on him and she will not bear guilt.

▥ Chapter 8
"God hates divorce" — slogan or scripture?

The words "I hate divorce, says the Lord God of Israel" which occur in many translations of Malachi 2:16 have frequently been paraphrased as the slogan "God hates divorce". At face value this slogan appears to condemn all divorce and all acts of divorcing, with no thought for who is the innocent, or less guilty, party. Understood like this, it might appear that God hates *all* divorce.

When Christians use the slogan "God hates divorce" they often have no idea how hurtful their words can be to those who might use divorce for disciplinary reasons — those who divorce adulterers, abusers or deserters. Christians who *do* realize that the slogan may cause pain to an innocent spouse often try to soften things by saying "God hates the sin but not the sinner" or "Divorce is a sin, but God forgives." However, such expressions may not make the innocent spouse feel much better, for every serious Christian knows that the forgiveness of sins is the forgiveness of *sins*. Defining all divorce as sin (albeit forgivable sin) makes the sensitive conscience of an abuse victim tremble with fear. How dare she divorce if it so displeases God? She does not want to be a hypocrite by knowingly and deliberately displeasing God, then asking him for forgiveness.

Victims of abuse whose partners have not committed adultery feel especially condemned and entrapped by the "God hates divorce" slogan. Adultery is an acceptable reason for divorce in most churches; desertion (abandonment) is an acceptable reason in quite a few churches. If an abuse victim does not have these "acceptable" grounds, she will almost certainly feel the slogan "God hates divorce" as a divine edict to stay in the terrible marriage, or (if she has left the marriage) as God's disapproval of her separation/divorce.

Accuracy about the meaning of this text is vital for our discussion. What does Malachi 2:16 actually say and require of us? In order to unpack this, we will circle the foothills of the mountain, so to speak, then climb the slopes, then tackle the summit (the slogan itself).

TREACHERY UPON TREACHERY

Malachi 2:10-17 condemns treachery — treachery against Israel's covenant with God when men were marrying pagan wives, and the treachery of men divorcing their first wives. These infidelities, each breaking a "oneness", are dealt with as two separate instances of treachery in the text, though they may have been "two parts of a coordinated event".[140]

The word "treacherously" is found five times in verses 10-17:

> [10]Have we not all one Father? Has not one God created us? Why do we deal **treacherously** with one another by profaning the covenant of the fathers? [11]Judah has dealt **treacherously**, and an abomination has been committed in Israel and in Jerusalem, for Judah has profaned the LORD's holy institution which He loves: He has married the daughter of a foreign god. [12]May the LORD cut off from the tents of Jacob the man who does this, being awake and aware, and who brings an offering to the LORD of hosts. [13]And this is the second thing you do: You cover the altar of the LORD with tears, with weeping and crying; so He does not regard the offering anymore, nor receive it with goodwill from your hands. [14]Yet you say, "For what reason?" Because the LORD has been witness between you and the wife of your youth, with whom you have dealt **treacherously**; yet she is your companion and your wife by covenant. [15]But did He not make them one, having a remnant of the Spirit? And why one? He seeks godly offspring. Therefore take heed to your spirit, and let none deal **treacherously** with the wife of his youth. [16]"For the LORD God of Israel says that He hates divorce, for it covers one's garment with violence," says the LORD of hosts. "Therefore take heed to your spirit, that you do not deal **treacherously**."
>
> [17]You have wearied the LORD with your words; yet you say, "In what way have we wearied Him?" In that you say, "Everyone who does evil is good in the sight of the LORD, and He delights in them," or, "Where is the God of justice?" (emphasis added)[141]

As well as treachery, the context repeatedly refers to hypocritical spirituality: insincere sin offerings, false tears, and those who say God delights in evildoers. The Lord may not be visibly exacting retribution, but this doesn't prove that everyone's conduct is righteous. God is wearied by the people's self-congratulation and audacious denial of sins.

Such self-justification can be observed in many abusers. One victim I know reported that her partner said to her, "Look — my behavior can't be bad because God hasn't struck me down!" In *Broken and Battered,* which recounts the lives of two battered Christian women, one of the husbands defended himself to his wife by saying: "Everybody sins — look at Adam and Eve. We all screw up and lie … God forgives sin as long as we say we're sorry. That's what the gospel is all about … You can't possibly be so self-righteous, judgmental and anti-Christian as to think God would kick anyone out of the kingdom who fails a little!"[142] Similar sentiments can be expressed by bystanders who favor the abuser: "He's such a good man, God approves of him; he's a good father, a good husband, and a fine member of the community and the church." (cf. Jer. 23:14, 17)

IT'S AS IF HE HAS BLOOD ON HIS HANDS

The NKJV translates the middle part of Malachi 2:16 with the words, *for it covers one's garment with violence.* We will look one by one at the words "garment", "violence and "covers".

The word "garment" is *lebush,* which is used both literally and figuratively in the Old Testament for garment, apparel or clothing. *Lebush* and its close relative *labash* are often used to signify the moral state of a person as something they have "put on" or are "wearing".[143]

The Jewish custom of tearing one's garments when in a state of great distress was a way of depicting one's inner state. There is a prefix attached to the word "garment" in verse 16 which indicates the garment is the thing covered, not the covering itself.[144]

The word "violence" is the Hebrew word *hamas.* It can mean physical violence or, more generally, any wrongdoing inflicting serious injury. In Genesis 16:5, when Sarai found that Hagar was despising her, she told Abram: *You are responsible for the wrong (hamas) I am suffering.*[145] Some translators render *hamas* as "crime" or "lawlessness" in Malachi 2:16.

The word "covers" is a third person masculine singular ("he covers"). This would suggest that the divorcing man soils his soul by the violence, harm or criminal injustice he has committed through his covenantal unfaithfulness.[146] The man who betrays the wife of his youth hypocritically portrays that he is doing no wrong, but God pronounces such a man guilty, using an idiomatic expression rather like "He's got blood on his hands."[147]

WHO FEELS THE HATRED?

In Malachi 2:16 the word "hates" *(śānē')* occurs next to *šallah* which means divorce. *Śānē'* is often used elsewhere in the Old Testament when describing a husband's attitude towards his wife.[148] In several ancient near-eastern[149] marriage documents, we find "hate" appearing in the context of divorce. For example, "the phrase 'hated, divorced' has a striking parallel in the Neo-Assyrian marriage contract ... 'If he hates, divorces, he must pay'."[150] There are good reasons to see *hates divorce (śānē' šallah)* as a compound term meaning "aversion divorce", that is, divorce without justification where the divorcing spouse simply has an aversion for the other spouse.[151]

In Malachi 2:16, the subject of the verb "hates" is not explicit: the Hebrew does not read "God hates" or "the husband hates". All we know from the verb is that the person who hates is third person masculine singular ("he", or "one"), just like "covers". It is certainly not the first person "I hate".

Now we come to our main point. Most Bible translations have taken the subject of the first verb to be God (God hates) and thereby changed *he hates* to the first person *I hate.* This is unfaithful to the Hebrew text and it creates an awkward grammatical shift between *I hate* and *he covers.* If Malachi says God hates divorce, this places Malachi in opposition to Moses, who condoned disciplinary divorce for cases of abuse or neglect. It also sets Malachi against Ezra, who required divorce of foreign wives when the continuation of the Jewish nation was in jeopardy. And it begs the question: If Malachi says that God hates (all) divorce, why did Jesus not quote Malachi when the Pharisees claimed that Deuteronomy 24 approved of divorce?[152]

Some translations try to overcome the grammatical disjunction between the different subjects of *I hate...he covers* by translating the passage as *I hate divorce...it covers...*We need not resort to such a solution. The subject of hates is third person, not first, and we should only depart from the plain sense of a text if compelled by something in the text. Nothing here compels such a departure.

It makes sense to maintain the same subject (the divorcing husband) for both verbs. The Holman Christian Standard Bible renders it *"If he hates and divorces [his wife]," says the Lord God of Israel, "he covers his garment with injustice," says the Lord of Hosts.*[153] The English Standard Version has *For the man who hates and divorces, says the Lord, covers his garment with violence, says the Lord of hosts.*[154] Since 1868 at least eighteen scholars have said that "he hates... he covers" is the most faithful way to render the Hebrew, with "he" being the divorcing husband. (See appendix 7 for a list of these translations.)

GOD DID NOT SAY "I HATE DIVORCE"!

What Malachi condemned was treacherous divorce, males who divorced their wives unjustifiably out of hatred and aversion.[155] On the authority of God, Malachi was saying, "Aversion divorce is unfaithfulness."[156] However, Malachi said nothing about disciplinary divorce.

God did not say "I hate divorce", nor did he condemn all divorce. We should therefore stop using the slogan "God hates divorce". If we still need a slogan, it would be better to say, "God hates treacherous divorce, but he does not hate disciplinary divorce."

The translation of Malachi 2:16 is an important matter. The mistranslation has bred a slogan that many ordinary Christians use (against themselves or others) like a blunt instrument, as if God hates *all* divorce. This has had such a big impact on the Christian community that more careful theologians, who have never claimed that God hates *all* divorce, have been fighting a losing battle against the slogan view.

The translation of Malachi 2:16 is also important for another reason. Some scholars seem to conclude that although "he hates" refers to the divorcing man (not God), this modification is not monumentally significant. After all (they say), isn't a condemnation of unjustified/treacherous divorce much the same as a condemnation of all divorce? I would ask male theologians in particular to try to put themselves into the shoes of victims and not diminish the significance of this translation issue. Let me reiterate that victims of abuse can feel immense fear and guilt if they believe God hates divorce. When a person empathizes with the pain of a scripturally-entrapped victim of abuse, they will appreciate the vast difference between the wrong translation and the right one.

It would do the Christian world a great service if future Bible translations take the same approach as the Holman Christian Standard Bible and the English Standard Version. Commentaries, scholarly papers and books like this one cannot hope to undo the misunderstanding that is so entrenched in the Christian community. Although the ESV and the HCSB have corrected matters,[157] there are many other Bible versions which, as yet, have not. We cannot afford to have such a minority of Christians knowing the real meaning of Malachi's statement on divorce.

part D ▦

JESUS' TEACHING

▥ Chapter 9
Isn't adultery the ONLY ground for divorce?

Matthew 19:9 *And I say to you, whoever divorces his wife, except for sexual immorality, and marries another, commits adultery; and whoever marries her who is divorced commits adultery.*

Jesus' divorce pronouncement in Matthew 19 is often taken to mean that the sole ground for divorce and remarriage is if the opposite spouse has sex with a third party. A less common interpretation is that while Matthew 19 gives sexual immorality as the sole ground for divorce, it does not permit remarriage. Much controversy has occurred between these two positions, involving debate over the question, "In a divorce for adultery, can the innocent party remarry?" This debate has somewhat drawn attention away from a third interpretation. The third view is that while Matthew 19 permits divorce and remarriage if one's spouse has sex with a third party, this is not the *sole* ground for divorce since Paul gave another ground.

Some Christians are not confident that Paul even mentioned grounds for divorce, because the words "divorce" and "remarriage" do not occur in 1 Corinthians 7:15 (as it is translated). Others are somewhat confused by the apparent contradiction between Jesus and Paul. If Jesus made a general ruling against divorce/remarriage, with sexual immorality as the "only" exception, how could Paul give another, apparently different, ground for divorce?

All these factors have meant that the Pauline ground has very much played "second fiddle" in the divorce debate. Thus, many Christians' views of divorce are primarily shaped by Matthew's divorce texts and in particular Matthew 19.

Up until recently, this interpretative landscape has acted like a straitjacket for many survivors of abuse. Those who take Matthew 19 as the preeminent rule commonly advise women, "If your husband has not had sex with a third party, you are not allowed to seek a divorce." For example, a wife wanted to divorce her husband who had attempted to rape the couple's daughter, but their minister forbade the divorce because the daughter had fought the husband off and no illicit intercourse had occurred. In another case, a husband, a mechanic, had a woman waiting in the wings but had not had sex with her, preferring to arrange for his wife's car brakes to fail on a winding road so he could "legitimately" marry the new woman after his wife's death. Fortunately, the wife discovered his sabotage without mishap. She also discovered the existence of the other woman. The church told her she had no grounds for divorce because adultery had not occurred.[158]

An abuse victim who seeks a biblically legitimate divorce finds her task very hard under these conditions. If the criterion for obtaining a divorce is that one's spouse has committed sexual infidelity with a third party, many victims of abuse will not qualify since many abusers do not have other sexual partners. While some abusers are philanderers, others are socially inept loners who are most unlikely to engage in sex with a third party.

There are some cases where the abuser is not guilty of "ordinary" infidelity (sex with another adult) but *does* sexually abuse his wife and/or children. It is difficult and embarrassing for a victim to seek divorce on the ground of her partner's abusive or perverted sex - far more difficult than seeking divorce because he has another woman. If a husband is addicted to pornography, commits marital rape, enforces gross sexual perversions, or re-enacts pornographic scenes on the wife, yet does not have sex outside the marriage, some Christians may still think of him as a "one-woman-man". If he commits incest with a child and pleads "not guilty" when charged by police, it is extremely difficult to get a criminal conviction. Under such circumstances it may be a daunting task to convince church officials that sexual immorality has occurred and thus divorce should be permitted.

Other factors also make it hard for the abuse victim who seeks a biblically legitimate divorce on the ground of her husband's sexual immorality. After prolonged separation, some abusers "vanish off the map" (perhaps to avoid paying child support), so whether they re-partner is unknown. And if an abuser does have sex outside the marriage, he may keep his unfaithfulness secret, like any other adulterer.

So a woman married to an abuser who seems sexually "faithful" (by the "sex with another adult" definition) usually believes her case does not fall within the special category of "permitted" divorce. She thinks — erroneously — that, for her, divorce is not permitted and remarriage would be adultery.

Such a survivor may condemn herself to living with the abuser until death, or living in "separation limbo" but never divorcing. If she does divorce, she may never remarry because she fears it would be adultery. She will constantly be at risk of being condemned by fellow Christians who (perhaps unintentionally) suggest that (1) her divorce was biblically unjustified, (2) she should reconcile with her estranged husband, and (3) remarriage is off-limits for her. If she is raising children, this means they will grow up without any possibility of having a godly step-father. (Step families sometimes have difficult relationships, but in some cases the step-father's presence enhances the children's lives.) The woman also knows that many single Christian men may not consider her as a potential wife, for they believe they would commit adultery if they married her.

THE JEWS' DISTORTION OF DEUTERONOMY 24

In order to arrive at the meaning of Matthew 19, we need to understand the cultural background. By the time of Jesus, the Jews were distorting the meaning of Deuteronomy 24 in order to "legitimize" treacherous divorce and disguise its hardhearted nature. The School of Hillel and the School of Shammai had different interpretations of Deuteronomy 24:

> The School of Shammai says: A man should not divorce his wife unless he has found unchastity in her, for it is written, *Because he hath found in her **indecency** in anything.* And the School of Hillel say: [He may divorce her] even if she spoiled a dish for him, for it is written, *Because he hath found in her indecency in **anything**.*[159]

The differing opinions revolved around the interpretation of *she finds no favor in his eyes because he has found some uncleanness in her* (Deut. 24:1). The Shammaites and Hillelites mistakenly believed that the term "some uncleanness" (Hebrew: *erwat dabar*) specified valid grounds for divorce, although they argued over the meaning of the term. The word *"erwat"* has connotations of "uncleanness", "nakedness", or "unseemliness", whilst *"dabar"* means "thing" or "matter". The School of Shammai understood *erwat dabar* to mean adultery and attempted adultery. The School of Hillel interpreted the two words *erwat* and *dabar* separately. They allowed divorce for adultery (which they derived from the first word *erwat*), but they also allowed divorce for "any matter" (which they derived from the second word *dabar*).[160] Thus they asserted that if the wife burnt a dish, the husband could legitimately divorce her.

Both schools placed great importance on the divorce certificate. If a certificate was issued according to accepted protocol (correct names, dates and method of serving the document), it was deemed a valid divorce.

To obtain a divorce, a man could go to a Hillelite or a Shammaite court (which meant selecting lawyers who represented the school of their choice).[161] The differences between the schools did not cause much difficulty for the general society. Both court systems coexisted because both recognized each other's divorces. The two schools disputed what *erwat dabar* could cover, but they did not dispute that *erwat dabar* designated legitimate grounds for divorce. Both approaches quite overshadowed the original significance of the text in Deuteronomy 24 — the prohibition in verse 4.[162]

In one sense, the differences between the two schools were like an academic debate — interesting only to teachers of the Law. But the differences were relevant to ordinary Jews in that each kind of divorce had different effects. If a man used a Shammaite divorce, there was a high burden of proof: he needed witnesses who could testify to existence of his wife's illicit relationship. The husband and wife were both humiliated because the matter was "made public". However, the advantage of using a Shammaite divorce was that if he did prove the accusation, he kept the wife's dowry. On the other hand, if he used a Hillelite divorce he did not have to call witnesses ("any matter" was so subjective that it did not need proof), but he had to pay the dowry back to the wife.[163] Thus, Jewish men weighed up which kind of divorce would be easiest/best for themselves. Some righteous Jews even weighed this up on the basis of what would be best for their wives. We may perhaps see an example of this with Joseph and Mary. Since Jewish betrothal was as binding as marriage, Joseph would have had to divorce Mary to sever their engagement. He suspected her to be guilty of premarital fornication but as a "just man" (Matt. 1:19) he did not want to humiliate her in a public trial, nor did he want to punish her by impounding her dowry. So it would appear that he determined to use a Hillelite divorce — *he was minded to put her away secretly*.[164]

Hillelite divorces had become available about the time of Jesus' birth. During Jesus' ministry, both Hillelite and Shammaite divorces were available to men.[165]

In addition, women as well as men could apply for divorce on the grounds of Exodus 21, from either a Shammaite or Hillelite court. We assume this because both legal schools detailed what spouses must minimally grant to each other in the provision of food, clothing and sexual intercourse — the three marital duties specified in Exodus 21:10-11. In addition, there are rabbinic rulings giving instances of marital disrespect, mistreatment, humiliation and sexual neglect, and setting out the appropriate penalty in each instance, with different schools setting the penalties slightly differently.[166] The accounts read like precedents established by actual court cases. They cover mistreatment by either sex and appear to give fairly equal treatment to victims regardless of their gender. In cases of cruelty, the penalty was divorce with the innocent partner keeping the dowry; in cases of sexual neglect, incremental changes were made to the dowry in favor of the innocent partner, to attempt to persuade the rebellious partner to resume sexual relations. The early rabbis clearly saw Exodus 21:10-11 as a case law which gave rights to both wives and husbands. A wife or a husband could appeal to the courts for a divorce on the principles of Exodus 21 if their partner was mistreating them.

The Hillelite interpretation of Deuteronomy 24:1 was influential at the time of Jesus' ministry, indeed it was probably the most popular method of divorce for men.[167] Although there was a financial disincentive for husbands (return of the dowry), a Hillelite divorce was an unproblematic legal process. Some men would have delighted in the ease with which it allowed them to get rid of unappealing wives. And a husband mistreated by his wife could readily issue a divorce using the Hillelite "any matter" interpretation of Deuteronomy 24:1, so he might elect not to use Exodus 21:10-11 as grounds for divorce if he had no difficulty returning the wife's dowry. In contrast, it appears that a wife's only way of seeking divorce under Jewish law was by requesting a court, according to principles that could be inferred from Exodus 21:10-11, to persuade her husband to sign a divorce certificate.[168]

Deuteronomy 24:1 was not a law setting out grounds for divorce.
Having examined the cultural background, let us return to the divorce discussion between Jesus and the Pharisees. This discussion has been greatly misunderstood by Christians, even though we have known about the Hillelite/Shammaite debate for many years. Naturally, Christians have been affronted by Hillel's self-serving concept of male-privileged entitlement and the extremity of his example (the "matter" can equal a spoilt dish). But they have tended to overlook Hillel's primary fault: namely, that he made the narrative detail of Deuteronomy 24:1 into a law. Shammai's major fault was the same. He made verse one a law.

To see this, we must examine Matthew 19:3-8.[169]

> [3]The Pharisees also came to Him, testing Him, and saying to Him, "Is it lawful for a man to divorce his wife for just any reason?" [4]And He answered and said to them, "Have you not read that He who made them at the beginning 'made them male and female' [5]and said 'For this reason a man shall leave his father and mother and be joined to his wife, and the two shall become one flesh'? [6]So then they are no longer two but one flesh. Therefore, what God has joined together, let not man separate." [7]They said to Him, "Why then did Moses command to give a certificate of divorce, and to put her away?" [8]He said to them, "Moses, because of the hardness of your hearts, permitted you to divorce your wives, but from the beginning it was not so."

In the first part of Jesus' rebuke, he drove their thinking back to Genesis. The creation ordinance of marriage in Genesis 2 indicates that God intended marriage to be a permanent, committed relationship. In the second part of his rebuke, Jesus returned to the issue with which the Pharisees opened the discussion: the interpretation of Moses' words *erwat dabar* in Deuteronomy 24:1.

As we saw in chapter six, Jesus explained that Moses wrote those words not to command or authorize divorces but because of the hardness of heart of some husbands: they had a callous disregard for their marriage covenants and were divorcing their wives for no good reason. The so-called "Mosaic concession" was not an indulgent concession; Moses simply described the undesirable sin of hardhearted divorce in order to regulate the worst outcome which might eventuate after that kind of divorce — the abuse of divorce and remarriage so that they resembled pimping and adultery. In effect, Jesus told the Pharisees: "Moses gave this passage in Deuteronomy 24 because of *your hardness of heart.* He did not license such divorce to indulge you in your selfishness and obstinacy. He did not give formal approval to men who wanted to divorce their wives treacherously. *From the beginning it was not so.* If you had interpreted Deuteronomy 24 in the light of Genesis 2, you would never have drawn the conclusions you have!"[170]

WHAT GOD HAS JOINED TOGETHER, LET NOT MAN SEPARATE

Some people read *what God has joined together, let not man separate* and think, "Maybe God hasn't blessed some marriages, or been involved in their formation. Maybe it is all right to separate *those* marriages." We have no indication that Jesus meant to distinguish "spiritual" marriages, where God united the couple, from merely human marriages where God was not involved in the union. There is no indication in the creation ordinance, or in Matthew 19 or Mark 10, that we may treat marriages differently, depending on whether or not God was involved in uniting the couple.

So what is the meaning of *what God has joined together*? God created male and female intending them to fit and complement each other in the committed relationship of marriage. Every marriage between a man and a woman is a divinely made union — it is "joined by God" in the sense that it has taken place as part of his providence and it follows the basic pattern created and ordained by him. (This is why homosexual relations should not be called "marriage" if the term is to be used biblically.) The fact that a couple may or may not invite God's blessing and involvement in their marriage does not change the fact that they are joined according to the design God used for Adam and Eve.[171]

The instruction "what God has joined together let not man separate" does not mean that it is metaphysically impossible to disjoin two people once they have been joined together in marriage. God prohibits stealing, but that doesn't mean it is impossible to steal. "Let not" is not the same as "can not". The marriage bond can indeed be broken — by sin — hence the command *let not man separate.*[172]

THE EXCEPTION CLAUSE

> Matthew 19:9 *And I say to you, whoever divorces his wife, except for sexual immorality, and marries another, commits adultery; and whoever marries her who is divorced commits adultery.*[173]

The words *except for sexual immorality* are authentic to Jesus and could not have been inserted later by Matthew (or some other editor of Matthew's Gospel) as some commentators have suggested. The Bible is divinely inspired and without error; men did not write (or edit) it merely by themselves. The beginning words *I say unto you...* emphasize that Jesus himself is making this statement. If we countenance the idea of Matthew or a later editor "adding" something that Jesus did not say, we are saying that someone deliberately and knowingly passed off his own inserted words as Jesus' words.[174] Rather than supposing that Matthew added words, it is better to suppose that in Mark's parallel account of this discussion between the Pharisees and Jesus, Mark omitted the exception clause.

It is wrong to say that the exception clause in Matthew must be interpreted in the light of Mark 10:11-12 and Luke 16:18, which have no exception clause. Thomas Edgar says that "to consider the less detailed account as determinative is abnormal interpretative procedure."[175] John Owen says, "It is a rule owned by all, that where the same thing is reported by several evangelists, the briefer, short, more imperfect expressions, are to be measured and interpreted by the fuller and larger."[176]

The exception is for sexual immorality (*porneia*)

The term "sexual immorality" in verse 9 is the Greek word *porneia*. It is a general term for illicit sexual activity and includes such things as pre-marital sex, adultery, rape, homosexuality, pedophilia, bestiality, incest and all sexual sins referred to in Leviticus 18.[177] Some authors have suggested that *porneia* could also cover domestic violence, but this is not really sustainable. *Porneia* is only used figuratively for spiritual infidelity (humans worshipping a false god). When it refers to human relationships it always refers to sexual sin, not some non-sexual variety of covenantal violation. It is important to recognize that Jesus did not use the word *moicheia* ("adultery") but the broader word *porneia* and therefore all forms of illicit sex (including sodomy, incest, enforced prostitution, bestiality, marital rape) qualify as exceptions as well as adultery. This is quite relevant to abusive marriages, as such practices sometimes occur in marital abuse scenarios.

Some say that *porneia* must include sexual intercourse with a third party, but that would rule out the sharing of nudity, caresses, masturbation and oral sex. These things can also involve the kind of emotional bonding, erotic stimulation and orgasm which should be reserved for one's marriage partner. Furthermore, we need to consider the question of cyber sex (explicitly sexual communication with a third party by telephone or internet). Videophones and computer cameras permit cyber conversations using both image and voice, and we can already project 3-D images into real world space. Perhaps cyber sex will extend to two people having dual-interactivity via projected 3-D images of each other's naked bodies in real world space. How meaningful will it then be to define *porneia* as "actual intercourse"?

A question we might ask today is: does *porneia* include pornography? The word "pornography" derives from *porneia*, yet we cannot necessarily leap to conclusions from this. Pornographic art was available in Gentile areas of the Roman Empire, but nothing like the flood of pornography available in our day. In our current context it is possible to argue that the *habitual* use of pornography might come within the term *porneia* for the purposes of our discussion of Matthew. This should not be taken to mean that a wife may divorce her husband if, for example, he is accidentally exposed to pornography and gets drawn into brief self-indulgence.

If a man does get drawn into pornography, we must distinguish between falling into sin and living in sin. The quality of a man's response to being "caught" by his wife will indicate a lot, as will the quality of any repentance he shows. A sincerely repentant person will "turn from his sin with grief and hatred, and turn to God with full resolve and effort after new obedience".[178] If the man who has fallen into pornography does not show real effort in struggling against this sin, then his repentance has to be questioned. Local church leaders may need to decide on individual cases, but surely if a man is addicted to pornography one could argue that this comes within the ground of *porneia.* If his indulgence in pornography defiles his wife and children (either by being exposed to the material themselves, or by becoming objects of the man's fantasy-directed lust), then this is probably an indication that the wife has put up with or hidden from the problem for too long.

With sexual immorality, the innocent spouse may divorce and remarry

In the seventeenth century the Puritan theologian, John Owen, stated the meaning of the exception clause very succinctly: "Every exception is a particular case that is contradictory to a general rule. The rule here in general is: 'He that divorces his wife and marries another commits adultery.' The exception here is: 'He that divorces his wife because of fornication and marries another does not commit adultery.'"[179] (Fornication is an old fashioned word for sexual immorality.)

The cultural context also tells us that the exception clause permits the innocent spouse to remarry. To the Jews of Jesus' day, divorce always implied freedom to remarry; they had never heard of "separation from bed and board" (without freedom to remarry). This means that if Jesus had intended to permit divorce for sexual immorality but not permit remarriage after it, he would have had to spell this out to the Pharisees much more clearly than he did.

This man's freedom has several aspects. Let us imagine he is married to a Christian who has an affair but then repents of her adultery. The husband, as a fellow Christian, must accept her repentance and forgive her sin, as Christ commands us. However, he is not obliged to reconcile with her as a husband. He may reconcile with her in marriage *or* he may divorce her, and he is free to marry another should he choose the latter. The exception clause is a genuine exception and gives liberty and relief to the innocent party.

The case of a Christian spouse contracting venereal disease during an extra-marital affair demonstrates the equity of the divine ruling. Even if such a person fully repents and remains within the church, the other spouse is not obligated to have them back *as a spouse.* The innocent partner does not have to suffer further hurt by being forced to reconcile with a contaminated partner.

The same liberty is given to a wife whose husband has committed adultery. She is not obligated to rejoin her husband in the marital relationship and is free to marry another should she so choose. We may be confident of this because in Paul's teaching on marriage he was careful to give similar liberties to a "sinned against" husband as to a "sinned against" wife.[180]

The only divorce Jesus condemns is treacherous divorce

The church has often read Jesus' exception for sexual immorality as if it were the one and only ground for divorce, but to his Jewish listeners it would not have sounded like this. For them, there were different types of divorce and they would all have known that divorce for "any matter" meant Hillelite divorce. The term "any matter divorce" was probably even more familiar to them than the term "no-fault divorce" is to us.[181] To the Jews, "Is it lawful for a man to divorce his wife for 'any matter'?" meant "What is your opinion about the Hillelite interpretation of Deuteronomy 24:1?"[182] The particular question of the Pharisees — about a man who wanted to divorce his wife, rather than a woman victim of abuse or abandonment who might want to divorce her husband — points to the fact that the conversation was not about *all* kinds of divorce.[183]

The Pharisees assumed Deuteronomy 24:1 was an entitling law, and they just wanted to know which school had the correct interpretation of that entitlement. But it was not an innocent inquiry: we know their question was a trap question. Whatever Jesus answered, some faction or other would be antagonized. In addition, their question might even lead to an order for Jesus' arrest, as had happened with John the Baptist when he denounced Herod's illicit marriage.[184] Facing this kind of interrogation, it is unlikely that Jesus would have delivered a comprehensive teaching on *all* aspects of divorce and remarriage, or touched on all the Old Testament passages. Blomberg notes that "The specific historical background that informs this debate, the particular way in which the question is phrased, and the unscrupulous motives behind the Pharisees' approach all warn us against the notion that Jesus was comprehensively addressing all relevant questions about marriage and divorce."[185]

In his answer, Jesus criticized the Hillelite system by cutting a line through the middle of it. He isolated divorce for *porneia* as legitimate (whether obtained under the Shammaite or Hillelite system), but said all trivial grounds were illegitimate. Jesus' remarks apply only to unjustified divorce and he phrased them in the way he did because he was reproving the Jews' distortion of Deuteronomy 24. He did not disallow all divorce grounds except for sexual immorality, he disallowed *all treacherous divorce*. In his day, this meant all use of the Hillelite "any matter" method as an excuse to divorce a wife on trivial grounds. He declared that the seventh commandment was violated when a man engaged in unjustified divorce and then remarriage. The Jews would have heard Jesus' teaching as a rebuke of the laxity of the Hillelite interpretation and the treacherous, male-privileged divorce system that had sprung from that interpretation.

Jesus said nothing to condemn disciplinary divorce. He specifically exonerated those men who used disciplinary divorce on the ground of their wives' adultery. Now we must be careful here, because many people have assumed that Jesus simply agreed with the Shammaites and disagreed with the Hillelites. It is not that simple.

• The Shammaites said "Porneia is a valid ground for divorce; Deuteronomy 24:1-4 tells us this." (The Shammaites said *erwat dabar* meant nothing except porneia.)

• In contrast, Jesus said "Porneia is a valid ground for divorce; Deuteronomy 24:1-4 does <u>not</u> tell us this. Deuteronomy 24 was given because of *men's* hardness of heart. Nothing in the Hillelite divorce system is valid except when they allow divorce for porneia."

Jesus agreed with the Shammaites that porneia is a valid ground for divorce, but disagreed with them about where we derive that doctrine from. From what Jesus said, and from reading Deuteronomy 24:1-4, we can deduce that Deuteronomy 24 was not given to set forth grounds for valid divorce (in *erwat dabar*, or in any other expression) but because some hardhearted men were so abusing the practices of divorce and remarriage that they made them resemble pimping and adultery (see chapter six).

The apparent identity between the Shammaites' expression "nothing except porneia" and Jesus' "except porneia" is only superficial. They are not using the expressions to refer to exactly the same thing. Shammaites used it to nail down what they thought to be the meaning of *erwat dabar*. Jesus used it to isolate the only Hillelite divorces that were acceptable before God. Jesus cannot be accused of deceitful word-play when he used the expression "except porneia" in a different way to the Shammaites. He had been asked about the legitimacy of Hillelite divorces, not the validity of the Shammaite interpretation. He answered the question that had been put to him, and in doing so he (a) condemned both schools for their presuppositional assumption that Deuteronomy 24:1 gave grounds for divorce,[186] and (b) condemned the Hillelites specifically for their licentious approach to divorce.

Jesus did not condemn other grounds for disciplinary divorce, such as abuse or severe deprivation. We know the Shammaites and Hillelites agreed that disciplinary divorce on the grounds of cruelty was justified, basing this on an extension of Exodus 21:10-11. Jesus had no qualms about raising a controversy when he disagreed with a prevailing view; if he had disagreed with the consensual application of Exodus 21 he would probably, at some stage, have said so. Moreover, both testaments uphold the principle that we should protect the weak and vulnerable; it would be totally inconsistent with this principle if the kingdom ethics did not protect a vulnerable spouse from a cruel or callous spouse.[187] Additionally, 1 Corinthians 7:12-15, which covers abuse under "constructive desertion", is in complete harmony with the disciplinary divorce teaching in Mosaic Law.

A MAN WHO TREACHEROUSLY DIVORCES AND REMARRIES IS GUILTY OF ADULTERY

If a Jewish woman became divorced in the first century she needed a certificate to remarry, to verify the former marriage was "over and done with". Should she remarry without a valid divorce certificate, she and the new husband would both be committing adultery. In contrast, a divorced man did not need a certificate to verify his freedom to remarry, for Jewish law allowed men to have two wives at the same time. If a divorced man married a woman who had never married before, he did not need a divorce certificate and the new marriage never counted as adultery. If he married a previously married woman, it did not count as adultery so long as the woman possessed a certificate of divorce.

Jesus took a radically different position about when remarriage was adultery. He indicated that a divorce certificate does not legitimize treacherous divorce, so a man who remarried after having divorced his wife for a trivial reason committed adultery.

The status of the new wife made no difference at all: he was guilty of adultery even if she possessed a divorce certificate, or had never been married before. This was unheard of to the Jews. It declared men guilty of adultery in cases where, by their own interpretation of the Law, they had never before considered themselves guilty of adultery. It challenged the system they had so carefully constructed on their distortion of Deuteronomy 24:1.

Is adultery-by-remarriage once or continual?
The vast majority of commentators have taken the view that the adultery-by-remarriage which Jesus discusses is a one-time act, not an ongoing adulterous relationship.[188] Matthew 19:9 could be called a "pronouncement story" — like many such biblical teachings it begins with a story and ends with a pronouncement. Pronouncement stories generally climax with a verb having a timeless sense — one that simply states the result of the story rather than emphasizing ongoing action.[189] It has been suggested that the translation "is guilty of adultery" is preferable to "commits adultery".[190] This is an excellent suggestion because it focuses on the fact that the seventh commandment is broken, without raising unhelpful speculation about the precise moment (or period in time) when the transgression occurs.

Divorce and remarriage were quite common in the ancient world. Yet Paul never advised new converts to divorce if they were on their second or third marriage.[191] If he had done so, the Roman authorities would certainly have taken action, for they were concerned to increase the number of legitimate children by encouraging and maintaining marriages.

CONCLUSION

It is not the case that Jesus simply abrogated the Mosaic divorce law and instituted a new, more stringent divorce rule for kingdom living. The Mosaic Law had always set forth the divine intention that marriage was a lifelong committed relationship. It had sought to protect a vulnerable, innocent spouse from a callous or unfaithful spouse, and had allowed the use of disciplinary divorce. It had sought to deter people from treacherous, cavalier and impulsive divorce and remarriage.

Jesus did not change any of this; he simply called for a full and proper adherence to God's standards for marriage. He condemned the legalistic approaches of his own day, which had legitimized treacherous divorce. And he declared that treacherous divorce with ensuing remarriage is equivalent to adultery and a breach of the seventh commandment. If this appeared to be changing the standard, it was only because the Jews had so poorly adhered to the standard.

▥ Chapter 10
What about where Jesus seems to forbid all remarriage?

There are a few places in the Bible where it might seem that Jesus forbids all remarriage and encourages divorcees to remain single. This chapter looks at those texts. We will first examine Mark 10, then the eunuch saying in Matthew 19 and lastly the divorce verse in Luke.

MARK 10: AN ABSOLUTE RULE WITHOUT ANY EXCEPTION?

> Mark 10 ²*The Pharisees came and asked Him, "Is it lawful for a man to divorce his wife?" testing Him. ³And He answered and said to them, "What did Moses command you?" ⁴They said, "Moses permitted a man to write a certificate of divorce, and to dismiss her." ⁵And Jesus answered and said to them, "Because of the hardness of your heart, he wrote you this precept. ⁶But from the beginning of the creation, God 'made them male and female.' ⁷'For this reason a man shall leave his father and mother and be joined to his wife, ⁸and the two shall become one flesh'; so then they are no longer two, but one flesh. ⁹Therefore what God has joined together, let not man separate."*
>
> ¹⁰*And in the house His disciples asked Him again about the same matter. ¹¹So He said to them, "Whoever divorces his wife and marries another commits adultery against her. ¹²And if a woman divorces her husband and marries another, she commits adultery."*

When the victim of domestic abuse reads this passage she naturally assumes that it condemns any woman who divorces her husband because of his abuse, and it prohibits all remarriage after divorce. However, the passage in Mark needs most carefully to be read in conjunction with Matthew 19, for they are parallel accounts and complement each other.

Each Gospel writer, under the inspiration of the Holy Spirit, selected or omitted certain narrative details. This resulted in a particular emphasis to suit the audience to whom that Gospel was initially addressed. In both Matthew 19 and Mark 10 the divorce dialogues show the marks of selective reporting for teaching purposes.[192] Selective reporting does not mean adding things that were not spoken by the original protagonists. It only means choosing what to leave in and what to leave out.

When we compare Matthew's and Mark's accounts we find there are three elements peculiar to Matthew that do not occur in Mark's version. One element peculiar to Matthew is a follow-up conversation about eunuchs that Jesus had with his disciples, which we will look at later in this chapter. We looked at the other two elements unique to Matthew's account in the last chapter: (1) the words *"for any matter"* from the Pharisees' question, and (2) the *porneia* exception. These two elements were of special relevance to the Jewish situation in that they pertained to the Hillelite/Shammaite controversy.[193]

Some people have made too much of the fact that Mark does not contain the exception clause, arguing that Mark's account must condemn *all* remarriage after divorce, so Matthew's exception must be interpreted in some way that diminishes its force. It is true that Mark 10:11-12 represents a general rule about divorce, but every general rule can be modified by an exception mentioned in another place in scripture.[194] The commandment *You shall not murder* is qualified by the commands concerning capital punishment and war; the instructions to obey parents and civil authorities are qualified by the precept that we ought to obey God rather than men (Acts 5:29).[195] Matthew 19:21, 9:15, and 13:57 may seem like exceptionless absolutes; nevertheless we do not claim that all Christians should sell what they have to give to the poor, that all should fast, and that prophets are *never* honored in their own locality.[196] A general rule may not mention the exception, yet it does not contradict that exception.[197] So the general rule in Mark about divorce does not contradict Matthew 19, and it should be understood as being able to be qualified by the exception in Matthew and the rule in 1 Corinthians 7:15.

It is worth noting that Matthew recorded another exception clause Mark omitted — the words *except the sign of the prophet Jonah*[198] — yet little significance is ever attributed to this difference between Matthew and Mark.[199] The inclusion/omission of the Jonah clause may be explained simply by the different audiences to whom the respective Gospels were initially addressed. It made sense for Matthew to include the exception about Jonah, since Jews were familiar with the story of Jonah and were used to the Jewish method of illustrating doctrine by typological teaching. Mark's predominantly Gentile audience was less familiar with the Jewish scriptures and the use of typology to illustrate doctrine, so it made sense to omit the clause.

Likewise, the inclusion of the *porneia* clause in Matthew 19 illuminated the particularly Jewish aspect of the dialogue with the Pharisees. Matthew's account shows that the dialogue was about the Hillelite interpretation of Deuteronomy 24:1, which hung on the words "any matter". Jesus was criticizing the unjust divorce condoned by the Hillelite system, and he mentioned the *porneia* exception expressly to exempt from his criticism those men who used the Hillelite system to obtain disciplinary divorce on the ground of *porneia*.

Mark 10 omitted these peculiarly Jewish aspects of the debate. His audience did not need to know the nuances of a Jewish controversy about the interpretation of Deuteronomy 24:1.[200] Furthermore, Gentiles did not need to be informed of the *porneia* exception for they would have assumed that sexual immorality was a legitimate ground for divorce.[201] Gentile societies universally acknowledged that a wife's adultery was grounds for divorce. Adultery was subject to criminal penalties under the Roman law *lex Julia de adulteriis*. This law, enacted by Augustus around 18 BC, applied for several hundred years. It specified criminal penalties for any respectable woman (i.e., virgin, married, or formerly married, but not slave women or prostitutes) who with intent engaged in extra-marital sex. The man who was the woman's partner in such acts was also subject to prosecution, whether or not he was married. A husband who did not prosecute an adulterous wife risked being prosecuted himself for pimping.[202]

Although Gentiles did not need to know about the rabbinic debate, they would have been aware that the Jewish legal system permitted divorce and that much of the Christian ethic was based on the Old Testament. Gentiles lived under Roman law, which permitted divorce whenever one or both parties wished to separate. Mark's account served to teach them not to accept any longer this easy divorce mentality, because God did not condone such easy, self-centered divorce.

Gentile converts could easily be misled by Jewish Christians (as were the Galatians over circumcision, dietary rules and holy days). Gentiles were especially vulnerable to such misguided teachers, for they might tend to think: "Jesus and his first followers were Jewish; Jesus' teaching was harmonious with the Law of Moses; therefore all things from Judaism must be okay." Despite Jesus' condemnation of Hillelite divorce, some Jewish Christians may still have subscribed to the Hillelite approach. (Christians sometimes do retain elements of the worldly mind-set in which they have grown up.)

It was vital that Gentiles learn the correct understanding of the Mosaic teaching on marriage and divorce, so they would not be misled into thinking that the Law of Moses was similar to Roman law, in that both laws permitted easy divorce. In order to learn this, Gentiles did not need to know the ins and outs of the Hillelite-Shammaite debate. But they did need to know that the Law of Moses, as displayed by the creation ordinance of marriage, did not condone divorce for slight or non-existent offenses, so it implicitly condemned dumping your spouse just to marry someone you might find more attractive. They needed to know that the teaching of Moses — and of Christ — called spouses to the high and demanding goal of faithfulness to one's partner.

These needs can explain why Mark's text simply records the Pharisees' question as *"Is it lawful for a man to divorce his wife?"* (omitting the phrase "for any matter"). Having omitted the allusion to the Hillelite system, Mark also omitted the *porneia* exception for it related particularly to Jesus exempting from criticism those who were using the Hillelite system to obtain a divorce on just grounds.

JESUS DID NOT OVERTURN THE MOSAIC "CONCESSION"

We saw in the previous chapter that Jesus did not overturn the Mosaic concession to divorce for Moses had not really *made* a concession to divorce, but rather, described divorce in order to regulate one of its most destructive outcomes. We now need to revisit this issue because the text in Mark has been used to argue that Jesus *did* annul the so-called Mosaic concession.

Some people have interpreted Mark's account in the following manner: (1) Jesus asked the Pharisees *What did Moses command you?* (2) When Jesus said this, the only Mosaic command he had in mind was Deuteronomy 24:1. (3) Jesus' words affirm that the divorce pictured in Deuteronomy 24 was, under Moses, a legitimate, permitted concession. (4) When Jesus said *What God has joined together let not man separate* he annulled this so-called Mosaic concession and disallowed divorce.

This interpretation is incorrect because point (2) is a dubious assumption. Jesus' question *What did Moses command you?* does not imply he saw Deuteronomy 24 as the only relevant Mosaic command regarding divorce. We know from the next few verses that Jesus saw other Mosaic principles as highly relevant to the Pharisees' question: the principles of *one flesh* and *do not commit adultery*. Jesus asked *What did Moses command you?* to expose the error of the Pharisees. He knew they would answer *Moses permitted us to divorce our wives*. He was giving them rope with which to hang themselves — getting them to clearly state their wrong emphasis, so he could proceed to demolish it.

The Pharisees said Deuteronomy 24:1 was a "permission", showing they paid lip service to the difference between what scripture commanded and what it allowed as a concession.[203] But Jesus knew that they actually downplayed the texts about marital faithfulness and elevated Deuteronomy 24:1 to an entitling law. So he told them the Deuteronomic regulation had only been given because their hearts were hard. They should have focused more on God's intention for permanency in marriage as expressed in Genesis.

MARK'S MESSAGE EMPHASIZED GENDER EQUITY

Mark's version emphasized the gender equity of Jesus' teaching regarding unjustified divorce. Under Greco-Roman law, both females and males were able to initiate divorce without any particular grounds. Mark's record omitted the gender specific language that Matthew recorded. For instance, Matthew wrote *Moses, because of the hardness of your hearts, permitted you to divorce your wives*, whereas Mark wrote *Because of your hardness of your heart, he wrote you this precept*, omitting the words "you to divorce your wives".

Also, Matthew's sentence is gender specific: *Why then did Moses command to give a certificate of divorce, and to put her away?* It shows the husband is the one doing the divorcing and the wife is the one put away. In Mark's sentence, *Moses permitted (a man) to write a certificate and to dismiss (her)*, the words in parentheses do not appear in the Greek but are added by translators to make the verse sound more natural to the English reader. In some translations these added words are italicized: "Moses permitted *a man* to write a certificate and to dismiss *her*." Read without these added words, Mark's language is gender free: "Moses permitted to write a certificate and to dismiss."

We know from Matthew's account that Jesus informed the Pharisees: *Whoever divorces his wife except for porneia and marries another commits adultery* (Matt. 19:9a). This meant that Jesus was closing the loophole of Jewish male privilege in regards to divorce rights. It was also notorious that some women of the ruling class, such as Salome and Herodias, had flouted convention and divorced their husbands in order to remarry.[204] We know from Mark's account that in a private house a little later the disciples questioned Jesus about his statement. We don't know their question, but possibly they asked him whether his condemnation of treacherous divorce and remarriage applied to both sexes. Jesus' answer clearly addresses gender equity: *"Whoever divorces his wife and marries another commits adultery against her. And if a woman divorces her husband and marries another, she commits adultery."* Our Lord divinely foreknew the future needs of his church, which was soon to include Gentiles. Jesus' gender-equity answer, recorded by Mark, would serve to guard converts of both sexes from groundless or selfish divorce.

The double standard of the day held that a wife's illicit sex was a crime against her husband, whereas a husband's extra-marital sex was not so much a crime against his own wife as a crime against another married man (the husband or future husband of the woman).[205] Jesus challenged this double standard with the words "against her", which are unique to Mark's account. By these words, Jesus declares that a husband's indulgence in treacherous divorce and adultery-by-remarriage is a crime against his first wife, so bringing an adulterous husband and an adulterous wife under identical condemnation.

SHOULD A DIVORCEE LIVE AS A EUNUCH?

> Matthew 19 *¹⁰His disciples said to Him, "If such is the case of the man with his wife, it is better not to marry." ¹¹But He said to them, "All cannot accept this saying, but only those to whom it has been given: ¹²For there are eunuchs who were born thus from their mother's womb, and there are eunuchs who were made eunuchs by men, and there are eunuchs who have made themselves eunuchs for the kingdom of heaven's sake. He who is able to accept it, let him accept it."*

Some divorcees think this passage means divorcees should remain as eunuchs for the rest of their lives, or at least until the ex-spouse dies. Victims of abuse may be particularly inclined to read this interpretation into the text. Being used to submitting to their husbands, no matter how much self-abnegation or renunciation of self this entails, they have a parallel readiness to submit to what they believe is God's will.

The eunuch passage is another follow-up conversation between Jesus and the disciples, different to the one recorded by Mark. This conversation follows through on the theme of Jesus' criticism of Hillelite divorce which was the focus in Matthew's record of the Pharisaic conversation. The eunuch passage opens with the reaction of the disciples: *If such is the case of the man with his wife, it is better not to marry.* The disciples seem to have thought: "If a man's right to divorce for 'any matter' is removed, and if after divorce for aversion remarriage is adultery, then a man would be better off never marrying!" This off the cuff response showed just how radical was Jesus' teaching on divorce compared to the popular assumptions based on the male prerogative. A Hillelite divorce allowed a husband to divorce for "any matter" that he might find objectionable in his wife. Jesus had just disallowed every excuse for divorce embraced by this Hillelite system except for the matter of *porneia*. And it was unheard of for a rabbi to say that remarriage was adultery![206] Even the Shammaites recognized remarriage made after "any matter" divorce as legitimate marriage, because the Shammaites and the Hillelites had a policy of mutual recognition of each other's rulings.[207] Jesus' divorce and remarriage teaching was different from anything the disciples had ever encountered.

Jesus responded *All cannot accept this saying, but only those to whom it has been given: For there are eunuchs who were born thus* [innate physical deformity] *and there are eunuchs who were made eunuchs by men* [castration or accidental injury] *and there are eunuchs who have made themselves eunuchs* [voluntarily renounced marriage] *for the kingdom of heaven's sake.*

Some theologians have taught that *All cannot accept this saying* refers to the "saying" of verse nine where Jesus pronounced on divorce and remarriage. They conclude that divorcees should make themselves eunuchs for the kingdom of heaven's sake in an act of obedient discipleship, as long as their former spouse remains alive.[208] Gundry has even made this obedience a criterion for salvation: "out of obedience to Christ's law concerning divorce, [his true disciples] do not remarry, but live as eunuchs, lest their righteousness fail to surpass that of the scribes and Pharisees and entrance into the kingdom be denied them (cf. verse 12 with 5:20)."[209]

This line of interpretation has to be questioned. The most natural referent for "this saying" is not verse nine but the saying uttered by the disciples in verse ten *"it is better not to marry"*. Firstly, this is the saying most immediately preceding Jesus' answer.[210] Secondly, Jesus' answer (about eunuchs, those who do not marry) corresponds to the disciples' statement (*it is better not to marry*). Both the disciples' question and Jesus' answer were primarily about first marriages, not remarriages.[211] And when Jesus says there are *eunuchs who have made themselves eunuchs for the kingdom of heaven's sake* there is nothing to tell us he refers to divorced people only.[212] He finishes his statement with *He who is able to accept it, let him accept it,* not "let all those who are divorced accept it". Thus, there is no indication that he is referring back to his teaching in verse nine.

Jesus does not agree with the disciples' generalization that it is better for a man not to marry. He says *All cannot accept this saying, but only those to whom it has been given.* In other words, the saying "it is better not to marry" is not true for everyone. Some people simply don't have a choice about whether it is better or worse to marry — for them, consummated marriage is not physically possible. Others choose to renounce marriage; but voluntary renunciation of marriage is not for all.

The disciples' remark gave a *negative* reason for remaining single: "If you rule out a man's general right to divorce for 'any matter', and if remarriage after most of those Hillelite-style divorces is adultery, then it would be better never to marry in the first place!" This was said unthinkingly, more an expression of their dismay over Jesus' teaching than a well thought out comment on singleness versus marriage. Jesus indicated their comment was rhetorical overstatement and did not apply to everyone. He then directed them to think about a *positive* reason for singleness: working for the kingdom. This would have been another surprising teaching to the disciples, for most Jews believed every man ought to marry because "go forth and multiply" (Gen. 1:28) required them to marry and procreate children.[213]

While Jesus said that singleness was a valid lifestyle and was not displeasing to God, he also said that voluntary celibacy is good only for those who are able to accept it. This implies that some of the never married, some divorcees, and some widows and widowers will live as voluntary celibates in kingdom service, while some will not. This in turn implies that some divorcees will remarry.

The idea of voluntary celibacy being "given" could mean a variety of things. It obviously refers to God's providence but it may also refer to such things as the strength of one's sexual drive, one's role of service in the kingdom, and whether it is difficult to find a compatible spouse who shares the intensity of one's Christian calling.[214] For example, a man who feels called to a difficult mission field and wants to take a wife with him would be seeking a wife who was prepared to undergo many trials and hardships.

LUKE 16: TOTAL PROHIBITION — OR CRITICISM OF MALE PRIVILEGE?

Luke 16:18 *Whoever divorces his wife and marries another commits adultery; and whoever marries her who is divorced from her husband commits adultery.*

Taken in isolation, the divorce pronouncement in Luke sounds like an absolute edict. It appears to condemn all divorce and remarriage without exception. How are we to understand this black and white condemnation of divorce and remarriage?

We must first note that (as for Mark above) the absence of the exception clause does not mean we may take the condemnation of divorce and remarriage in Luke as a full, final and absolute decree. We have to read Luke's record alongside Matthew's, which gives the *porneia* exception. Luke's audience, like Mark's, was composed of Gentiles who would have taken for granted that *porneia* was ground for divorce. Furthermore, Jesus did not cover everything necessary for a Christian understanding of divorce, as Paul recognized in 1 Corinthians 7:12.

Why does the exception clause not appear in Luke? It has been argued that Mark omitted the "except for *porneia*" phrase because it pertained to a rabbinic divorce system remote from Gentile thinking. The conversation documented by Luke is a different conversation from that documented by Mark and Matthew. It is reasonable to assume that Jesus, in the conversation recorded by Luke, simply did not say anything about the exception for *porneia,* so the question of whether Luke omitted any of Jesus' words simply does not arise.

We can understand Jesus not mentioning the exception clause when we look at the context. Luke's verse about divorce comes in the middle of one of our Lord's wide-ranging denunciations of Pharisees. The key points of this rebuke are [13]*No servant can serve two masters ... You cannot serve God and mammon...* [15]*You ... justify yourselves before men, but God knows your hearts...* [16]*The law and the prophets were until John. Since that time the kingdom of God has been preached, and everyone* [except proud people like you Pharisees] *is pressing into it.* [17]*And it is easier for heaven and earth to pass away than for one tittle of the law to fail.* [Here is an example of how you are breaking the law:] [18]*Whoever divorces his wife and marries another commits adultery; and whoever marries her who is divorced from her husband commits adultery.* Verses 19-31: You Pharisees are like the rich man who ended up in the place of torment after he died: you do not hear Moses and the prophets, neither will you be persuaded if one [Lazarus, or even I myself] rise from the dead.

Verse 18 may be understood as an illustration of the previous verse: Jesus was showing how the Pharisees were constantly and repeatedly breaking the law.[215] The verb forms in Luke 16:18 suggest continuous or repeated action in contrast to Mark 10:11 where the verbs suggest simple, undefined action.[216] Jesus in Luke's account is talking about men who are constantly divorcing and remarrying, whereas in Mark he is talking about the simple act of divorce and remarriage.

In Luke's account Jesus was not untangling the strands of rabbinic controversy over a Mosaic text. Nor was he setting out measured and qualified ethical interpretive principles about divorce. His concern was not with legal definitions but with moral exhortation.[217] He was rebuking the Pharisees, delivering a general statement condemning divorce and remarriage without muffling it in the circuitous language of qualifications and conditions.[218] Because of this context, we are justified in assuming that it was the Pharisees' characteristic teaching on divorce/remarriage which Jesus was condemning.

Jesus was pointedly criticizing the Pharisees for condoning a type of divorce which resulted in adultery. Those who committed this sin were injuring the institution of marriage and repeatedly defying God's law. Luke's record says nothing about whether the woman bore any guilt. In the second part of verse 16 (*whoever marries her who is divorced from her husband commits adultery*), the man is explicitly stated to commit adultery whereas the woman is not explicitly stated to be guilty of anything. Jesus' words in Luke highlight only the guilt of men — men who engaged in treacherous divorce and remarriage, and men who condoned the system that enabled treacherous dismissal of wives and who self-servingly took advantage of this system by marrying cast-off divorcees. The Samaritan woman in John chapter 4 was possibly a victim of this kind of behavior. Implicit in Jesus' emphasis is that he wants to protect women from cavalier divorce, not to punish those who have already been betrayed by it.[219]

▥ Chapter 11
If I'm the innocent party, why do I still feel guilty?

> Matthew 5 [31]*"Furthermore it has been said, 'Whoever divorces his wife, let him give her a certificate of divorce.'* [32]*But I say to you that whoever divorces his wife for any reason except sexual immorality causes her to commit adultery; and whoever marries a woman who is divorced commits adultery."*

Note: I will discuss verse 32 as if it contains two sentences (a+b) rather than one sentence bisected by a semicolon.

RACKED WITH GUILT!

When a victim of abuse reads this passage, the thing that jumps out at her is that a husband divorces his innocent wife and the woman commits adultery. She knows scripture says God will judge adulterers and they will not inherit the kingdom of God (1 Cor. 6:9; Heb. 13:4). Being already racked with guilt and self-doubt as a result of the abuse, she may feel that Matthew 5:32 speaks dire condemnation towards her and maligns her personally.

She may believe that the verse teaches one or more of the following ideas: (1) remarriage after divorce equals adultery, so remarriage must be prohibited; this is so even for an innocent spouse who has not been the cause of the divorce. (2) A woman divorced by her husband, despite her not having committed an offense in the marriage, will nevertheless be too depraved to maintain chastity once she is divorced. (3) Such women will commit adultery-by-remarriage because they lack the self-control necessary to remain single. (4) Even if such women do *not* remarry, they are always on the brink of committing adultery and so are guilty before the act. (5) Therefore they are a liability to every church, because they represent a perpetual temptation to every man in the congregation. These kinds of interpretations have prompted many divorced abuse victims to remain determinedly *un*married.

Some Christian bystanders read the verse in similar ways and treat divorcees with suspicion. One victim reported to me that some months after separation her pastor's wife said to her, "Are you going to reconcile with your husband, or are you going to go on being a floozy?" At the time, my friend was seeing all men as threatening and was purposefully wearing dowdy clothes to deflect male attention. She had previously disposed of her wedding ring but was wearing a cheap ring in order to make men think she was unavailable. While not all bystanders show such negative attitudes to victims as this pastor's wife, many do not quite know what to say when separation or divorce occurs. Their silence can inadvertently exacerbate the negative projections of the abuse victim who imagines that the silence is a polite attempt to mask a judgmental attitude.

The divorce saying in Matthew 5 should be read in the light of Matthew 19, which gives more background to the divorce debate. However, Matthew 5 is not simply an abbreviated version of Matthew 19. In Matthew 5:32a Jesus deals directly with the remarriage of an innocent party, something he does not do in any other divorce sayings. This woman has been unjustly dismissed; she has been divorced despite the fact that she seems to have done nothing to cause the divorce. Reading verse 32a in isolation, it is easy to draw the inference that remarriage must be forbidden to an innocent party. But how do we reconcile this interpretation with the generally held view that an innocent party, in a case of adultery, is at liberty to remarry? For if we grant remarriage to the innocent party when divorce is occasioned by the adultery of the other spouse (Matt. 19:9) yet prohibit remarriage to a person who has suffered unjust dismissal (Matt. 5:32a), we uphold a contradictory morality. This is the contradiction: one kind of innocent party has liberty to remarry, but another kind of innocent party does not.

ALL IMPORTANT CONTEXT: THE SERMON ON THE MOUNT

Matthew 5:32 is part of the Sermon on the Mount, a sermon where Jesus' purpose is to correct distortions, traditions and legalisms that had encrusted community morality like a coating of barnacles. Jesus is addressing a crowd of ordinary people and his disciples. He says the moral law of the Old Testament is not to be abrogated (verses 17-18) and he denounces the Pharisees' and scribes' legalistic beliefs which opposed the spirit of the moral law (verse 20). To crush these legalistic beliefs, he expounds the deeper meaning of two of the Ten Commandments as well as some other parts of the moral law.

The passages that surround his divorce teaching can be summarized as follows. The sixth commandment, murder, is broken not only by the deed of murder, but by unjustifiable anger and thoughts of hatred. It is wrong to emphasize the taking of oaths as a way of convincing others that one will keep one's word; we ought to be people of our word with a simple "yes" or "no".[220] The "eye for an eye" law was meant to set upper limits on vengeance, not authorize us to resist people who oppose us or who make unreasonable demands on us. The command to "love your neighbor" never included the words "hate your enemy"; we should love and pray for our enemies. In addition, charity, prayer and fasting should be practiced secretly, not ostentatiously.

In relation to the seventh commandment, adultery, Jesus said it is broken not only by intercourse that breaks the exclusive commitment of marriage, but also by several other kinds of behavior. The dominant authorities in Jesus' day believed adultery occurred when a married woman had or attempted to have intercourse with a man who was not her husband. It was not necessarily seen as adultery when a married man had intercourse with a woman other than his wife; such a man was only seen to be guilty of adultery if the woman he had sex with was the wife of another man. The legalistic reasoning behind this was that if a married man had sex with an unmarried woman, he would always, in theory, marry her and have two wives.

Jesus criticizes this narrow, gender-biased definition of adultery by expanding the application of the seventh commandment in two distinct but related ways. His first point is that the law against adultery is broken when a man dwells on lustful thoughts or indulges in seductive conduct with a woman other than his wife. This implies that a man can be guilty of adultery in the heart or attempted seduction without any guilt attaching to the woman who is the object of his lust. It also implies that a husband who womanizes is guilty of adultery regardless of the marital state of the woman he seduces. His second point is the divorce pronouncement, which we will now consider piece by piece.

WHAT DOES MATTHEW 5:32A MEAN?

Jesus begins this divorce saying by referring to the significance being given to divorce certificates: *"Furthermore it has been said, 'Whoever divorces his wife, let him give her a certificate of divorce'..."* The Old Testament does not contain this expression (despite the misleading suggestion in some Bible footnotes that it is a quote from Deuteronomy 24:1). Jesus is quoting not scripture, but a common expression of his day.

Hillelites and Shammaites both taught that divorce certificates were essential in divorce. The Shammaites required two elements for a divorce to be legitimate: a wife's sexual immorality had to be established at court, then the certificate had to be issued. The Hillelites did not require proof of immorality since they accepted "any matter" as ground for divorce. For them the certificate was all important: it was the only requirement for a morally legitimate divorce.

What kind of divorce is Jesus criticizing?
Jesus focuses his blowtorch exclusively on the unjust divorces condoned by the Hillelites. When he refers to the saying *"Whoever divorces his wife, let him give her a certificate of divorce",* he is quoting a maxim that could have been used by either Shammaites or Hillelites, but would especially have been used by those who subscribed to the Hillelite style of divorce.[221] His next sentence begins: *But I say to you that whoever divorces his wife for any reason except sexual immorality...* The phrase *for any reason except sexual immorality* is a translation of the Greek words *parektos* (except, apart from[222]) *logou* (matter, thing) *porneias (sexual immorality)*. A literal translation might read "apart from / a matter of / sexual immorality". Since Jesus' subject was the moral significance being given to divorce certificates, the word "matter" would have been an echo of the "any matter" catch cry of the Hillelites under which not only sexual immorality but any other more trivial matter could be grounds for divorce.

Therefore, it is suggested that the beginning clause in verse 32a means, "Whoever divorces his wife for any reason except sexual immorality (using the Hillelite 'any reason' method, but apart from the reason of sexual immorality)...." By the exception phrase, Jesus excludes disciplinary divorces (obtained using the Hillelite system) from his criticism. This is similar to the significance of the exception phrase in Matthew 19:9.

From this platform, Jesus delivers his stinging pronouncement: whoever divorces his wife for a trivial matter (in the style of Hillel) *causes her to commit adultery.* This immediately raises several questions. What is the adultery? What is it about the scenario in verse 32a that constitutes a breach of the seventh commandment? Does the text condemn *all* remarrying divorcees, even those who did not cause their divorce? Or is there a valid interpretation which does not unfairly malign or blame the innocent party and does not block the permission of an innocent divorcee to remarry?

That terrible word — adultery

We must note firstly that the NIV's translation "become an adulteress" is incorrect. It is wrong because it renders the verb for adultery (*moicheuo*) as a noun, and it wrongly suggests a permanent state. The tense of the verb actually suggests that "Jesus wishes to avoid characterizing the adultery as an ongoing, continual state. He rather wishes to say merely that the adultery occurs, and leave it at that."[223]

Let us "walk through" the situation that Jesus describes to find out the nature of this adultery. When a man marries he promises to be joined to his wife, which implies he will meet her need for sexual relationship. She for her part commits to sexual fidelity, promising to have no other partner but him. If the husband then unjustly divorces his wife, he breaks his side of the promise, making it impossible for her to maintain active sexual relations with him.

Jesus describes the situation where an unjustly dismissed woman remarries. We can deduce this from the second sentence in verse 32, for the two sentences are coordinated and parallel.

We need not understand Jesus to be saying that *all* divorcees would remarry, only that the case he describes is the common one — where the divorcee *did* remarry. This is not surprising when we consider that while divorced women in Israel could sometimes remain single,[224] many did remarry. The economic pressures in that era for women to remarry were much greater than in the modern Western world. Most women had to rely on men for financial support. The only way to be respectable and have children was to be married, and it was best to have several children so that at least one male child would live to adulthood and be able to look after his elderly mother.

Not quibbling with the rightness of the woman's remarriage, Jesus simply states that when she does so her hitherto inviolate chastity is adulterated.[225] Let us most carefully seek to understand what this might mean. Chastity is not restricted to virginity; it means being pure from unlawful intercourse. Therefore a wife is chaste if she is sexually faithful to her husband. This woman started off married life intending and expecting to be sexually faithful to her original husband and to enjoy the benefits of such commitment: continuity, security, stability. She had given herself to this man in the fullest way possible — by sexually bonding with him — and had remained chaste in that relationship. Now the husband's breaking of the marriage covenant has required her to make adaptations. The first marriage bond is null and void; the husband broke that bond when he treacherously divorced her, so she can no longer be said to be under an obligation to remain sexually loyal to him.[226] She commits herself to a sexual bond with a new husband. This new marriage does not break the old marriage bond because the old bond had already been broken. But the new marriage does entail entering in to a new sexual relationship which involves profound emotional and psychological adjustments on her part, for sexual relationships involve the deepest parts of our being. It is these deep changes, affecting the core of her being, which constitute an adulteration to her hitherto inviolate chastity.

Possibly a woman might feel more deeply the adulteration of having two husbands than a man if he had successive wives. God created woman with a submissive and responsive nature (Gen. 2:18). This woman has received a certain man into herself and "tuned" herself to him, rather like a harp whose strings have been tuned to resonate in sympathy with notes from another instrument. Now she has to tune herself to a new man. A husband who had successive marriages might not find the adjustment quite so difficult, since man's nature is to lead rather than to respond.

Injury to the dismissed woman

The treacherous husband bears the guilt for the adultery. His wife is the injured party. It was stated above that when the woman remarries, her hitherto inviolate chastity is adulterated. It is quite hard for us to understand this without blaming the woman, because we are used to the English language where "adultery" is always conceived of as an active, culpable sin on the part of the adulterer. In the Greek language, however, the word "adultery" can sometimes take the passive voice.

In the first sentence in Matthew 5:32, the verb "he causes" is in the active voice, meaning the husband is the author of the action, whereas the verb "adultery" is in the passive voice, meaning that the woman receives the action of the verb. The first husband has actively brought about a situation where the woman undergoes adultery. The passive voice of the woman's verb probably underscores the fact that she is a victim.[227]

Most English translations of verse 32 say the man causes his wife to *commit* adultery. This translation is inaccurate because it gives an active sense to the verb. So it unfairly lays guilt upon the woman: "she *commits* adultery" implies she is *guilty* of adultery. It also misleads the reader because it obscures the woman's victimization.

It is preferable to give a passive sense to the verb, one which illuminates the woman's victimization. Some have suggested that the adultery is merely a stigma, a subjective perception in the eyes of others.[228] However, this idea is not inherent in Greek passive verbs[229] and we must wonder why Jesus did not use similar language to Romans 7:3 (*she will be called an adulteress*) if he had meant to convey the idea of stigmatization in Matthew 5:32.[230] In first century Israel, women were divorced for many reasons, so the fact that a woman became divorced did not necessarily imply she had been unfaithful in her former marriage.[231] Instead of saying "he causes her to *commit* adultery," we can legitimately convey the passivity of the woman's verb by saying the husband causes her to *experience* adultery, to *undergo* adultery, or to *suffer* adultery.[232]

Jesus is careful to blame the treacherous husband in this situation.[233] By unjustly dismissing his wife he makes her sexual commitment to him meaningless and he exposes her to a sexual relationship with a different man. It is she who decides to remarry, but it was her husband's action that made her unmarried (and perhaps also impoverished) in the first place. We must be cautious about attributing blame to the woman for the text does not do so — it is silent about whether she bears any guilt in the remarriage.

We must turn to the wider scriptures to discover whether the woman bears any guilt in such a remarriage. The teaching on women's vows in Numbers 30 indicates that she cannot be held guilty for breaking the promise of sexual fidelity made to her former husband, since he has already broken his promise to be faithfully joined to her. Ultimately, Paul's teaching in 1 Corinthians 7 is decisive. The only instance in which an unjustly dismissed spouse should bear guilt for remarrying is the instance where both spouses are truly Christians. If church discipline were done properly, such instances would be relatively rare; usually a person who employs treacherous divorce is either an unbeliever, or will eventually be judged to be "as an unbeliever" if due disciplinary procedures are carried through.

Thus, most victims of treacherous divorce are *not under bondage* and free to remarry, since their ex-spouses will (sooner or later, if churches are doing their job) be deemed to be unbelievers. In this situation, the guilt for the adultery-by-remarriage lies with the person who employed treacherous divorce, and with the social system that condones and enables treacherous divorce.

Jesus' teaching on guilt and injury would have been appropriate to his audience. The mixed crowd at the Sermon on the Mount probably would have contained not only those who were disposed to engage in Hillelite treacherous divorce, but also their victims. Jesus highlighted the sin of treacherous men[234] *and* the plight of women who have been unjustly dismissed. (We may contrast this with Matthew 19 and Luke 16. On those occasions, where Jesus was speaking to hostile male Pharisees, he highlighted only the sin of treacherous men.) In other words, Jesus is not confronting the woman in the scenario of Matthew 5, but the man who unjustly divorced her. Jesus is confronting him with the consequences of his sin in its impact upon her, and hence with his responsibility. He is saying that a man cannot walk away from his sin by hiding behind a certificate of divorce.

"Adultery by affair" and "adultery by remarriage"

With the above explanation of adultery-by-remarriage, it is now possible to distinguish adultery-by-remarriage from common adultery (having an affair while currently married).

The two kinds of adultery are alike because in each of them a person who had been in a one-on-one sexually exclusive and committed relationship becomes sexually involved with someone else. But the two kinds of adultery differ in important ways. Adultery by affair occurs while the marriage is still intact and often results in the dissolution of that marriage. Adultery-by-remarriage does not dissolve a marriage, for it occurs after divorce on unbiblical grounds has already dissolved the marriage.

In an affair, the guilty partner is the spouse having the affair. In adultery-by-remarriage the only guilty partner (in the vast majority of cases) is the person who dissolved the marriage on unbiblical grounds. Someone who employs treacherous divorce and takes another spouse is guilty of adultery-by-remarriage. If an unbeliever employs treacherous divorce and the cast-off partner takes another spouse, the unbeliever is guilty of causing adultery-by-remarriage.

What if I don't remarry?

Not every victim of treacherous divorce will remarry. Those remaining unmarried will not undergo adultery-by-remarriage. However, those who employ treacherous divorce are always guilty because they expose their partners to the likelihood of adultery-by-remarriage.

Jesus' phraseology does not resemble precise statute law, where all possible outcomes and eventualities are carefully accounted for. In the construction "Whoever unjustly divorces his wife causes her to undergo adultery", the word "whoever" delivers an absolute censure to *all* men who use unjust divorce. But the entire pronouncement need not be read as an exceptionless absolute.[235] It does not have to mean *all* women so divorced will undergo adultery. It only means that *if* the woman remarries she undergoes adultery.[236]

Jesus stated the general truth: every husband who unjustly dismisses his wife breaks the seventh commandment, because he causes his ex-wife to undergo adultery-by-remarriage. This general truth allows that there will be some instances where the outcome does not fully eventuate, when a divorcee does *not* remarry; but the absolute censure still applies, even if the divorcee does not remarry. Every husband who unjustly dismisses his wife breaks the seventh commandment.

Like all good preachers, Jesus employed rhetoric — his language was designed to persuade. There is a rhetorical reason why he stated only the general truth about treacherous divorce: he did not want to diminish the impact of his censure by surrounding it with qualifications. If he had said, "Such husbands expose their ex-wives to adultery, but not all of the ex-wives will suffer adultery since not all of them will remarry," treacherous men would have easily been able to retort, "Well it's not *our* fault our ex-wives experienced adultery! They chose to remarry!" Jesus was not going to give them such an easy "out".

What about the man who marries me — is he committing adultery?

We have previously noted that the Jews held a man guilty of adultery if he had sex with a currently married woman. They believed that if a man married a divorced woman (one who possessed a correctly worded divorce certificate) he would not be guilty of adultery. They gave undue and inordinate moral significance to divorce certificates.

In the second sentence of verse 32 Jesus attacks this false view by saying *Whoever marries a woman who is divorced commits adultery*. This is arresting language. We could paraphrase Jesus like this: "Your teachers of the law have been wrong! The divorce certificate does not automatically legitimize things. It does not exonerate you from a charge of adultery. When a woman has undergone unjust divorce, the man who marries her will be guilty of adultery."[237]

This second part of verse 32, out of all the divorce texts in the Bible, is perhaps the most difficult to understand. A small minority has argued that it is eminently easy to interpret because it simply tells us that all remarriage after divorce, even remarriage by the innocent party, is sin. However, this "simple" interpretation has a fatal defect. For it means that while Jesus' purpose was to protect women from the injury of treacherous divorce, his teaching intensifies the injury of innocent parties who *have* been treacherously divorced, by condemning them to a life of singleness unless their ex-spouse dies. On this ground alone we must surely reject the "no remarriage of the innocent party" interpretation.

It is difficult to be definitive, but it is suggested that the following interpretation accounts most successfully for all the facts. Jesus' purpose was to protect women from the injury of treacherous divorce. He said, "A man who marries such a woman is guilty of adultery-by-remarriage," using arresting language to burst the bubble of men's self-righteous and self-serving reliance upon divorce certificates. However, this strong language must not be taken as implying that all remarriage is prohibited for the innocent party and that no one may marry a divorcee. The key must surely lie in the man's heart attitude and beliefs. If a man endorses an unbiblical system that, by the mere issuing of certificates, purports to legalize treacherous divorce, and he marries an unjustly dismissed woman, he is guilty of adultery-by-remarriage *in that he supports a system which endorses treacherous divorce*. However, another man might marry a divorcee without coming under this condemnation. He might marry an unjustly dismissed woman without endorsing the system by which she was dismissed. He might be showing compassion in taking to wife a woman whose previous marriage covenant had been broken by a wicked husband. He might detest the unbiblical system and feel kindness for its victims. Jesus did not feel it was necessary to state that the divorced woman had the right to remarry, since this right was so completely taken for granted in that culture and was enshrined in the very wording of the divorce certificate ("you are free to marry any man").

Does this apply to disciplinary divorce?

Jesus specifically exempted from his criticism those divorces occasioned by sexual immorality, because the words *"except sexual immorality"* exclude *porneia* divorces. Logic demands that other kinds of disciplinary divorce — those occasioned by the other partner's abuse or desertion — are also exempt from criticism.

We cannot say that disciplinarily divorcing spouses bear moral responsibility for causing their ex-spouses to undergo adultery-by-remarriage. Let us suppose a victim of abuse has used the discipline of divorce against her husband. We cannot blame her for making her ex-husband suffer adultery-by-remarriage when he marries another (hapless) woman. Nor can we accuse an unlucky woman of adultery-by-remarriage simply because she enters into marriage with a hardened abuser whose first marriage has already failed because of the way he treated his wife. Such a woman would probably not even know that her prospective husband abused his previous wife. Many a person has married a divorcee, believing the divorcee's story about their "terrible" first spouse, and then discovered that the divorcee had victimized their previous spouse. Sometimes the two victims eventually swap notes and even become good friends and allies.[238]

In the case of desertion, the deserted party must turn a *de facto* divorce into a legal divorce, because the deserter has failed to furnish the abandoned partner with the certificate or formalities required for a legal divorce. We cannot blame this victim of desertion for making the deserter undergo adultery-by-remarriage when the deserter marries another spouse. And a person marrying someone who had negligently deserted a previous spouse cannot be condemned for adultery-by-remarriage, but might rather be pitied, for this alliance may end in desertion too.

IMPLICATIONS

In the first century, the Jewish legalists' narrow definition of adultery always included a guilty female. Jesus' expanded definition means a man can be guilty of adultery without any guilt attaching to a woman. A man who indulges in lustful thoughts and conduct is guilty of adultery — without any guilt necessarily attaching to the woman who is the object of his lust. A man who unjustly dismisses his wife is guilty of causing her to undergo adultery-by-remarriage — without any guilt attaching to the woman for that remarriage. Adultery is forbidden by the seventh commandment, so illicit lust and unjustified divorce are also forbidden.

Jesus did not criticize the woman-friendly wording of divorce certificates. Rather, he criticized men who used divorce certificates to break promises they had no right to break, and the system which allowed them to do this. Jesus carefully limited his rebuke only to treacherous divorce.

Since Jesus taught that the Hillelite system of easy divorce for males was sinful, we may apply this judgment to any system which permits treacherous divorce for either sex, such as the no-fault systems that we have in the Western world today. But we may not apply his teaching to any form of disciplinary divorce. People who employ disciplinary divorce but have to do so under a system that only recognizes "no fault" divorce should not be condemned. Such people have no choice: the only way they can achieve a godly outcome is to use the ungodly system, because their government offers them no other system. They should, however, verify the godliness of their divorce by submitting it to a church court, for although that "court" has no legal power, it does have spiritual authority.

part E

CONCLUSION

▥ Chapter 12
Fitting it all together

In this final chapter, we will examine all the points of harmony between the various divorce passages in the Old and New Testaments. After that we will look at how Moses, Jesus and Paul, in their various cultural settings, addressed different facets of the divorce and remarriage issue. We will conclude by reviewing the erroneous assumptions that have obscured the divorce texts and the findings of this book which rebut each false assumption.

DO THE OLD AND NEW TESTAMENTS SPEAK AS ONE?

Both the Old and New Testaments disapprove of hardhearted divorce and approve of disciplinary divorce. Both testaments also harmonize in their views of remarriage after divorce. Let us examine all the points of harmony.

The Old Testament indicates that hardhearted divorce is wrong by teaching that a married couple become "one flesh" (Gen. 2:24), by forbidding adultery (Exod. 20:14) and by saying that he who hates and divorces sullies his soul with wrongdoing (Mal. 2:16). The Old Testament also says not to use divorce and remarriage in a way that is analogous to pimping and adultery by voiding your bond to each other but then re-committing to it (Deut. 24:1-4). The New Testament condemns hardhearted divorce when it says *What God has joined together, let not man separate* (Matt. 19:6; Mark 10:9). It also teaches that a believing spouse is not to divorce a believing partner (1 Cor. 7:10-11) and that if a believer has a spouse who does not believe, and the unbeliever is willing to live in the marriage with goodwill towards the believer, the believer should not initiate divorce (1 Cor. 7:12-13).

If a hardhearted person does initiate divorce, both testaments condemn that person's taking a new spouse or lover. The Old Testament teaches this explicitly and by implication as evidenced by the following: the death penalty for those convicted of adultery (Deut. 22:22); the need to remind men *let none deal treacherously with the wife of his youth* (Mal. 2:15); and the metaphorical parallel between adultery and apostasy (Mal. 2; cf. Jer. 3; Hos. 1-2). In the New Testament, Jesus condemned a treacherous divorcer's remarriage by saying that a man commits adultery if he divorces his wife without valid grounds and marries another woman (Matt. 19:9) and he said the same for a woman who groundlessly divorces her husband in order to remarry (Mark 10:12).

In the Old Testament, if a second marriage follows divorce, this rules out any possibility of renewing the first marriage (Deut. 24:1-4). In the New Testament, this rule is applied to prohibit two believers who are mutually divorced from entering second marriages with new partners (1 Cor. 7:10-11).

When it comes to disciplinary divorce, there are many points of correspondence between the Old and New Testaments. In regard to adultery, the Old Testament enables disciplinary divorce for proven adultery, because execution of the adulterer amounts to a divorce for the innocent party. The New Testament permits disciplinary divorce for adultery by the words *except for sexual immorality* in Matthew 19 and Matthew 5.

In regard to other violations of the marriage covenant, the Old Testament instructs divorce rather than victimization or enslavement of a vulnerable spouse (Deut. 21:10-14) and it approves of disciplinary divorce in cases where a husband is depriving his wife of her basic needs (Exod. 21:7-11). The New Testament says not to deprive your spouse sexually: there should be mutual giving and receptivity because each spouse has authority over the other's body (1 Cor. 7:3-6). The New Testament also approves the use of disciplinary divorce by a believing spouse against an unbelieving spouse when the non-Christian is unwilling to show goodwill in the marriage (1 Cor. 7:15).

In regard to remarriage, the Old Testament does not explicitly state that remarriage is permitted for the innocent party, but neither does it contradict the idea. Although the Old Testament implicitly condemns the remarriage of a hard-hearted divorcer, it does not condemn the overall idea of remarriage after divorce. The New Testament goes into a lot more detail about remarriage. When a husband treacherously divorces his wife and she then remarries, the guilt for the adultery-by-remarriage is laid at the feet of the treacherous first husband (Matt. 5:32). When either spouse commits adultery, remarriage is permitted for the innocent spouse (implied by Matt. 19:9). Similarly, when an unbeliever has willfully repudiated the marriage covenant, the innocent believer is permitted to remarry — for such a believer is not enslaved to the marriage bond (1 Cor. 7:15). Willful repudiation of the marriage covenant can take the form of unjust dismissal (treacherous divorce), adultery, abuse or abandonment. These last three offences may lead to the employment of disciplinary divorce as just punishment for the offending party.

WHY DID MOSES, JESUS AND PAUL ADDRESS DIFFERENT ASPECTS OF DIVORCE?

While the teachings of Moses, Jesus and Paul harmonize in their approach to divorce and remarriage, each one addressed a slightly different facet of the issue. The different facets relate to the different religious and cultural settings in which each taught.

Moses focused on adultery, disciplinary divorce and certain types of remarriage

Moses legislated in the Old Covenant era, where not every member of the covenant community was responsive to the Holy Spirit. Some Israelites were faithful believers and some were not, so Mosaic divorce law was tailored for a community whose moral conduct covered a very wide range. Moses made it clear that adultery was a serious crime by requiring divorce by execution for proven adultery. He also approved of divorce for cases of abuse or serious neglect. At the same time, he regulated the worst case outcome of male divorce for aversion (divorce that sprang from mere hardness of heart). And he did not prohibit men from divorcing their wives for serious offences such as unwitnessed adultery, which was verified by the trial of bitter water.

The Mosaic Law did not comprehensively address the rights and wrongs of remarriage after divorce. The Law did not prohibit remarriage after divorce except for two rather special cases: (1) revival of a first marriage after a second marriage had terminated; and (2) a priest marrying a divorced woman. Most persons who remarried after divorce were neither explicitly condoned nor explicitly condemned, the law merely took for granted that some divorcees *would* remarry. However, the law on women's vows (Num. 30:14-15) said that if a husband made null his wife's vow after having previously given it his approval, the guilt for not fulfilling her vow fell on his shoulders. This implied that if a wife could not fulfill her marriage vow because her husband had willfully repudiated their marriage covenant, she would not bear guilt if she remarried.

Jesus focused on treacherous divorce and the morality of remarriage
Jesus was responding to a system that had been developed to legitimize male, treacherous divorce. A Mosaic text — which had originally been written to restrain the hardhearted misuse of divorce and remarriage — had been twisted by the Jews to add a veneer of righteousness to their practice of hardhearted divorce. Jesus attacked this system by teaching that remarriage after hard-hearted divorce is equivalent to adultery. He said the guilt for such adultery-by-remarriage lies with the person who employs treacherous divorce. He also indicated that the victim of an adulterous spouse is permitted to remarry.

Yet adultery is not the only sin that creates victims of divorce. Jesus did not touch on cases of disciplinary divorce where the grounds for divorce are the *non*-adulterous (but similarly destructive) sins of the other party. And although he did touch on victims of treacherous divorce (i.e. unjust dismissal), he left unexpressed certain moral aspects of their situation. He did not positively state that the victim of an unjustly dismissing spouse is free to remarry without bearing any guilt whatever. Nor did he state whether it might ever be *wrong* for such a victim to remarry.

Paul combined and applied the teachings of Moses and Jesus
Paul applied Jesus' teaching about hardness of heart to the Church. The hardness of a person's heart became a determining factor in his delineation of the ethics of remarriage after divorce. Unbelievers are hardhearted, whereas believers, since the coming of the Church age, should have softer hearts for they are in-dwelt by the Holy Spirit. This new situation enabled Paul to divide the domain of divorce into two, not according to whether the grounds were adultery or "non-adultery", but whether the divorcing parties were believers or unbelievers. He taught that (1) two believers are exhorted not to divorce, but if they do divorce, they are prohibited from marrying other partners; and (2) remarriage is not prohibited to a believer whose unbelieving spouse has caused the divorce because he has not shown goodwill towards the marriage. Paul (in 1 Corinthians 5:11) also explained the criteria for determining when a so-called believer should be treated as an unbeliever. Taken altogether, Paul's teaching meant that an unjustly dismissed spouse is free from guilt and able to marry again *if* the dismissing partner rejects the call of Christ to repentance and faith. This effectively clarified whether it was sinful for victims of treacherous divorce to remarry (a point unexpressed by Jesus).

Hardness of heart was also the criterion for determining whether or not a marriage to an unbeliever should be maintained. If the unbelieving spouse was sufficiently soft of heart to "think well of in common" (*syneudokeo*) with the believing spouse, the believer ought to remain in the marriage. But if the unbelieving spouse declined to "think well of in common" with the believing spouse — had failed to show approval and goodwill toward the believing spouse — divorce and remarriage were permitted. This wording moved things out of the reach of legalists who in the Old Testament era had tried to regulate disciplinary divorce by setting "minimum requirements" of food, clothing and sexual provision.

The criterion for goodwill in the marriage was a useful, general one that covers various expressions of hardheartedness toward the other spouse. The goodwill of an unbelieving spouse is manifestly lacking in instances of unjust dismissal, desertion, abuse, and sexual immorality. Paul thus clarified the validity of disciplinary divorce for the *non*-adulterous offenses of desertion and abuse (a matter not addressed by Jesus, but touched on by Moses), yet he did not open the floodgates to divorce for such excuses as "mutual incompatibility".

By stating the regulations so they applied equally to males and females, Paul extended the teaching of our Lord that Mark had recorded about the sexes having parallel rights and responsibilities in divorce and remarriage.

Why didn't Paul mention the *porneia* exception?

Paul did not mention Jesus' exception for *porneia,* but the exception must be understood in the apostle's teaching, for he would not overthrow a rule that Jesus had made.[239] There are several good reasons why Paul did not mention the *porneia* exception. It was abundantly clear that Christians should avoid sexual immorality. All Gentile believers would have been aware that *porneia* was forbidden for Christians (Acts 15). Paul had taught that a so-called believer practicing unrepentant sexual immorality should be excommunicated (1 Cor. 5). The Corinthians almost certainly knew that Jesus permitted divorce for sexual immorality — Paul had, after all, spent 18 months with them when he first founded the church (Acts 18:11). The way he says *"yet not I but the Lord"* suggests that he knew the Corinthians to be familiar with Christ's teaching on divorce.

In addition, we must remember that Jesus mentioned the *porneia* exception because he was severing an acceptable use of the Hillelite "any matter" system from the unacceptable uses of that system. Paul did not have the same need to mention *porneia* because, writing to a predominantly Gentile audience, he was not specifically rebutting the Hillelite system. Indeed he had good reason to leave it out, since to restate it would complicate his exposition and thereby lessen the contrast he wanted to make between those divorcees who were obliged to remain unmarried, and those who were free to remarry. Adams suggests that "Paul omitted the exception [sexual immorality] in order to set up the contrast between verses 1 Corinthians 7:10-11 and verses 12-16 more sharply. Surely he would have understood the exception, but *here* it would not serve his general purpose to mention it. To do so would (unnecessarily) complicate what he wished to say."[240]

Furthermore, Paul's permission for divorce comprehended and included Jesus' permission of divorce for sexual immorality. It is not a matter of Jesus' ground versus Paul's ground, because the grounds expressed by Paul and Jesus really overlap.[241] A sexually immoral spouse jeopardizes the well-being of his or her spouse and does not show the loyalty and respect characteristic of someone who "thinks well of in common" with the faithful spouse. Sexual immorality may also be accompanied by desertion, since adulterous spouses frequently abandon their marriage and live with their lover. A so-called believer who commits sexual immorality and fails to repent should be treated as an unbeliever. For all these reasons, sexual immorality would usually meet Paul's criteria for disciplinary divorce. There is only one instance where Jesus' ground of sexual immorality would not be completely congruent with the Pauline criteria: the instance where a believer commits sexual immorality but then repents and remains legitimately within the church. In this instance, while reconciliation is certainly desirable, it is not mandated, and disciplinary divorce (with freedom to remarry for the innocent partner) would be permissible solely on the ground of Matthew 19:9.

In applying the essential teachings of Moses and Jesus, Paul used wording that would be applicable in every New Testament church, whatever its local cultural setting might be. His mastery of doing this in the space of six or seven verses is mind-boggling. Only the Holy Spirit could have been so precise and so concise at the same time.

ERROR AND TRUTH

By way of conclusion, here is a list of the false assumptions that have clouded interpretation of the divorce texts. Each false assumption is numbered; after each assumption is its counteracting truth in bold type.

1. Adultery is the only ground for divorce permitted in the New Testament.

Adultery, abuse and abandonment are the three grounds for divorce in the Bible. This kind of divorce can be called "disciplinary divorce".

2. Jesus condemned all divorce, except divorce for adultery.

Jesus condemned treacherous divorce, but not disciplinary divorce.

3. The exception for adultery is Jesus' sole exception to his otherwise global condemnation of divorce.

The exception for adultery is Jesus' sole exception to his otherwise global condemnation of the Hillelite interpretation of Deuteronomy 24:1 — the "any matter" system which legitimized treacherous divorce.

4. Paul allowed two believers to separate, but not to divorce each other.

Paul recognized that divorce might occur between two believers, but if so, they could not marry new partners. (While remaining unmarried they could pursue biblical discipline; should it be determined that the opposite partner was to be treated as an unbeliever, the believer would be free to marry a new partner.)

5. Whatever Paul said about desertion as a ground, it cannot be a ground for full divorce; it must mean something less.

Paul's teaching means that adultery, abuse, or abandonment by an unbelieving spouse are grounds for divorce and remarriage.

6. Remarriage after divorce equals adultery. Remarriage is a breach of the seventh commandment.

Remarriage to new partners is not allowed if married believers become divorced from each other. Biblical discipline may be necessary to verify whether a person should continue to be treated as a believer.

If one spouse is an unbeliever and the divorce is disciplinary (for the unbeliever's adultery, abuse, or abandonment), remarriage by the believer is not a breach of the seventh commandment. If one spouse is an unbeliever and has unjustly employed

divorce, remarriage by the treacherous party is a breach of the seventh commandment. The treacherous party's victim may remarry without sin, as the guilt for the breach of the seventh commandment falls on the treacherous divorcer.

Not all divorcing couples fall neatly into the "guilty party/innocent party" category. Where the cause of divorce is mutual sin, these principles would suggest that remarriage by either party would be a breach of the seventh commandment.

7. If a divorced person's remarriage equals adultery, divorce must not "work", it must be an empty procedure. The first marriage must still exist in the sight of God.

Divorce does "work"; it truly ends a marriage.

8. Moses allowed divorce for hardness of heart.

Moses suffered hardhearted divorce but he did not approve of it. He only described it in order to regulate an abominable situation which could sometimes ensue from it — the use of divorce and remarriage in a way that was analogous to pimping and prostitution. (Pimping means acting as a go-between in extramarital affairs or prostitution, by ministering to the baser passions or evil designs of others.)

9. Jesus revoked the Mosaic allowance of divorce and remarriage. The Old Testament law did not always set forth the ideal, but was an accommodation to what the nation could bear. In the New Testament, Jesus set a higher ethical standard.

Jesus did not overturn or change any Mosaic laws regarding divorce. The Mosaic Law had always set forth the divine intention that marriage be a lifelong committed relationship: 1) it had sought to protect a vulnerable or innocent spouse from victimization; 2) it had sought to deter people from treacherous, selfish and impulsive divorce and remarriage; and 3) it had prohibited people from using marriage and divorce in a way that was analogous to pimping and adultery. Jesus did not change any of this; all he did was more clearly spell out the meaning of the Law. He condemned the legalistic approach of his own day which had legitimized treacherous divorce. And he declared that treacherous divorce/ remarriage is equivalent to adultery and a breach of the seventh commandment.

Jesus appeared to be changing the standard, but only because the Jews had so poorly adhered to it. Jesus simply called them back to a full and proper adherence to the Mosaic Law.

10. Since Jesus allowed porneia as ground for divorce, and Moses appeared to allow erwat dabar as ground for divorce, there must be an equivalence: porneia equals erwat dabar.

***Porneia* means sexual immorality. The phrase *erwat dabar* might sometimes have been used to refer to sexual immorality, but it had a much broader usage; it was used by men to refer to any thing they found objectionable about their wives, thus it could be an excuse for treacherous divorce.**

11. Moses allowed the practice of divorce because wives were being hardhearted in their adultery.

According to Jesus, Moses described and regulated the practice of treacherous divorce because it was being practiced by hardhearted husbands.

12. Jesus only condoned divorce for adultery where one's spouse had been really hardhearted in infidelity (repeated, prolonged and unrepentant adultery).

Jesus allowed divorce for any case of adultery. Although his overall teaching encourages forgiveness and reconciliation, he did not specify that one had to remain married to a spouse whose adultery was "minor".

13. Since Jesus agreed with Shammai that divorce was permitted for sexual immorality, Shammai must have been completely right in his interpretation of Deuteronomy 24:1 and Hillel must have been completely wrong.

Shammai was right on some things but wrong on other things; Hillel was more wrong than Shammai, but he was correct on some things. Jesus disagreed with both rabbis in quite a few areas.

14. God hates divorce.

The correct translation is "He who hates and divorces … covers his garment with violence." God condemns treacherous divorce, but he does not condemn disciplinary divorce.

A CLOSING PLEA

It is not uncommon to read a magazine article or hear a talk where a Christian leader states "God hates divorce". The expression is true if we are talking about treacherous divorce, and its use may be understandable in the age of the ten-second sound byte. However, these three words are potentially damaging to those who must employ disciplinary divorce. Many Christians have felt so intimidated by the slogan "God hates divorce" that they put up with abuse, adultery or horrendous neglect rather than employ disciplinary divorce.

If I could make one plea it would be that teachers and speakers evaluate what they plan to say by imagining how a victim of marital abuse would be likely to hear their message. Teachers need to ask themselves: "How would a victim interpret my teaching? Is there anything in what I plan to say that would further entrap a person who is subordinated in an abusive marriage? Would they feel I have condemned and cut off their hope for freedom?" It takes only eleven words to say "God hates treacherous divorce, but he does not hate disciplinary divorce."

Appendix 1
Augustine on his parents' marriage.

The great theologian, Augustine of Hippo, made an almost unrivalled contribution to the Christian church, particularly in respect of the doctrine of the Trinity. However, like many esteemed Christians, he did not understand the dynamics of domestic abuse very well and so made statements that could be taken to inadvertently condone it. In the following account from his *Confessions*[1] he praised the way his mother Monica put up with her husband Patricius:

> She arrived at a marriageable age, and she was given to a husband whom she served as her lord. And she busied herself to gain him to thee [Christ], preaching thee to him by her behavior, in which thou made her fair and reverently amiable, and admirable to her husband. For she endured with patience his infidelity and never had any dissension with her husband on this account. For she waited for thy mercy upon him until, by believing in thee, he might become chaste.
>
> Moreover, even though he was earnest in friendship, he was also violent in anger; but she had learned that an angry husband should not be resisted, either in deed or in word. But as soon as he had grown calm and was tranquil, and she saw a fitting moment, she would give him a reason for her conduct, if he had been excited unreasonably. As a result, while many matrons whose husbands were more gentle than hers bore the marks of blows on their disfigured faces, and would in private talk blame the behavior of their husbands, she would blame their tongues, admonishing them seriously — though in a jesting manner — that from the hour they heard what are called the matrimonial tablets read to them, they should think of them as instruments by which they were made servants. So, always being mindful of their condition, they ought not to set themselves up in opposition to their lords. And, knowing what a furious, bad-tempered husband she endured, they marveled that it had never been rumored, nor was there any mark to show, that Patricius had ever beaten his wife, or that there had been any domestic strife between them, even for a day. And when they asked her confidentially the reason for this, she taught them the rule I have mentioned. Those who observed it confirmed the wisdom of it and rejoiced; those who did not observe it were bullied and vexed.

From this account we cannot be sure that Patricius was a true abuser, although by our standards he certainly was an adulterer (in those times it was customarily accepted for a husband to engage in extramarital sex with prostitutes or slaves). Although he had dreadful temper outbursts, he perhaps did not thrive on power and control. Perhaps he really did

---

1 Augustine, *Confessions and Enchiridion,* trans. & ed. Albert C. Outler, Library of Christian Classics, vol. 7 (London: SCM Press, 1955), pp. 190-1.

become friendly and reasonable again, once his outburst had run its course and he listened to Monica's explanations.

However, if a woman was married to a true abuser, who thrived on power and control, Monica's advice would have been worse than useless. It would have made her into a doormat and entrapped her in horrendous situations. Her patient explanations would have fallen on deaf ears, or would have been used against her. Her submission to sin would have been interpreted as license to commit more sin.

Augustine, as is natural for children growing up in abusive households, adopted the viewpoint of one of his parents. Augustine and his mother imply that women who get beaten deserve it, because they "set themselves up in opposition to their lords". He does not even class his father's furious anger as domestic strife — it is only classed as strife if the wife resists. He puts all the responsibility for preventing strife onto the wives.

Augustine's viewpoint was probably no more invidious than that of many other Christians (including Christians in our own age) who are blind to the true dynamics of domestic abuse. Such views can best be challenged by posing questions such as: Should women *never* oppose their husbands? Should we applaud women staying while their husbands practice domestic terrorism, send the family into extreme poverty, or commit incest with their children?

Appendix 2
Constructive desertion

Several theologians in the sixteenth and seventeenth century saw 1 Corinthians 7:15 as covering constructive desertion.

The reformer Theodore Beza (1519-1605) wrote:

> ... we know him also to be a deserter who does not refuse cohabitation, but obstinately demands impious conditions. ... another question occurs: what should the faithful spouse do when indeed cohabitation is not denied, but either hazard of life is incurred or something is either to be done or endured against the true religion. I respond that these two distinctions are to be observed. First, either the unfaithful [spouse], whether intentionally or unwittingly, persecute the faithful spouse, or the persecution arises from some other direction. If the former, the faithful spouse really has a suitable excuse for shunning her domestic enemy for no other reason than that she should consider her life and conscience, and I would decide in this case nothing other than if the unfaithful spouse himself had departed for another. To depart from someone and to drive the other away by threats or force are the same thing. But if such persecution should assail [the faithful spouse] from some other direction, the faithful spouse should act at length more moderately than if she should cherish an enemy in her home and bosom. Nor is its to be doubted that if the unfaithful spouse should attend the faithful with conjugal love, should provide for her life in every way, in this case the faithful spouse rather should bear whatever you will than that it should be her duty to abandon the unfaithful spouse. But if the unfaithful spouse does not care as is right that the faithful spouse is in peril, no one does not see, I think, not only that he is a deserter, but also that he may be shunned with a good conscience as a traitor.[1]

The Puritan William Perkins (1558-1602) said:

> Like unto desertion is malicious and spiteful dealing of married folks one with another. Malicious dealing is, when dwelling together, they require of each other intolerable conditions ... Here it may be demanded, what a believer should do, who is in certain and imminent danger, either of loss of life, or breach of conscience, if they both abide together.
>
> If [this danger is] from the stranger, then the husband either takes upon him the defence of his believing wife, or not; if he doth, then she ought to abide with him. If not, she may depart and provide for her own safety. Again if the husband threateneth hurt, the believing wife may flie in this case; and it is all one, as if the unbelieving man should depart. For to depart from one, and drive one away by threat, are equipollent [equivalent].[2]

---

1 Beza, *De Repudiis et Divortiis, Tractationes Theologiae*, vol. 2, cited in The Presbyterian Church in America's "Report on Divorce and Remarriage", ch. 1, pp. 199-200.

2 Perkins, *Christian Oeconomie*, p. 88, cited in The PCA Report (ibid.), p. 194.

Another Puritan, William Ames (1576-1633), wrote:

> For if one party drive away the other with great fierceness and cruelty, there is cause of desertion, and hee is to bee reputed the deserter. But if hee obstinately neglect, that necessary departure of the other avoyding the eminent danger, hee himselfe in that playeth the deserter.[3]

David Clyde Jones suggests that paragraph 24.6 of the Westminster Confession, which was written during the Puritan era, should be reworded to read: "Although the corruption of man be such as is apt to study arguments unduly to put asunder those whom God hath joined together in marriage, yet, nothing but adultery, or such wilful ~~desertion~~ *repudiation of the marriage covenant* as can no way be remedied by the church, or civil magistrate, is cause sufficient of dissolving the bond of marriage".[4]

This rewording would comprehensively embrace all that Paul means to say in 1 Corinthians 7:15. Willful repudiation of the marriage covenant covers desertion, constructive desertion and treacherous divorce (legalized desertion).

---

3 Ames, *Conscience with the Power and Cases Thereof,* cited in the PCA Report (ibid.), p. 197.

4 Jones, "The Westminster Confession on Divorce and Remarriage", p. 28.

Appendix 3
Jay Adams' advice on complex church discipline procedures

The following is Jay Adams' advice to church leaders and church members when dealing with complicated cases of church discipline after marriage break-up, where one of the spouses has gone to another church without discipline procedures having been conducted properly. The present author has taken the liberty of inserting a couple of remarks in square brackets; otherwise the text (including footnotes) is Adams'.

From pages 88-91 of *Marriage, Divorce, and Remarriage in the Bible*, by Jay Adams:

> Sometimes complications also arise from the sin of the church in failing to do what God requires; this always comes back to haunt the church in days to come. Many of the difficulties that result could have been avoided if the church had done what it ought to do at the outset.
>
> Let us take, for example, what could have been a relatively simple situation but which was muddied by the church's poor advice and inaction. (Usually it is the hands-off stance of the church that accounts for the problems. But difficulties rarely ever "go away" if we do nothing.) In this case, Mary and Joe are professed Christians. Neither has committed adultery. Joe divorces Mary because he is "tired of arguing and fighting about everything." The ground of the divorce is incompatibility (a non-biblical ground). The church got involved only after the divorce occurred. Joe, in unrepentant anger,[1] left the church and when the pastor called to see why, he read him the riot act, said that he didn't care to remain in a church where people said such things, and demanded that his letter be transferred to a congregation up the street. The first church, in fact, did send a letter of his good standing to the second church (the pastor and church officers actually breathed a sigh of relief when they did so). But now the chickens finally have come home to roost: Mary has met another Christian man and wants to marry him. (Joe has not remarried.) The first church has what they call a "strong stand" against remarrying divorced persons under circumstances where the former spouse is alive and unmarried;[2] what should the pastor do?
>
> Well, because of his own failures, and the failures of the officers of the church, the pastor and officers have brought this complication on themselves. Originally, the church should have entered the picture early — at the very latest, when Joe went to see the lawyer (good shepherding usually picks up problems of this magnitude much sooner). On the basis of 1 Corinthians 6 (and other passages) Joe should have been required to disengage the lawyer since to file for divorce [without biblical grounds — author] is sin. Among other points he should have been instructed that:

---

1 A member (not the pastor or an officer) told him that he had sinned in divorcing Mary.

2 This is typical of many churches in which this "strong stand" actually grows from great weaknesses in the care and discipline of members. The place to be "strong" is where the Bible is; not where it isn't!

1. God has forbidden him to take his wife — a professed believer in Jesus Christ — to court. All such problems as he and Mary have must be resolved by the church within its jurisdiction and not before pagans at court. [The present author would qualify this statement by saying that it is not sin to take a professing believer to court in order to obtain a protection order. The church cannot wield the sword to protect a believer from assault or harassment, but the state is ordained by God to provide protection for all citizens who are vulnerable to the predations of others (Romans 13). A protection order does not prove criminality: it merely requires good behavior in the future, and signals consequences if that good behavior does not eventuate.]

2. God has required him to take the Matthew 18:15ff. route in order to resolve these problems.

3. God does not allow divorce on the grounds of incompatibility.

4. There is no reason why the marriage cannot be *transformed* if both parties desire it for God's glory.

If Joe had agreed to these admonitions, then there would have been no divorce, reconciliation could have been effected and counseling toward a new sort of lifestyle could have begun. It would have been work; but the situation would have remained fairly simple.

If Joe had failed to respond positively, this sin would have complicated matters a bit more, but if Mary (and the church) had pursued the Matthew 18:15ff. procedure faithfully then — assuming (as does Matt. 18:15ff.) that Joe stubbornly refused to cease and desist from his sinful plans to divorce Mary on unbiblical grounds — at length (after all attempts had been made to bring about reconciliation) Joe would have been excommunicated and the whole matter would fall under 1 Corinthians 7:15. Mary's position, and that of the church would be clear — she would be free to marry another. The outcome, once more, would be clear and uncomplicated.

However, because the church (both congregations were wrong in different ways) failed to advise and act as they ought (a typical scene in evangelical churches today), many new complications have arisen making it harder for everyone concerned. Here are some of these complications:

1. Mary isn't free to remarry.

2. Joe had been deprived of his rights to church discipline.

3. Joe hasn't been confronted at all levels according to the requirements of Matthew 18:15ff. and is still considered a member of Christ's church in good standing despite his rejection of Christ's authority in the Bible.

4. A sinful divorce has been ignored.

5. Joe (and Mary) stand in peril of committing adultery.

Now, can anything be done to rectify the situation? Yes, but it will be complex, messy and harder on all concerned. Avoiding the original mess — as it always does — has brought on a far worse one (Spurgeon once said "It is easier to crush the egg than it is to kill the serpent"). How does one bring order out of chaos? Here is (among other things that may arise along the way) basically what must be done to bring about a peaceful settlement of all the issues:

1. The first church must seek God's forgiveness, forgiveness from Joe and Mary, and from the second church for failing to handle matters scripturally. This step cannot be omitted without destroying everything.

2. Next, Mary must be advised to go seek reconciliation with Joe faithfully following the procedures of Matthew 18:15ff. step by step.

3. Joe should be called upon to repent and seek reconciliation with Mary and his former church (and the member against whom he expressed such anger).

4. If all goes well, Mary and Joe will be reconciled, remarry and build, under proper care in counseling, a new and better marriage (not go back to the same old things[3]).

5. But, let us suppose Joe sinfully refuses to be reconciled. Accordingly, his sin further complicates. But that should not stop the process.

6. In that case, Mary should pursue Matthew 18:15ff.

7. But this time she must ask Joe's new church to become involved (at least in the final stage of the Matthew 18:15ff. procedure) since he is now under their discipline.

8. By this time, of course, they would be aware of what was happening since Mary's congregation (sometime before) should have contacted them, seeking forgiveness and alerting them to the new action that Mary has been advised to take, and the possibility of involving them in discipline should Joe not respond to the early steps of the procedure.

9. If Joe's church does what it should, well and good. Joe will repent or will be excommunicated, setting the matter to rest.

10. But what if Joe's church fails to assume its responsibilities and will not excommunicate Joe even though he fails to heed advice? This sin on the part of the church further complicates matters. Nevertheless, we still have recourse.

11. Then, the officers of Mary's church must humbly confront the officers of Joe's church (it might begin with pastor confronting pastor; but if that fails, officers confronting officers) to try to resolve the matter, offering help, support, direction, encouragement, etc.

12. If Joe's church agrees, well and good. All will flow naturally to one of the two presented ends: reconciliation or discipline. But what

---

3 See Adams' book *More Than Redemption,* pp. 174-83.

if Joe's church refuses? Obviously, as it has all along, their sin further complicates matters.

13. Mary's church, at that point, has only one alternative left — only to be used with great caution when *every* effort has failed — to declare (by a functional judgment) Joe's church to be as no church since it refuses to hear Christ's authority, and Joe (as a part of the organization) to be as a heathen and a publican.

14. At long last, all threads have been pulled; the matter is set to rest, and on the basis of 1 Corinthians 7:15 Mary is eligible to marry another.

I have gone through this elaborate process, not to discourage church discipline, but (rather) to encourage its use at an early point for the benefit of all. Only then, can many of the complications be avoided. Nevertheless, since churches have been failing to discipline (and presumably many will continue to), you will need to know what to do (as Mary, as a pastor, as a church officer) in order to clean up the many messes that you may encounter along the way. The basic principles, with variations to meet each case, can be used in any number of situations.

Appendix 4
Giving advice to unbelieving couples

Sometimes a non-Christian couple (or one of the partners) comes to a minister seeking moral direction regarding divorce. The following explanation sets forth the general principles that a minister might use in such counseling. It starts with the highest standard of godliness, but recognizes that one partner may have goodwill towards the marriage while the other partner may not.

The creation ordinance of marriage — one man, one woman, until death brings an end to the relationship — applies to all mankind.

Genesis 2:24: says *...therefore a man shall leave his father and mother and be joined to his wife, and they shall become one flesh.* This verse contains two principles of covenantal marriage: being joined to one's spouse (a vow of loyalty, a faithful, committed relationship) and one flesh (sexual union, but also intimacy, mutual communication).

God's command to every married person is, do not be the one who causes a divorce. If someone offends someone else, God calls the offender to repent, and the offended one to forgive.

But God permits a person to divorce his or her spouse on certain grounds: sexual immorality, desertion, or abuse. These grounds represent violations of the covenantal promises to *be joined* in *one flesh.*

If separation or divorce takes place for some reason, one should, initially, abstain from extramarital sex or remarriage, and seek godly counsel. One should give calm consideration to whether the grounds for divorce are accepted by God (see above), and whether repentance and forgiveness should be sought and by whom. Abstaining from remarriage allows for the possibility of reconciliation.

If sexual immorality has occurred, the innocent party is permitted, but not obliged, to divorce. Christian values encourage repentance and forgiveness, so the innocent partner may choose to forgive and to reconcile, but the Bible does not say there *must* be reconciliation of the marriage.

In the case of obstinate desertion or persistent abuse, the behavior of the sinning partner shows that they are not willing to live as a spouse ought to live, so the victim may consider the marriage ended. Divorce is upheld by the Bible in such cases. This may entail turning a "*de facto*" divorce into a legal divorce.

Appendix 5
Mosaic Laws prohibiting divorce

The Mosaic Law prohibited divorce in only two circumstances: where a husband falsely accused his new wife, and where a man had sex with an unbetrothed virgin and subsequently married her. In both situations the woman had been unjustly treated and so was given special security in her marriage, with the attendant financial security, as a form of compensation.

> Deuteronomy 22 *13 If any man takes a wife, and goes into her and detests her, 14and charges her with shameful conduct, and brings a bad name on her, and says, "I took this woman, and when I came to her I found she was not a virgin," 15then the father and mother of the young woman shall take and bring out the evidence of the young woman's virginity to the elders of the city at the gate. 16And the young woman's father shall say to the elders, "I gave my daughter to this man as wife, and he detests her; now he has charged her with shameful conduct, saying, 'I found your daughter was not a virgin', and yet these are the evidences of my daughter's virginity." And they shall spread the cloth before the elders of the city. 18Then the elders of that city shall take that man and punish him; 19 and they shall fine him one hundred shekels of silver and give them to the father of the young woman, because he has brought a bad name on a virgin of Israel. And she shall be his wife; he cannot divorce her all his days.*

In this passage a man slanders his new wife, accusing her of not having been a virgin when he married her. If the accusation is unjust, he is not allowed to divorce her. The purpose of this legislation is to award the injured woman exceptional security in her marriage. It makes no sense to think that this security would entitle her to commit any subsequent marital violation with impunity. Nor does it make sense to think that the prohibition on the man from divorcing his wife would prevent her obtaining a disciplinary divorce should that become necessary because of more bad conduct on his part. We may assume that either spouse could use disciplinary divorce if genuine grounds arose.

> Deuteronomy 22 *28If a man finds a young woman who is a virgin, who is not betrothed, and he seizes her and lies with her, and they are found out, 29 then the man who lay with her shall give the young woman's father fifty shekels of silver, and she shall be his wife because he has humbled her; he shall not be permitted to divorce her all his days.*

Commentators are divided about whether this text is a case of seduction or rape. The verb in verse 28 contains the idea of grasping but not necessarily that of overpowering. It stands in contrast to verse 25 where a different verb definitely means overpowering. Verse 28 also contains the phrase "they are found out". If verse 28 is about seduction it may be another version of Exodus 22:16-17 and the father's veto applies. If Deuteronomy 22:28 is about rape, we may still probably suppose that the father can veto the marriage (and might well do so at his daughter's request). Philo said that the choice whether to marry lay with the woman.[1] Josephus taught that the father could veto the marriage and, if he did, the man had to pay fifty shekels as compensation for the outrage.[2]

---

1 See Instone-Brewer, *Divorce and Remarriage in the Bible*, p. 28.

2 See Josephus, *Judean Antiquities*, 4.253; also Clark, *Putting Asunder*, pp. 218-9.

To us it seems bizarre for a virginal, unbetrothed woman to marry the man who had (perhaps forcefully) taken her virginity. However we need to bear in mind that the woman might have considerable difficulty in finding another husband in a society where virginity was much more highly prized than it is today. Some women were willing to marry the man who violated them, as we see in the story of Tamar and Amnon (2 Sam. 3:16).

If such a marriage took place, the man was forbidden from ever divorcing the woman. By his lack of sexual restraint, the man could find himself married to that woman for the rest of his life. This law probably acted as something of a deterrent to illicit sex. However, as with all of God's laws, we may (indeed must) interpret this rule in conjunction with other laws that deal with the subject. Thus, although he was forbidden from divorcing her "all his days", we cannot take this to mean that he could not divorce her if there were proper disciplinary grounds such as the wife's adultery or her abuse/neglect/desertion of her husband.[3] Rabbinic Judaism recognized the right of such a husband to divorce his wife if she was unchaste after the marriage.[4]

---

3 See Instone-Brewer, *Divorce and Remarriage in the Bible*, p. 27; Clark, *Putting Asunder*, p. 38.

4 See Mishnah, Ket. 3.5

Appendix 6
Philo on the remarriage prohibition in Deuteronomy 24:1-4

The first century Hellenistic-Jewish philosopher Philo commented on Deuteronomy 24:1-4 as follows:

> *Special Laws* III (30-31): Another commandment is that if a woman after parting from her husband for any cause whatever marries another and then again becomes a widow, whether this second husband is alive or dead, she must not return to her first husband but ally herself with any other rather than him, because she has broken with the rules that bound her in the past and cast them into oblivion when she chose new love-ties in preference to the old. And if a man is willing to contract himself with such a woman, he must be saddled with a character of degeneracy and loss of manhood. He has eliminated from his soul the hatred of evil, that emotion by which our life is so well served and the affairs of houses and cities are conducted as they should be, and has lightly taken upon him the stamp of two heinous crimes, adultery and pandering [*proagogeian*]. For such subsequent reconciliations are proof of both.

Liddell and Scott's dictionary says *proagogeian* means "pandering, procuring". Pandering is an old-fashioned word for pimping. The Oxford Dictionary defines "pander" as "a go-between in clandestine amours; a male bawd or procurer; one who ministers to the baser passions or evil designs of others".

Appendix 7
Translations of Malachi 2:16

This appendix presents eighteen translations of Malachi 2:16 where the one who hates is the divorcing husband. The date of each translation is shown.

• 1868 (Ewald) **For he who from hatred breaketh wedlock, saith Yahweh Israel's God, — he covereth with cruelty his garment, saith Yahweh of Hosts.** To arrive at his translation, Ewald repointed the perfect verb *śānē'* as a Qal participle *śōnē'* and the infinitive construct *šallah* as an infinitive absolute *šallēah*.[1]

• 1908 (van Hoonacker) **Quand quelqu'un répudie par aversion, dit Jahvé le Dieu d'Israël, il se couvre d'injustice par-dessus son vêtement, dit Jahvé des Armées.** Hoonacker repoints *śānē'* to the Qal active participle *śōnē'* (like Ewald), but repoints the infinitive construct *šallah* as a Piel perfect "to send away, divorce" to match the perfect "covers" in the latter part of the verse.[2]

• 1927 (J. M. P. Smith) **"For one who hates and divorces,"** says the Lord God of Israel, **"covers his clothing with violence,"** says the Lord of Hosts.[3]

• 1934 (Lattey) **For he that putteth away with hatred...**[4]

• 1970 (New English Bible) **If a man divorces or puts away his spouse, he overwhelms her with cruelty, says the Lord of Hosts the God of Israel.**

• 1981 (René Vuilleumier) **En effet, répudier par haine, c'est couvrir son vêtement de violence, dit YHWH Sabaot.** (In fact, to repudiate through hatred is similar to covering one's garment with violence says YHWH Sabaot.)[5]

• 1986 (Westbrook) **For he has hated, divorced ... and covered his garment in injustice...** Westbrook follows J. P. M. Smith and takes the two verbs as finite.[6]

• 1987 (Glazier-McDonald) **"For one who divorces because of aversion,"** says Yahweh, the God of Israel, **"thereby covers his garment with violence."** Glazier-McDonald says "making Yahweh the subject is wholly arbitrary and requires too many inferences."[7]

---

1 H. Ewald, *Die Propheten des Alten Bundes,* (2nd ed. 1868, Gottingen: Vandenhoeck & Ruprecht, 3. 224). I have quoted the English edition *Commentary on the Prophets of the Old Testament* (trans. J. F. Smith, London: Williams, 1881) cited by David Clyde Jones in "A Note on the LXX of Malachi 2:16", 1990.

2 A. van Hoonacker, *Les Douze Petits Prophètes,* J. Gabalda & Cie., 1908, cited in Beth Glazier-McDonald, *Malachi: The Divine Messenger* (Atlanta: Scholars Press, 1987), p. 110. A. S. van der Woude notes that Junker, Nötscher and Chary have each advocated similar repointing to Hoonacker's.

3 J. M. P. Smith, *The Old Testament, An American Translation,* University of Chicago, 1927, cited in Jones, *Biblical Christian Ethics,* p. 191.

4 Lattey, *The Book of Malachy* (London, New York, Toronto: Longmans Green & Co., 1934), p. 12.

5 Réné Vuilleumier, "Malachie" in *Commentaire de L'Ancein Testament XIc,* eds Delachaux & Niestlé, (Paris: Neuchatel, 1981), p. 237.

6 Westbrook, "The Prohibition on Restoration of Marriage", p. 403.

7 Glazier-McDonald, *Malachi: The Divine Messenger,* pp. 82, 110.

- 1994 (Hugenberger) **If one hates and divorces, says Yahweh, God of Israel, he covers his garment with violence, says Yahweh of hosts.** Hugenberger spends thirty-five pages analyzing the various interpretations and translations of verse 16 made prior to his time of writing, and presenting reasons why his translation is the most supportable. He leaves both *śānē'* and *šallaḥ* unchanged, suggesting that *šallaḥ* be interpreted "as a Piel infinitive absolute functioning as a substitute for a finite form, in this case a perfect ... in the Piel conjugation the infinitive construct often provides an alternative form for the infinitive absolute."[8]

- 1994 (D. C. Jones) Translation of the Septuagint (the Greek version of the Old Testament made in the intertestamental period). The Septuagint has the first clause in the verse in the second person: **If you divorce out of hatred, says the Lord God of Israel, then ungodliness covers your thoughts.** Jones says:

> The Septuagint ... is widely and mistakenly assumed to have the same rendering as the Targum and the Vulgate: "If you hate, divorce!"... Correctly parsed, however, the Septuagint is not a subjunctive and an imperative, but a participle and a subjunctive. It does not say, "If you hate, divorce!" It says, "If hating you divorce," with the apodosis [result] still to come, as in the Hebrew. ...This rendering is congruent with Malachi's general style as Malachi often inserts "says the Lord" before completing the thought (1:10, 14; 3:10, 17). In one other verse he places it as here, between the protasis [condition] and the apodosis [result] of a conditional sentence (2:2).[9]

Jones notes how two distinct Septuagint readings dating from the fifth century have been confused. One reading said "If you hate, divorce!" the other said "If hating you divorce...". The former came to be regarded as "the LXX" of Mal. 2:16 to the neglect of the other reading. Jones says there is overwhelming manuscript evidence for the latter reading.[10]

- 1994 (C. John Collins) renders the Septuagint as **If having hated you should divorce...** because "the participle is an aorist, and an adverbial aorist participle before the main verb normally denotes action prior to that of the main verb."[11]

- 1994 (C. John Collins) translates the Hebrew: **For he hated, he divorced [his wife] ... and he will [consequently] cover his garment with wrongdoing.** Collins suggests that *šallaḥ* (divorce) be taken "as a Piel perfect, with a rare but not wholly unattested *a* in the first syllable rather than the usual *i*." This suggestion would give two perfect verbs (hated, divorced) denoting consecutive past action. He concludes: "Taken this way, Malachi 2:16 shows how the sin condemned but not named in verses 13 and 14 is a violation of the marital unity described in verse 15."[12]

---

8 Hugenberger, *Marriage as Covenant*, pp. 69, 72-3, 83.

9 Jones, *Biblical Christian Ethics*, p. 191.

10 See Jones, "A Note on the LXX of Malachi 2:16". Also Russell Fuller, "Text Critical Problems in Malachi 2:10-16" *Journal of Biblical Literature* 110/1 (1991): 54-7.

11 C. John Collins, "The Intelligible Masoretic Text of Malachi 2:16", p. 40.

12 Ibid., pp. 37-9.

- 1997 (Sprinkle) **When he hates so as to divorce, says the LORD God of Israel, then he covers himself with lawlessness.** Sprinkle says *I hate divorce* is "an impossible translation of the MT, one that can only be retained on the basis of conjectural emendation without any manuscript support." He takes the infinitive *šallaḥ* as a result clause.[13]

- 1998 (Stuart) **If one hates and divorces (Yahweh, Israel's God, said), he covers his clothes with crime (Yahweh of the Armies said).** Stuart sees both Hoonacker and Hugenberger's suggestions as reasonable and does not arbitrate between them. He describes Malachi 2:16 as a conditional sentence with a typical "if ... then" structure. The condition (if he hates and divorces) reflects the reference to divorce for aversion in Deuteronomy 24:3. The result (then he covers his clothes with crime) is the consequence of divorce for aversion.[14]

- 1999 (Holman Christian Standard Bible) **"If he hates and divorces [his wife]," says the LORD God of Israel, "he covers his garment with injustice," says the LORD of Hosts.**

- 1999 (Shields) **For the one who hates and divorces, says Yahweh, the God of Israel, covers his garment with violence, says almighty Yahweh.**[15]

- 2001 (English Standard Version) **For the man who hates and divorces, says the LORD, covers his garment with violence, says the LORD of hosts.** [16]

- 2003 (Zehnder) **For the one who hates and divorces, covers his garment with violence, says YHWH of hosts.** Zehnder says "The widespread rendering of the clause with 'For I hate divorce' is … untenable." He interprets *śānē'* as "either a verbal adjective or (with revocalization) as a Qal participle, *šallaḥ* as an infinitive Piel or (with revocalization) as a third person singular perfect Piel." He also gives, as an alternative translation, the same wording used by Hugenberger.[17]

These translations supply a weight of evidence against the common rendering "I hate divorce" and they all read the text as condemning a husband who both hates and divorces his wife. Since 1986, when the wave of these new translations began in earnest, an impressive degree of agreement has been developing amongst scholars.

DIFFERING VIEWS

There is not complete unanimity, however. For the sake of fairness, the scholars who have taken differing views will now be briefly canvassed. It will be seen that their various solutions have far less unanimity than the scholars listed above.

- Wilhelm Rudolph did not emend or revocalise *śānē'* but argued that it could be construed as a verbal adjective acting as a participle, with an elided first person singular pronoun "I" as the

---

13 Sprinkle, "Old Testament Perspectives on Divorce and Remarriage", p. 539.

14 Stuart, "Malachi", pp. 1339, 1343-4.

15 Martin A. Shields, "Syncretism and Divorce in Malachi 2:10-16", *Zeitschrift für die Alttestamentliche Wissenschaft* 111 (1999): 76.

16 Heth, "Jesus and Divorce, How my mind has changed", p. 7, comments that the ESV is "the most probable translation".

17 Zehnder, "A Fresh Look at Malachi 2:13-16", pp. 251-2.

subject. He read "sallah" as the object and arrived at "Because I hate divorce".[18] Hugenberger refuted this, saying there are "no other first person pronouns in the context, and ... a verbal adjective of *śānē'* is otherwise unattested".[19] Rudolph also repointed "covers" as an infinitive construct and added a prepositional prefix to it. Martin Shields refuted this by saying, "When a participle constitutes the predicate of a verbless clause, the subject is usually explicitly represented in the clause. The absence of such explicit representation in Malachi 2:16 is a serious difficulty for this view."[20]

- In 1984, Ralph L. Smith emended *śānē'* to the first person perfective form ("I hate") as found in Malachi 1:3.[21]

- In 1986, A. S. van der Woude rejected the "I hate divorce" reading because it required emendation of "he covers". He recognized the third person of "hates" but rejected Hoonacker's translation on the grounds that "it must sincerely be doubted whether in Old Testament times even a prophet would have denounced divorce as a crime. Deuteronomy 24 tells against this interpretation." His solution was to translate *šallah* not as divorce, but as "a morally detestable hostile act".[22]

- In 1987, Pieter Verhoef rejected the translation "he hates" because he thought it must lead to "if he hates, let him send away" — which would contradict all that the prophet was seeking to convey. He argued for "I [God] hate divorce", positing an elided "I" and repointing *śānē'* to make it the Qal participle *śōnē'*.[23]

- In 1993, Andrew Cornes echoed Verhoef and Rudolph. He rejected a posited translation, "if he hated when divorcing it would be as bad as covering his garment with violence", because "it would imply that divorce was perfectly acceptable if there were no hate involved and that would undermine all that Malachi is wanting to say about not breaking faith with your partner..."[24]

- In 1994, Eugene Merrill argued for "I hate divorce", simply because he claimed that that translation seemed to be preferred by the majority of scholars. He saw no difficulty in rendering "he hates" as "I hate" because "one must allow for fluidity in such grammatical forms".[25]

---

18 Wilhelm Rudolph, *Haggai, Sacharja 1-8, Sacharja 9-14, Malachi*, Kommentat zum Alten Testament (Gutersloh: Gutersloher Verlagshaus Gerd Mohn, 1976) p. 270; ibid., "Zu Mal. 2:10-16" *Zeitschrift fur die Alttestamentliche Wissenschaft* 93 (1981): 90.

19 Hugenberger, *Marriage as Covenant*, p. 64.

20 Shields, "Syncretism and Divorce in Malachi 2:10-16", p. 82.

21 Ralph L. Smith, *Micah: Malachi*, Word Biblical Commentary Series vol. 32 (Waco, Texas: Word Books, 1984), p. 320.

22 A. S. van der Woude, "Malachi's Struggle for a Pure Community: Reflections on Malachi 2:10-16", in *Tradition and Re-Interpretation in Jewish and Early Christian Literature* ed. van Henten, de Jonge, van Rooden, & Wesselius (Leiden: E. J. Brill, 1986), pp. 65-71.

23 Pieter A. Verhoef, *The Books of Haggai and Malachi* (Grand Rapids: Eerdmans, 1987), p. 278.

24 Cornes, *Divorce and Remarriage*, p. 167.

25 Eugene Merrill, *An Exegetical Commentary: Haggai, Zechariah, Malachi* (Chicago: Moody Press, 1994), pp. 420-25.

- In 1995, David Petersen translated verse 16a as "Divorce is hateful!" reading *ki* as asseverative and *šallah* as either a Piel imperative or an infinitive absolute. However, he read the passage as a metaphorical comment about Yahweh's relationship to Israel rather than taking a literal divorce interpretation.[26]

- In 1995, John J. Collins reviewed Hugenberger's book, applauding the new translation, but questioning the conclusion that Malachi was making a distinction between divorce based on aversion and divorce that is justified:

> He [Hugenberger] is surely right to reject the traditional translation "for I hate divorce," since the term "hate" is very widely associated with divorce in the extrabiblical sources. Despite the support of Westbrook, however, the term "hate" does not imply that divorce is "merely on the ground of aversion". In the context of divorce, to "hate" means to repudiate without further qualification. The term is used as a technical term for divorce in the Elephantine papyri and the technical sense is reflected in such expressions as "silver of hatred" = divorce money, and "judgment of hatred" = divorce proceedings. The fact that the longer expression "hate and divorce" is also used at Elephantine does not prove that "hate" implies something beyond mere divorce. Marriage formulae are often redundant (cf. "to have and to hold, to love and to cherish"). We need not conclude that Malachi condemned divorce without qualification. Prophetic speech does not lend itself to legal niceties. We can only conclude that he was unhappy with the current practice of divorce in his day. We cannot attribute to him, on the basis of the verb "to hate", a distinction between divorce based on aversion and divorce that is justified.[27]

Against John J. Collins, the view of Douglas Stuart may be relevant:

> For those who recognize the overt dependency of the prophets on the Pentateuch and of Malachi specifically on Deuteronomy, it is entirely reasonable to expect that Malachi would be careful in the process of condemning what his contemporaries were doing — divorcing their first wives to marry pagans — not to state that all divorce was illegal. He might do this in the most semantically economical way (by the use of a single adjective ["hating"] to pin down the type of divorce under attack), but he would certainly want to do it.[28]

- In 1998, Andrew Hill argued that: "*śānē'* makes excellent sense if one presumes that the subject, *hā'ehād* ['The One,' i.e., Yahweh], of the verb has been gapped from verse 15 ('Indeed, *The One* hates divorce...')." Yet Hill seemed to contradict himself by implying that the divorcing husband was the one doing the hating: "The occurrence of the verbs *śn'* and *šlh* [hate/divorce] in Deuteronomy 24:3 gives rise to the interpretation that 'hating' or 'aversion' was the motive for divorce."[29]

---

26 David L. Petersen, *Zechariah 9-14 and Malachi: A Commentary* (Louisville: Westminster John Knox Press, 1995), pp. 194-5.

27 John J. Collins, "Review of *Marriage as Covenant* by Hugenberger" *Journal of Biblical Literature* 114/2 (1995): 307.

28 Stuart, "Malachi", p. 1342.

29 Andrew E. Hill, *Malachi: A New Translation with Introduction and Commentary,* The Anchor Bible (New York: Doubleday, 1998), pp. 250-1.

Appendix 8
Where Jesus agreed and disagreed with Shammai and Hillel

Shammai and Hillel were both Jewish religious teachers who lived about two decades before Jesus. A school of followers developed around each man's teachings. One difference between the schools was their interpretation of Deuteronomy 24:1-4.

> The School of Shammai says: A man should not divorce his wife unless he has found unchastity in her, for it is written, *Because he hath found in her* **indecency** *in anything.* And the School of Hillel say: [He may divorce her] even if she spoiled a dish for him, for it is written, *Because he hath found in her indecency in* **anything**.[1]

Christians have often assumed that Shammai was right about Deuteronomy 24 and Hillel was wrong, but this is mistaken and simplistic; the truth is far more complex. Yes, Jesus allowed divorce for *porneia,* but this does not mean that Shammai was completely correct in his interpretation of Deuteronomy 24:1, nor that Hillel was completely wrong. Shammai and Hillel held some points in common. Jesus agreed with some of these points, and disagreed with others. Shammai and Hillel were in controversy about their specific differences. Jesus agreed with Shammai on some of these distinctions, and agreed with Hillel on others. What exactly did Jesus agree with, and what did he disagree with?

Jesus agreed with both schools that sexual sin was ground for divorce. He opposed both schools by teaching that the mere existence of a divorce certificate did not automatically legitimize remarriage. Most importantly, he disagreed with both schools where they presumed that Deuteronomy 24:1, and in particular the term *erwat dabar,* spelled out "approved grounds" for divorce.

Probably Moses had used the term as a general expression in describing a situation where a man objected to his wife and so divorced her. He did not use it to indicate anything about what constituted *legitimate* grounds for divorce. According to Jesus, Moses knew divorce was occurring hard-heartedly and although he "permitted it" (i.e., reluctantly tolerated it), he did not condone it. Rather, he described it because he sought to prohibit the worst case outcome of such divorces.

As to the distinctive features of the Shammaite interpretation, while Jesus agreed that sexual sin was a ground for divorce, he rejected the idea that we know this from Deuteronomy 24:1's use of the expression *erwat dabar.* He also held a stricter attitude than Shammai on the question of remarriage. Shammaites did not denounce remarriages that took place after unjustified Hillelite divorces, whereas Jesus *did* denounce such remarriages.[2] Jesus was also more forbearing than Shammai, for Shammaites said a man *must* divorce his wife if she had been sexually unfaithful whereas Jesus did not make divorce obligatory in the case of adultery.

---

1 Mishnah git. 9.10 (trans. Danby; translator's emphasis).

2 See Keener, *A Commentary on the Gospel of Matthew* p. 463; Clark, *Putting Asunder*, p. 87.

As regards the distinctive features of Hillelites' interpretation, they said Deuteronomy 24:1 *indulged* men by giving them permission to divorce their wives for "any matter". They justified this from the word *dabar* ("matter" or "thing") in *erwat dabar*. Jesus did not argue against the notion that *erwat dabar* was vague enough to mean "anything a man might find objectionable about his wife". However, he strongly rejected the idea that *erwat dabar* (or *dabar* on its own) was necessarily a legitimate ground for divorce. These results are summarized in the following table.

BELIEF	SHAMMAI	HILLEL	JESUS
Severe neglect of the other partner's needs for food, clothing and sexual intimacy is ground for divorce.	Yes	Yes (All rabbinic schools believed Exodus 21:10–11 gave grounds for divorce to either sex.)	We may assume that Jesus agreed with the rabbis, because he never challenged them on this point, and because this would be consistent with his defense of the vulnerable.
Sexual sin is ground for divorce	Yes; adulterous wives must be divorced.	Yes	Yes, but it isn't obligatory to divorce a wife for adultery.
Deuteronomy 24:1 (and in particular the phrase *erwat dabar*) spelled out approved grounds for divorce.	Yes	Yes	No; Moses did not authorize those divorces, he suffered (or tolerated) them because men were so hardhearted. Deuteronomy 24:1–4 prohibited a certain hard-hearted behavior involving divorce and remarriage; it didn't validate a certain ground for divorce. Therefore, *erwat dabar* does not indicate anything about permissible grounds.
Erwat dabar equals and is limited to the sin of wifely adultery. (*erwat dabar = porneia*)	Yes	No; *erwat dabar* covers sexual sin, but isn't limited to that.	Jesus did not specify what *erwat dabar* meant in Deuteronomy 24.

BELIEF	SHAMMAI	HILLEL	JESUS
Erwat dabar is vague enough to cover "anything a man might find objectionable about his wife".	No; erwat dabar only means sexual sin.	Yes; erwat means sexual sin, and dabar means "matter", so erwat dabar means "any matter".	When we read Deuteronomy 24:1-4 in light of Jesus' commentary, we may conclude that erwat dabar was simply one way Moses indicated that a hypothetical man found his wife objectionable.
A man may not divorce a woman he had raped before marriage, or one he had wrongly accused of fornication.	We may assume that Shammaites, Hillelites and Jesus all agreed with these rules.		
Apart from the above cases, a man engaging in divorce fulfils righteousness so long as he issues his ex-wife a certificate of divorce. He is then free to remarry without incurring sin.	Yes; they did not condemn the remarriage of men who had engaged in "any matter" divorce under the Hillelite system	Yes	No; a man who treacherously divorces and then remarries is guilty of adultery-by-remarriage (a breach of the seventh commandment).
A man does not break the 7th commandment unless he has sex with a woman who is still legally married to another man.	Yes	Yes	No; men are guilty of adultery when they take advantage of a system that legalizes treacherous divorce, and when they gaze lustfully at a woman to whom they are not married.

Appendix 9
Remarriage of an adulterous spouse

If an adulterous spouse remarries, is the new marriage adultery? Can you further nullify a covenantal connection if that covenant has already been nullified?

It would seem illogical to claim so. Let us take the instance of a woman whose husband divorces her because of her adultery. If a new man (not the illicit lover with whom she had committed adultery) chooses to marry her, he cannot be participating in the violation of any covenant. Therefore we cannot say he will be committing adultery (although he may be unwise in marrying a woman who has a history of being unfaithful to her previous husband). The same conclusions would apply if the genders were reversed. John Murray says we do not have a warrant to declare such a marriage legitimate *or* illegitimate.[1]

A slightly different question is, may a person divorced for adultery marry his or her partner in adultery? Would the sinful couple simply be continuing and compounding their shared guilt? The Jews believed an adulteress should be forbidden from marrying her lover.[2] While this rule is understandable, the Jews were going beyond scripture in making it.

Crispin has made the point that if we forbid remarriage to all those divorced for adultery, it implies that a person guilty of adultery can never be forgiven — yet scripture says the only unforgivable sin is blasphemy against the Holy Spirit. King David, after all, married the woman with whom he had committed adultery, and although God chastised him in many ways for this sin (and the sin of murdering Uriah), it is clear that God forgave David when he sincerely repented. Instone-Brewer has also made the point that the rule against marrying one's partner in adultery is very difficult to apply, for it is sometimes impossible to tell precisely how intimate the new couple were before one of them became divorced from a previous spouse.[3]

---

[1] Murray, *Divorce*, pp. 100-2.

[2] See Instone-Brewer, *Divorce and Remarriage in the Bible*, p. 287.

[3] Ibid. p. 28

Appendix 10
A brief history of doctrines on divorce and remarriage

LOSING TOUCH WITH THE JEWISH DEBATE

After the fall of Jerusalem in AD 70 the only rabbis to survive were the Hillelites, so Hillelite divorce became the sole method of divorce within Judaism. As the church spread and the apostolic era passed, Gentiles outnumbered Jews within the body of believers. This resulted in the church gradually losing touch with the significance of the phrase "any matter" as Jesus had used it in the context of the Hillelite/Shammaite debate.[1] Another understanding was lost: that Judaism had permitted divorce for disciplinary reasons other than sexual sin (i.e. for abuse or for persistent and serious neglect of marital obligations). Christians became unaware that Jesus had not censured divorce in general, but only treacherous divorce (as endorsed by the Hillelite system). Somewhere in the early centuries AD, Paul's teaching must become misunderstood and de-emphasised. Jesus' mention of sexual immorality came to be read as the solitary, monolithic exception to an otherwise global condemnation of divorce.

THE CHURCH FATHERS

Following the apostolic age, celibacy was increasingly idealized. By the end of the fourth century, clergy and monks were expected to be totally celibate and widows were strongly encouraged not to remarry. This trend influenced views about divorce and remarriage.

All the church fathers allowed divorce (that is, separation from bed and board) for adultery and a few said the innocent party *must* divorce in such a case. Some stated that adultery was the only ground for divorce. Many fathers did not explicitly discuss the meaning of 1 Corinthians 7:15. Basil taught that a woman ought to endure being beaten by her husband, or suffer his financial mismanagement, rather than separate from him.[2]

To explain Deuteronomy 24, Ptolemaeus and Origen said that Moses' divorce legislation was not divinely authorized and was contrary to the law of God but was ordained by Moses on his own authority as a lesser evil, divorce not being as bad as other kinds of unrighteousness that might ensue from an unhappy marriage. Tertullian stated that Jesus had abrogated the Mosaic concession and outlawed remarriage.

It would seem that most of the fathers forbade remarriage while an ex-spouse remained alive.[3]

---

1 See Instone-Brewer, *Divorce and Remarriage in the Bible*, pp. 238-9, 303; ibid., *Divorce and Remarriage in the Church,* pp. 130-4,142.

2 Letter CLXXXVIII, in *Saint Basil: The Letters,* trans. Roy J. Defarrari, vol. 3 (London: Heinemann; New York: Putnam, 1930).

3 Henri Crouzel claims that almost all the fathers prohibited remarriage by the innocent party after divorce for adultery; Pierre Nautin says that many Latin fathers from the second to the fourth centuries read Matthew 19:9 as allowing remarriage to the innocent husband of an adulterous wife. See Blomberg, "Marriage, Divorce, Remarriage and Celibacy", pp.180-81; Instone-Brewer, *Divorce and Remarriage in the Bible,* p. 258; Atkinson, *To Have and to Hold,* p. 39.

A few discouraged or even forbade remarriage after the death of a spouse (e.g. Tertullian, Athenagoras). The Council of Elvira said that a woman who remarried while her adulterous husband still lived could only be given communion when the first husband had died, or when she herself was on her deathbed. However, if a man had unjustly deserted his catechumen wife (one undergoing Christian instruction but not yet admitted to baptism), she might later remarry and be admitted to baptism. Jerome (c. 400) taught that if a woman divorced an adulterous husband and her family forced her to remarry, she must desist from any further intercourse because that intercourse was adultery.

Ambrosiaster was unusual in saying that if an unbeliever deserted because he did not revere God, the marriage was invalid and this meant the deserted party could remarry. He taught that a man whose wife was sexually immoral could divorce and remarry; however, a woman with an adulterous husband could divorce but she must remain unmarried. He explained this by a rather wooden reading of 1 Cor. 7:10-11, arguing (from male headship and female submission) that the law does not restrict the man in the same way as it binds the woman.

The only record we have of a church father explicitly recognizing constructive desertion in 1 Corinthians 7:15 is Chrysostom who gave two examples: a violent and combative husband, and a husband who compelled his wife to participate in pagan sacrifices. "For it is the other party who furnished the ground of separation, even as he did who committed uncleanness [fornication]."[4] However, this was not recognition of full divorce, for, according to Chrysostom, if a man dismissed his wife, or if a wife wished to leave her husband, the separated wife could not marry another since she was bound by the law of marriage just as an escaped slave still carries his chain. If a wife separated from her husband but was unwilling to master her sexual desires, her only recourse was to return to the husband or wait till he died.[5]

Origen held adultery to be the only scriptural ground for divorce but he wondered why the Bible did not allow a man to divorce his wife for crimes like poisoning, murder, pillaging the house, or killing the couple's newborn baby while the husband was absent. He believed remarriage during the lifetime of a spouse equaled adultery, yet he observed that some church rulers *had* allowed the innocent wife of an adulterous husband to remarry during the lifetime of the ex-husband. He surmised that they made this concession as the lesser of two evils. Epiphanius said remarriage of the innocent spouse during the lifetime of the guilty spouse was tolerated by the church on account of human weakness.

Justin Martyr described the case of a Roman woman who had converted, but her husband would not abandon the immoral life they had previously enjoyed together. She stayed with him against her feelings, because some friends encouraged her to hope for his conversion. Eventually, when he was away in Alexandria, having heard that his behavior was worse than ever, and not wanting to be a partaker of his wickedness, she sent him a divorce certificate. In response the husband got the local official to persecute Christians, and her Christian teacher was executed. Justin did not mention what happened to the woman.

---

4 Chrysostom, Homilies on 1 Corinthians, hom. XIX.

5 See Chrysostom's Second Homily on Marriage, cited by Instone-Brewer in *Divorce and Remarriage in the Bible*, p. 253. Also Chrysostom's discussion of Matthew 5:32 in his Homilies on the Gospel of Saint Matthew, iii. XVII.

INDISSOLUBILITY: MARRIAGE CONTROLLED BY THE CHURCH AND SEEN AS A SACRAMENT

Augustine of Hippo consolidated the idea that remarriage was adultery because marriage bonds were a permanent obligation that ought to last (or in fact did last) until death. In the case of adultery he first said he was unsure that the innocent partner's remarriage was a sin and if it was he thought it was not a grievous sin. Later, he wrote that this innocent spouse *would* commit adultery by remarrying.[6] He said the term *"sacramentum",* from the Vulgate translation of Ephesians 5:32, referred to the symbolic stability of marriage.

The decline of the Roman Empire meant the disintegration of the secular judicial system that had regulated marriages. By the sixth and seventh centuries the church had taken on the legal regulation of marriages.[7] Frankish regions in the eighth century tolerated (officially or unofficially) some instances of a man's remarriage (no mention is made of a woman's remarriage). Instances when a man's remarriage would be permitted are: (1) when a husband had been obliged to go abroad, and his wife, out of attachment to home and relatives, refused to accompany him; (2) if a wife had engaged men to kill her husband and he had foiled the plot by killing her accomplices in self-defense; also the wife's (3) willful desertion or (4) adultery; (5) being enslaved as punishment for a crime; (6) being taken prisoner in war.[8]

From the twelfth century onward the idea of Christian marriage as a sacrament was elaborated and systematized as doctrine by Thomas Aquinas and others. This system became canon law for the Roman Church. Marriage was declared sacramental because it enabled the Christian couple to have sexual relations without sin, it conformed to the Creation ordinance, it produced offspring which enlarged the church, and it reminded the couple of Christ's taking the church as his bride.

Building upon Augustine's idea of symbolic stability, Aquinas claimed that marriage between Christians brought sanctification, that is, it caused and conferred "grace" upon the individuals. The Roman Church taught (and still teaches) that Christ's death on the cross while paying the price for sin did not make sufficient payment for all of a person's sins, so a person must also build up their own fund of "grace" by doing works such as baptism, confirmation, the eucharist, confession, penance, and good deeds. This fund of grace was supposed to help a person pass more quickly through the fires of purgatory, a place where, according to Rome, believers go after death for their remaining sins to be burnt up before they can go to heaven. (The doctrine of purgatory is not held by Protestant denominations.)

Aquinas taught that the marriage bond between two Catholics must be indissoluble because the union between Christ and his church is indissoluble. Once this channel of sacramental grace had been opened it remained permanently open while both parties remained alive. If two believers became divorced because one spouse committed adultery, the innocent party could not remarry during the lifetime of the guilty party. In the case of an unbelieving spouse who was not willing to cohabit without insult to the Creator or without inciting the believing spouse to mortal sin, a believer could divorce the unbelieving spouse and remarry.[9] This was known

---

6 See Jones, *Biblical Christian Ethics,* p. 187.

7 See Theodore Mackin, S. J., *Divorce and Remarriage* (New York/Ramsey: Paulist Press, 1984), p. 367.

8 See "Divorce in Moral Theology", Catholic Encyclopaedia, www.newadvent.org.

9 See Aquinas, Summa Theologica, supplement, question 59 http://www.newadvent.org/summa/505900.htm .

as the Pauline privilege. Nevertheless, for most people abuse was only grounds for separation from bed and board, and only if body or soul were endangered. This was because Rome taught that infant baptism made one a Christian and they routinely baptized all babies, so the vast majority of people in Catholic countries were deemed to be believers.

A marriage could be annulled if Rome deemed it invalidly made in the first place. Remarriage after annulment was not considered adultery; but adultery, desertion and abuse were not grounds for annulment. Inevitably, some people used their wealth or influence to sway church officials into granting annulments.

THE EASTERN CHURCH

The Byzantine Church (also known as the Eastern Orthodox Church) did not take the monolithic approach of canon law. Each local church could deal with particular cases according to pastoral discretion while seeking to uphold both the sacredness of marriage and the moral growth of its individual members. Ideally marriage was held to be indissoluble with the marriage bond persisting even after death, but (on the basis of Christ's words) adultery was ground for divorce. Adultery represented moral death and so destroyed the marriage tie. In like manner other types of conduct might destroy a marriage: different types of sexual immorality including sodomy of the wife, treacherous actions, death threats, abortion without the husband's consent, prolonged disappearance, premarital and continuing impotence, contagion, incurable insanity, apostasy and heresy. Divorce might be granted in such cases and remarriage allowed.

THE PROTESTANT REFORMATION

As soon as the reformation began in 1517 marriage and divorce became hotly contested issues. Priests, monks and nuns were converted from Roman Catholicism and renounced their vows of celibacy to become married. People were prosecuted by Catholic courts for violating the canon law of marriage. Luther expressed his distress and perplexity over questions of divorce and remarriage, especially cases of desertion.[10] Reformed theologians and civil jurists produced tracts, sermons, legal briefs and pamphlets denouncing Rome's doctrines and affirming more biblical views of marriage and divorce.

The Reformers argued against the idea that marriage was a sacrament. The only two sacraments mentioned in scripture (baptism and the Lord's Supper) each carry with them a promise of God's salvation for those who would believe. Protestants said that marriage could not be considered a sacrament because it did not carry with it a promise.

Reformers said the church might advise and counsel about marriage and divorce but that legalities ought to be the province of the civil magistrate. Regions that became Protestant passed civil laws on marriage and divorce in defiance of Rome. Rome responded by reaffirming all the Catholic doctrines (indissolubility, separation from bed and board, etc.) at the Council of Trent (1563).

All Lutheran reformers and civil jurisdictions allowed divorce and remarriage for the innocent partner of an adulterous spouse, with criminal sanctions imposed upon the adulterer. Most also allowed willful and malicious desertion as a ground for divorce and remarriage.

---

10 See Mackin, *Divorce and Remarriage*, pp. 383-4.

Some allowed willful and persistent abstention from sexual intercourse as a ground. Other grounds were accepted by some jurisdictions: "impotence, grave incompatibility, sexually incapacitating illness, felonies, deception, serious threats against the life of the other spouse ..., confessional differences between the couple, defamation of a spouse's moral character, abuse and maltreatment, conspiracies or plots against a spouse, incest and bigamy, delinquent frequenting of 'public games' or places of ill-repute, and acts of treason or sacrilege".[11] Although the statutes named certain grounds, divorce was not necessarily easy to obtain. The person seeking a disciplinary divorce had to prove the offences had been committed, and pastors and magistrates often did not grant a divorce unless the appellant had positively demonstrated a willingness to reconcile.

These reforms brought marriage and divorce law more in line with the Bible's teaching, but some misunderstandings and inconsistencies lingered on. We may take John Calvin and the City of Geneva as an example. In cases of adultery, the innocent party was allowed to remarry, with the civil court applying criminal penalties to the adulterer. Calvin also taught that the guilty party may remarry after an interval of time, for he believed more sin would arise from prohibiting remarriage than from allowing remarriage. He saw malicious desertion or mutual separation as tantamount to adultery. However, he did not always allow remarriage for the victim of separation. In this Calvin represents those Protestants who grant full legitimacy to the ground of adultery but only a shadowy legitimacy to the ground of desertion. For the ground of constructive desertion the legitimacy was even more doubtful. Calvin only granted divorce for abuse and religious persecution by one's spouse if the innocent party's life and soul were imperiled (see appendix 11).

Divorce rates were very low in Calvinist Geneva because adultery and malicious desertion were the only grounds and the burden of proof was very high. This led to the Genevan Council, much against Calvin's wishes, reviving the practice of separation from bed and board in cases of "severe wife or child abuse, perennial fighting between couples, habitual desertion, contagious disease, habitual frigidity, and the like ... if all efforts at reconciliation failed".[12]

In the late sixteenth century the northern provinces of the Netherlands became Calvinist. They made marriage and divorce a matter for civil magistrates but they carried over the practice of separation from bed and board, ordering it frequently for such matters as adultery, abuse (including defamation), contagious disease, religious differences, sexual offenses, alcoholism and gambling. Yet they also permitted divorce with right of remarriage for adultery or desertion, and they included sexual and emotional desertion within the concept of desertion.

THE ANGLICAN SYSTEM

Wherever evangelical communities developed across the northern half of Europe and in the New World, marriage and divorce laws took on, to some degree or other, a Reformed model, with one outstanding exception. The Anglican Church started in the sixteenth century when Henry the Eighth (desiring to have his first marriage annulled) split with the Pope and declared himself head of the English church.

---

11   John Witte Jr, *From Sacrament to Contract: Marriage, Religion and Law in the Western Tradition* (Louisville: Westminster John Knox Press, 1997), p. 69. There was no one jurisdiction that accepted all these grounds.
12   See Witte, *From Sacrament to Contract*, p. 126.

In 1552, during the reign of Edward VI, the church attempted to reform marriage laws. The proposed statutes included clauses allowing divorce and remarriage to the innocent partner in cases of violence or secret plots such as to endanger life, and in cases where a husband was persistently cruel to his wife and had ignored the magistrate's order that he desist from such conduct. Paul's teaching was given as the authority for these rules.

However, Parliament did not pass the reforms so Anglicanism remained stuck in a system that (apart from allowing priests to marry, and rejecting the doctrine of marriage as a sacrament) resembled the early sixteenth century canon laws of Rome. Rulings were made by church courts, not civil courts. Annulment was allowed for marriages between close relatives (as per Leviticus 18), for pre-contract to an earlier party, or when a party was frigid, impotent or had not reached puberty. Divorce was allowed for proven adultery, for desertion of more than seven years, and for severe maltreatment. Each method of ending a marriage had its positives and negatives. Annulment permitted remarriage, but it affected inheritance and dowry rights, and made children of the annulled union into bastards. Divorce did not mean forgoing inheritance or dowry rights, but Anglican divorce only permitted separation from bed and board, never remarriage. In either method child custody belonged to the father.

The Westminster Confession (1646) was a doctrinal statement agreed upon by English, Scottish and Irish churchmen during the brief period of the Commonwealth in England. The section on divorce read:

> Although the corruption of man be such as is apt to study arguments unduly to put asunder those whom God hath joined together in marriage, yet, nothing but adultery, or such willful desertion as can in no way be remedied by the church, or civil magistrate, is cause sufficient of dissolving the bond of marriage: wherein a public and orderly course of proceeding is to be observed; and the persons concerned in it not left to their own wills, and discretion, in their own case. (Article 24.6)
>
> In the case of adultery after marriage, it is lawful for the innocent party to sue out a divorce and, after the divorce, to marry another, as if the offending party were dead. (Article 24.5)

These principles were not in conflict with Scottish divorce law, which already permitted divorce for both adultery and desertion when fully proven with the right to remarry. Many Puritans interpreted desertion to cover all behavior that nullified the marriage relationship, sometimes specifying examples such as when spouses require of each other intolerable conditions, long absence without news, malicious desertion, cruelty, contagious disease, and insanity.[13] But the English Parliament and the Anglican Church did not adopt the Confession's statement on divorce. A century later John Wesley, the father of Methodism, said that adultery is the only ground for divorce and remarriage, all other remarriage is adultery, and cruelty is not a ground for divorce.

By infinitesimal steps, English divorce law became more like the rest of the Protestant world. In 1658 divorce on grounds of adultery with the right to remarry became available to those with the means and influence to obtain a private Act of Parliament. In 1857 annulment,

---

13 See J. I. Packer, *A Quest for Godliness: The Puritan Vision of the Christian Life* (Wheaton: Crossway, 1990), p. 269.

divorce and separation from bed and board became obtainable by a private civil suit, while remarriage was allowed if adultery could be proven. Liberalization of English divorce law progressed further in the early twentieth century, reducing the cost, simplifying the procedures, and widening the grounds to include "desertion, cruelty, frigidity, habitual drunkenness, criminal conduct and other forms of fault".[14]

THE MODERN ERA

In the last third of the twentieth century, civil divorce across most of the Western world became transformed into "no fault" divorce. The question of who or what had caused the marriage breakdown was deemed virtually irrelevant in this secular system except where it might affect custody and property issues. Immoral conduct received minimal or no penalty. Churches were left articulating principles to their own congregations but having little influence on civil marriage and divorce laws — and often little influence on their own members who sometimes followed the trends of the wider (non-Christian) community.

Within modern Protestantism there is continuing debate about the Bible's teaching on marriage and divorce. However, this debate has been overshadowed by other controversies, for the fundamentals of the faith have been under attack. Vital doctrines have been assailed by higher criticism, modernism, Darwinism, experiential theology, paganism and Eastern religions. Able minds in theology have been working to defend the doctrines of creation, the Trinity, the deity of Jesus, the resurrection, heaven and hell, the full inspiration of the Bible, and the roles of the sexes. Most recently the doctrine under heaviest attack is the doctrine of God. All this has affected the amount of energy that could be devoted to clarifying the doctrine of divorce.

A large section of the divorce debate in recent decades has focused on whether Matthew's exception actually permits remarriage, along with the related question of whether *porneia* means "sexual immorality". Until recently, this has meant that relatively little energy was being devoted to 1 Corinthians 7.

Evangelicals have been attempting to find specific scriptural grounds for divorce and remarriage on the ground of cruelty. In part, this has been prompted by the recognition of domestic violence, which began in the 1970s as part of the feminist movement. There has been much dead wood to clear away from centuries of doctrinal misunderstanding — many old assumptions have hung on for a surprisingly long time. Churches that care about maintaining Biblical standards of behavior are now working at the hard task of granting ethical fairness to the innocent party in marriage breakdown whilst also interpreting the scriptures faithfully.

---

14 Witte, p. 204.

Appendix 11
Case study of a noblewoman

In 1552, a Protestant noblewoman wrote to the Geneva Consistory, headed by John Calvin, asking whether she had biblical grounds for leaving her Catholic husband. The woman's letter and the reply from the Consistory can be found on pages 193-198 of *The Register of the Company of Pastors of Geneva in the Time of Calvin*[1] and are reproduced below.

Letter from an unknown lady persecuted by her husband because of her faith

> Sirs, in the name of God and our Lord Jesus Christ may it please you to listen to the affliction of an unfortunate Christian woman who is subject to a husband that is an idolater and persecutor of Christians, not just at this moment, but for more than ten years now. Will you please excuse her if for the present she does not disclose her name, for with the help of the Lord it will shortly be revealed to you if you approve her leaving him with whom she has been placed through the power of her father and brothers, whom she did not dare to disobey. It is true that at that time she had no knowledge of the Gospel, but some time after the marriage it pleased the Lord to open her eyes to know her God, so that her husband and nearest relatives noticed it. Thereupon, torn by conflicting loyalties, she came to the point of speaking out openly for her God, who gave her a little more liberty in confessing her faith, which was taken well enough by her husband. He, however, held her all the time to the papal idolatry, forcing her to go to mass and to undertake journeys and pilgrimages and make vows to the saints. After six years of this he became so enraged that he sought other means for persecuting Christians because of the Gospel. Some he threw into prison; others he charged before the judges and nobility, of the kingdom, for he is a powerful nobleman with an income of ten thousand francs, and his word is well received among our robed and mitered bishops. He also forbids his wife to speak to any whom he suspects of listening to the Gospel. Knowing his fury, she keeps silent when she sees him blaspheming against Jesus Christ and His members in this way. This has the effect of making him still more frenzied, for he complains to all his household that she speaks no evil of those whom he calls Lutherans, that she belongs to their sect, and that he needs no further evidence. She admits this, knowing how displeasing it is to God to keep silence before men. He also threatens to throw her into the water or to commit her to perpetual imprisonment or to some other secret death, with the result that she has had to continue in this papal idolatry.
>
> She requests you in the name of the Lord Jesus to inform her whether the law of marriage compels her to live with her husband, or whether the Gospel permits her to leave him and to seek liberty to live to the glory of God in a place

1 Edited & trans. by Philip Edgcumbe Hughes (Grand Rapids: Eerdmans, 1996). Footnotes within the reproduced text are by Hughes.

where she can publicly call upon His name. Knowing, moreover, the family to which she belongs and the nobles of the realm with whom she is connected and who enjoy great favor with the king, she requests you most affectionately to let her know whether, if she were to withdraw herself to you and her return were demanded by the king or by her husband, you would give her up; for it is certain that he would not come to look for her, unless it were for the purpose of amusing himself by having her burnt or doing her slowly to death in a permanent dungeon.

She sends this gentleman to you, Sirs (hoping that you will show that charity which has the approval of the Lord Jesus Christ). He will describe to you the rest of her sad life; and, in order that you may give all the more credence to what she says, she has asked one of her closest friends to write to several persons of her acquaintance assuring them that this letter is not a fabrication, but truthful, as she herself knows it to be. If, further, it is permitted to speak and complain of grievous and severe assaults, be assured, Sirs, that no creature could have endured more than she for she suffers every kind of affliction of both spirit and body: apart from the strict servitude in which she is held, so that she does not dare to confess her God, so many unpleasantnesses are heaped upon her that the enumeration of them would take too long; but the carrier of this letter can tell you of them, if you wish to take the trouble to ask him, Sirs.

There are, besides, close relatives of her husband who have made confession of faith with her and have frequently spoken of the things of the Lord together, but who have banded against her, giving themselves over to sensual living and deserting Jesus Christ. In their revolt they perpetrate numberless persecutions, even against those who in time past have declared their faith to them, bringing accusations against them, causing them to be thrown into prison, and forcing them to offer themselves in military combat. In addition to all this, Sirs, her husband is their accomplice, ordering and attempting to compel her with all his power to incite others against one of our brothers in Jesus Christ, whom he is holding prisoner, because she has more friends than her husband, and he wishes her to engage them immediately for the execution of what he calls justice. She would rather die, Sirs, than do this. Even when he notices her pretences to conform to papal idolatry he resorts to extreme cruelty. Once, Sirs, when she was very seriously ill he required her to confess herself, which she was unwilling to do except to one whom she knew to be a believer. He then became so enraged with her that he refused to let her speak to the person whom she had requested, saying that they were both of them heretics. After she had recovered, one Easter Day, when she was still very weak from her illness she was compelled to receive her Easter communion from the hand of a priest, and in order to escape further idolatry she remained in the chapel of her home, keeping with her a small number of faithful servants. Her husband was so greatly enraged against her, and against her servants even more than her, that he was unwilling to see them, saying that they were all heretics and that he would have them burnt, cursing and blaspheming the name of Jesus Christ, so much so that his poor wife was compelled to keep away from him. If she wished to perform any charitable acts, such as visiting the sick or giving to the poor, he would never permit it; nor would he allow her to sing psalms or hymns or anything in praise of the Lord, since he hated this more than anything else in the world, with the result that neither she nor her servants dared to possess the psalms in French nor any books speaking of Jesus Christ; indeed, persons were appointed to keep a watch on her. He himself needed only to catch her at this to use it as an occasion for causing her further vexation. If any of his or her relatives die, he compels her to pay for masses to be sung for them and to be present at them, and if he suspects the beliefs of any he tries to compel her to slander and speak evil of them and to praise idolaters with him.

For the concluding part of her long and sad life, she entreats you humbly, Sirs, both you Messieurs of the Church and you Messieurs of the City, to meet together to formulate a reply to her sad request so that she may have a resolution of her case, for she has no desire to live any longer in this idolatry being deprived of all means of serving Jesus Christ, of obeying His commandments, and of confessing her faith. She would prefer the condition of a servant with you, Sirs, rather than to continue in an exalted position in this idolatry. Will you, then, be so kind as to give a ruling under your seal as to whether a woman is permitted to leave her husband for the reasons described above, and for others also which you may learn from the carrier of this letter; and also whether, if she were with you and the king or other great noblemen demanded it, you would deliver her up? These things she commends most humbly to your goodness.[2]

From France, 24 June 1552

Received 22 July 1552

REPLY TO THE PRECEDING LETTER [3]

With reference to the appeal made to us by a noble lady who because she wishes to follow the true and pure religion is ill treated by her husband and held in most severe and cruel servitude, and with reference to the inquiry contained in her letter, namely, whether it would be lawful for her to leave her husband and withdraw herself here, or to some other church, where she could live with peace of conscience, we have unanimously agreed to give the following reply.

In the first place, we bear in mind the perplexity and anguish in which she must be, and we are affected with such pity and compassion that our heart goes out to her, praying God that it may please Him to grant her such relief that she may have cause to rejoice in Him.

---

2 Ordinary precaution required that this letter should bear no signature.

3 The original of this letter is lost, but a copy has been preserved in the Register. Its composition may with reasonable certainty be attributed to Calvin, and it has been published in all the editions of the Reformer's letters. It is reproduced in Calvini Opera, X, coll. 239ff.

Since, however, she requests advice as to what she may be permitted to do, it is our duty to state in reply purely and simply what God shows us by His Word, closing our eyes to all else. We pray her, therefore, not to be exasperated if our counsel does not conform entirely with her desire; for it is imperative that both she and we should follow the Master's orders without mingling our feelings with them.

It must be remembered that the situation in marriage is such that a believing spouse cannot voluntarily leave an unbelieving partner, as St. Paul shows in the 7th chapter of the First Epistle to the Corinthians [v. 13]; and there is no doubt that St. Paul intends this even when the believing husband or wife has to suffer a great deal, for in his day the pagans and the Jews were no less inflamed against the Christian religion than are the papists today. But St. Paul enjoins that the believing partner should endure bravely and persevere with constancy in the truth of God, and should not desert the partner who is hostile.

In brief, we ought to prefer God and Jesus Christ to all the world in such a way that fathers, children, husbands, and wives are of no account to us, with the result that if we can be loyal to Him only by renouncing all, then this is what we must do. But this is not to say that Christianity should abolish the order of nature when the two are able to exist together. It is fitting rather that a Christian wife should redouble her efforts to fulfill her duty to her husband who is an enemy of the truth, so that if possible she may win him, as St Peter says in the 3rd chapter of his first canonical epistle [v. 1].

Moreover, as things are today in the papacy, a believing wife is not fulfilling her duty if she does not use every endeavor to lead her partner into the way of salvation. Even when she is met with extreme obstinacy, there should be no semblance of her turning from the faith, but she should rather affirm her resolution and constancy, whatever the danger it may involve.

On the other hand when persecution arises it is permissible for a partner to flee, after she has fulfilled what is her duty. For when husband or wife have made confession of faith and have shown, if necessity demands, that they ought to and can in no way consent to the abominations of the papacy, then, if persecution arises against them for this reason and they find themselves in extreme danger, they may justifiably avail themselves of a means of escape, should God provide one. For flight from persecution when one is compelled to it is not the same thing as a voluntary divorce.

Now, the noble lady who requests our advice is very far from having reached this point in the performance of her duty. For according to what she herself says in her letter she is only silent and dissimulates. When pressed to defile herself with idolatry she yields and complies. This being so, she has no excuse for leaving her husband, without having made a more adequate declaration of her faith and without having endured and resisted greater compulsion.

She must pray God, therefore, that He will strengthen her, and then she must battle with more constancy than hitherto, in the power of the Holy Spirit, both with all sweetness and humility to show her husband what faith she holds, and also to make it clear to him that for her to comply with his demands would be to sin against God. We do not overlook her husband's roughness and cruelty of which of which she has told us; but all this does not prevent her from being courageous, while commending the outcome to God. For we may be assured that when, because governed by fear, we do not dare to put our vocation to the test, this proceeds from lack of faith; and this is not a foundation on which to build.

If, after having put to the proof the things we have said, she finds herself in grave peril, and her husband is persecuting her to the death, then she may avail herself of the liberty which our Savior grants to His followers for escaping from the fury of the wolves.

As for the question of personal security, the gentleman who carries this letter will inform her what we have said by word of mouth, giving the reason why we have not gone further.

22 July 1552[4]

This case has been given in detail not from a desire to particularly comment on Calvin, but because it contains elements that can be found in many other cases of abuse of a Christian spouse by an unbeliever. For one thing, it is not uncommon that the husband's threats are at least partially discounted by those in authority, while the victim's godly conduct is overlooked and she is emphatically told that she is in sin. To his credit, Calvin took the view that the woman's sin was her complying with some of her husband's wicked demands. This contrasts with many other church leaders who have taken the (more damaging) view that the wife's sin is because "she provokes her husband".

The woman gives a fair amount of detail about the techniques of abuse used by her husband, more detail than many victims often give when applying for support from a person in authority. However, it would have been possible for her to give more. In particular, she could have described in detail some of the "grievous and severe assaults" — which may in fact have already endangered her life, the criterion required by the Consistory for legitimate separation. Such details may not have swayed the Consistory, of course, but it may have made them less ready to declare her declaration of faith inadequate. The Consistory only faintly acknowledged the fact that she had borne with ten years of persecution precisely *because* she wished to obey the scriptures about marriage. It is clear that they had little appreciation of the effects of traumatic stress, especially prolonged stress where the victim believes she cannot escape and/or it is her duty to remain in the stressful situation. Such stress can sap moral courage. It is possible that this letter galvanized the woman into determined refusal to attend Mass, but it is also possible that she felt such strong condemnation from the letter that she never could have mustered the strength to take a decisive stand against all idolatry.

The Consistory required that the abuse be life-endangering before escape was permitted. This condition would make it easy for an abuser whose methods of abuse do not run to extreme violence. If a wife refused to comply with any Papal idolatry, her husband could punish her with emotional abuse, restriction of liberty, threats, sexual abuse and other forms of control, yet the

---

4 The Register carries no record of the signatories to this letter.

Consistory would require the victim to stay in the marriage. Furthermore, a clever abuser could imprison his victim before embarking on conduct that endangered her life. According to the Consistory's guidance, such a victim was not allowed to flee from the impending imprisonment because, at that stage, her life had not yet been endangered.

The reader may like to try a simple exercise. Make a list of all the things the husband had done and all the things the wife had done, according to this woman's letter. Also list the significant points of the Consistory's response. Then compare your list with the list over the page. It is easy to miss the full force of what the victim is saying, especially when she expresses herself so graciously and makes her request with such politeness.

The husband had:

- persecuted her for ten years, with increasing severity over that time

- grievously assaulted her on numerous occasions

- forbidden her to speak to her co-religionists

- forbidden her to possess Christian books

- censored her letters

- forbidden her to sing Psalms

- forbidden her to perform deeds of charity

- tried to make her slander or denounce other Christians and to praise idolaters

- compelled her attend Mass

- made her receive the Catholic eucharist when she was very weak from illness

- demanded that she pay for Masses for the dead when any of their relatives died

- appointed people to keep watch on her

- threatened to imprison, drown or otherwise secretly murder her

- threatened to have her, and her servants, all burnt

- The husband's threats needed to be taken seriously because he had caused another Christian to face unjust trial or be imprisoned, and shown complicity in forcing Christians to offer themselves in military combat.

The wife had:

- spoken out about her faith before her husband

- refused to confess herself to a priest

- refused to denounce or slander other Christians

- kept silent when her husband blasphemed (as Peter instructs wives in 1 Peter 3:1)

- sometimes not dared to confess her God before her husband

- under coercion, complied with her husband's demand that she pay for Masses for dead relatives

- under threat of imprisonment or death, sometimes complied with her husband by attending Mass, receiving the eucharist, undertaking pilgrimages and making vows to the saints

- not relied upon her own counsel in separating from the marriage, but sought counsel and safe harbor from one of the most respected Christian authorities in Europe .

The Consistory said:

- 1 Corinthians 7:13 tells a spouse not to desert an obstinately hostile, unbelieving spouse (they thus ignored, or did not realize, the condition in verse 13 that he be willing to live in goodwill with her)

- flight from marital persecution was only permitted when one's life was endangered (they did not specifically mention verse 15, and they added a condition about "life endangerment" that does not exist in Paul's epistle)

- because the woman dissimulated in attending Mass, she had not made an adequate declaration of her faith

- she needed to " redouble her efforts" to win her husband to Christ

- they acknowledged her "perplexity and anguish" but never praised her for the efforts she had already made: her endurance, her quietness before her husband's blasphemy, her refusal to betray fellow Christians, etc.

- they ignored the fact that her life had already been endangered inasmuch as her husband had threatened to murder her or have her burnt by the papal authorities .

Endnotes

Notes to Introduction

1 See, e.g., Augustine's testimony concerning his parents in appendix 1.

2 *Christianity Today*, Dec. 14, 1992.

3 Ibid.

4 Al Miles, *Domestic Violence: What Every Pastor Needs to Know* (Minneapolis: Augsberg Fortress Press, 2000), p. 35.

5 Anne L. Horton, Melany M. Wilkins & Wendy Wright, "Women Who Ended Abuse: What Religions Leaders and Religion Did for These Victims", in *Abuse and Religion: When Praying Isn't Enough,* ed. Horton & Williamson (Lexington, Mass.: Lexington Books, 1988) pp. 235-46. The study participants (187 battered victims, 97% female) were sought through public service announcements in US newspapers. Fifty-four percent of religious victims and 38% of nonreligious victims sought help from clergy.

6 For example, Stephen Clark, *Putting Asunder: Divorce and Remarriage in Biblical and Pastoral Perspective* (Bridgend, Wales: Bryntirion, 1999); David Instone-Brewer, *Divorce and Remarriage in the Bible: The Social and Literary Context* (Grand Rapids: Eerdmans, 2002); ibid., *Divorce and Remarriage in the Church: Biblical Solutions for Pastoral Realities* (Carlisle, Cumbria: Paternoster, 2003); Craig S. Keener, *...And Marries Another* (Peabody: Hendrickson, 1991), pp. 106-7; David Clyde Jones, *Biblical Christian Ethics* (Grand Rapids: Baker Books), pp. 203-4.

7 See James & Phyllis Alsdurf, "A Pastoral Response", in *Abuse and Religion: When Praying Isn't Enough*, eds Horton & Williamson (Lexington, Mass.: Lexington Books, 1998), pp. 167-8. There have been, to my knowledge, no recent surveys of ministers' views on the permissibility of divorce or remarriage for victims of spouse abuse.

8 This reasoning is paraphrased from Jones, *Biblical Christian Ethics,* pp. 203-4. See also Craig L. Blomberg, "Marriage, Divorce, Remarriage and Celibacy", *Trinity Journal* 11n.s./2 (1990):192; ibid. *1 Corinthians* (Grand Rapids: Zondervan, 1994), pp. 138-9; ibid. *Matthew*, New American Commentary Series, vol. 22 (Nashville: Broadman Press, 1992), p. 293; Craig S. Keener, *Matthew,* IVP New Testament Commentary Series, ed. G. R. Osborne (Downers Grove: InterVarsity Press, 1997), p. 123.

9 See Vicky Whipple, "Counseling Battered Women from Fundamentalist Churches", *Journal of Marital and Family Therapy* 13/3 (1987): 251-8.

Notes to chapter one
What is Abuse?

10 Partnerships Against Domestic Violence, *Two Lives, Two Worlds: Older People and Domestic Violence* (Canberra: Australian Commonwealth Government, 2000), vol. 1, p 33.

11 "World Report on Violence and Health - Summary", WHO, 2002. See also Eleonora Dal Grande, Jacqueline Hickling, Anne Taylor & Tony Woolacott, "Domestic Violence in South Australia: a population survey of males and females", *Australian and New Zealand Journal of Public Health* 27/5 (2003): 547; Marc Dubin, "Men as Victims of Intimate Violence", www.xyonline.net/menasvictims.

12 US National Institute of Justice/Centers for Disease Control and Prevention, "Prevalence, Incidence and Consequences of Violence Against Women: Findings From the National Violence Against Women Survey," 1998. This survey sampled both men and women.

13 US Department of Justice, National Crime Victimization Survey, 2001. This nationally representative survey asks men and women about events they perceive as crimes against themselves.

14 Dale Bagshaw & Donna Chung, *Women, Men and Domestic Violence* (Canberra: Australian Commonwealth Government, Partnerships Against Domestic Violence, 2000), p. 13.

15 With physical assault by intimates in the US, the injury rate for women is 41%, for men 19%. See National Institute of Justice/Centers of Disease Control and Prevention (USA), "Prevalence, Incidence and Consequences of Violence Against Women: Findings from the National Violence Against Women Survey" (1998), pp. 7, 9.

16 Bagshaw & Chung, *Women, Men and Domestic Violence,* p. 13.

17 See Colin Phillips, "Equipping Religious Professionals to Engage Effectively with Domestic Violence", *Journal of Religious and Theological Information* 4/1 (2001): 55.

18 For example, Nancy Nason-Clark's study of evangelical clergy in Canada found that 83% had counseled women who had abusive partners, with 43% counseling two or more such women per year. Of the same clergy, only 40% had counseled men with abusive partners and only 10% encountered such men two or more times per year. See N. Nason-Clark, *The Battered Wife: How Christians Confront Family Violence,* (Louisville: Westminster John Knox, 1997).

19 A good discussion and overview of this subject is Michael Flood's "Domestic Violence Against Men", 2003. www.austdvclearinghouse.unsw.edu.au/RR docs/Flood-DV against men.pdf See also Michael Kimmel, "Male Victims of Domestic Violence: A Substantive and Methodological Research Review", 2001. www.xyonline.net/downloads.malevictims.pdf

20 Partnerships Against Domestic Violence, *Two Lives, Two Worlds: Older People and Domestic Violence,* (Canberra: Australian Commonwealth Government, 2000), vol. 1, p 17. This volume includes information about 22 male victims' experiences.

21 See Bagshaw & Chung, *Women, Men and Domestic Violence,* p. 11.

22 See Eva Lundgren, "I am endowed with All the Power in Heaven and on Earth: When men become men through 'Christian' abuse", *Studia Theologica* 48 (1994): 33-47.

23 Ibid., 35.

24 Many of these examples are taken from Marge Cox, "Reflections of an Abuse Survivor", in *Healing the Hurting: Giving Hope and Help to Abused Women,* ed. Catherine Clark Kroeger & James R. Beck (Grand Rapids: Baker, 1998), pp. 75-81.

25 This does not mean all weak men are abusers.

26 Al Miles, *Domestic Violence,* p. l22. The British Crime Survey of 1996 found that only one third of (male and female) victims saw themselves as "victims of domestic violence", with females being much more likely than males to identify with that label. Only 17% of all incidents (involving male and female victims) were considered to be crimes by their victims, but virtually no male victims saw themselves as "victims of crime". Women were more likely to say "it was wrong, but not a crime" whereas men were more likely to say "it was just something that happens".

27 Victoria Police (Australia), *A Way Forward-Violence Against Women Strategy*, August 2002.

Notes to chapter 2
Biblical Action Steps

28 I want to record my gratitude to Rev. John Stasse who mentioned the biblical principle of fleeing the first time I disclosed my own situation to him.

29 The wider context of the epistle also addresses the importance of a person not taking the Lord's Supper if he or she is in a state of unrepentant sin (11: 27-30).

30 1 Kings 13:9, where the man of God from Judah was commanded not to eat with anyone in Israel, is another instance of mealtime fellowship being a sign of acceptance of the beliefs and practices of one's meal companions.

31 See John MacArthur, *1 Corinthians* (Chicago: Moody Press, 1983), p. 130.

32 Schreiner, "Loving Discipline", *Southern Baptist Journal of Theology* 4/4 (2002). www.sbts. edu/resources/sbjt/2000

33 See James & Phyllis Alsdurf, *Battered into Submission: The Tragedy of Wife Abuse in the Christian Home* (Downers Grove: InterVarsity Press, 1989; Guildford UK: Highland Books, 1989), pp. 43-4.

34 Nason-Clark, Fisher-Townsend, & Ruff, "An Overview of the Characteristic of the Clients at a Faith-Based Batterers' Intervention Program," *Journal of Religion and Abuse* 5(4) as cited in Nason-Clark, "When Terror Strikes at Home: The Interface Between Religion and Domestic Violence," *Journal for the Scientific Study of Religion* 43:3 (2004): 303-310.

35 See Kimmel, "Male Victims", p.16.

Notes to chapter 3
Does the Apostle Paul Permit Divorce for an Abused Spouse?

36 See Murray, *Divorce* (Phillipsburg: Presbyterian & Reformed, 1961), pp. 62-3; Jay E. Adams, *Marriage, Divorce and Remarriage in the Bible* (Grand Rapids: Zondervan, 1980), pp. 36-8; Stephen Clark, *Putting Asunder,* p. 242; Andrew Cornes, *Divorce and Remarriage: Biblical Principles and Pastoral Practice* (Grand Rapids: Eerdmans, 1993), p. 245; Blomberg, *1 Corinthians,* pp. 135, 139. Paul states several times in 1 Corinthians that he wrote with apostolic authority (7:17, 25, 40; 14:37).

37 See Instone-Brewer, *Divorce and Remarriage in the Bible: The Social and Literary Context,* p. 140.

38 Although this rendering makes the second "separate" masculine, this is only because Greek reverts to the masculine when either gender applies. The context indicates that the unbeliever may be female or male.

39 See Jones, *Biblical Christian Ethics*, p. 201.

40 See Adams, *Marriage, Divorce and Remarriage in the Bible,* p. 48.

41 See Clark, *Putting Asunder,* p. 155.

42 *The Oxford Companion to Law*, p. 353.

43 See Clark, *Putting Asunder,* p. 289.

44 William F. Luck, *Divorce and Remarriage: Recovering the Biblical View* (San Francisco: Harper & Rowe, 1987), pp. 82-4, employs the contrasting terms "treacherous divorce" and "disciplinary divorce".

45 Bauer, Arndt, Gingrich & Danker, *Greek English Lexicon of the New Testament*; Thayer, *Greek-English Lexicon of the NT;* Horst, Balz & Schneider *Exegetical Dictionary of the NT;* Zodhiates, *Complete Word Study Dictionary of the NT.* The Strong's concordance number for *syneudokeo* is 4909.

The word *syneudokeo* is used in Romans 1:32 in relation to the unrighteous: ...*who, knowing the righteous judgment of God, that those who practice such things are worthy of death, not only do the same but also approve* (syneudokeo) *of those who practice them.* The KJV translates *syneudokeo* here as "have pleasure in".

46 A new convert can enter a marriage before she understands the teaching about not being unequally yoked. Take my own case for example; see "About the Author" in the front of this book.

47 For example, a Christian woman may be in an abusive marriage, receive no support from fellow Christians, yet eventually flee from her husband. In post-traumatic stress, and the belief that God no longer cares what she does, such a woman may fall away from the Christian walk and be easy prey for another abuser who entices her into a second marriage.

48 See Clark, *Putting Asunder,* p. 182.

49 Dale Bagshaw, Donna Chung, Murray Couch, Sandra Lilburn & Ben Wadham, *Reshaping Responses to Domestic Violence Final Report* (Canberra: Australian Commonwealth Government Partners Against Domestic Violence & University of South Australia & Department of Human Services, 2000), p. 39.

50 Horton, Wilkins & Wright, "Women who ended abuse".

51 See Jones, *Biblical Christian Ethics,* p. 201; Adams, *Marriage, Divorce and Remarriage in the Bible,* p. 41. For helpful guidelines on discipline in divorce cases see appendix 3, also the Presbyterian Church in America's "Report of the Ad-Interim Committee on Divorce and Remarriage to the 20th General Assembly", (Atlanta: Georgia, 1993) http://www.pcanet.org/history, ch. 3, pp. 243-8).

52 Bauer, Arndt, Gingrich & Danker, *Greek English Lexicon of the New Testament.*

53 See Presbyterian Church in America, "Report on Divorce and Remarriage", pp. 228-9. This report reflects the pious advice of that particular assembly and has no constitutional force.

54 This telling phrase comes from a woman who stayed with her abusive husband; see email reproduced by Instone-Brewer, *Divorce and Remarriage in the Church: Biblical Solutions for Pastoral Realities* (Carlisle, Cumbria: Paternoster, 2003), p. 166.

55 Email to the author from Michael Hill, Moore College, Sydney.

56 See Clark, *Putting Asunder,* pp. 157-8; Lenski, *The Interpretation of St Paul's First and Second Epistles to the Corinthians* (Minneapolis: Augsburg, 1963), p. 297.

57 See MacArthur, *1 Corinthians,* pp. 93-4.

Notes to chapter 4
May I Remarry if I have Suffered Divorce?

58 See Murray, *Divorce,* p. 62; Adams, *Marriage, Divorce and Remarriage in the Bible,* ch. 7; Clark, *Putting Asunder,* pp. 147-148, 152; MacArthur, *1 Corinthians,* p. 90; Fee, *The First Epistle to the Corinthians,* p. 291; Lenski, *1st and 2nd Corinthians,* p. 285.

59 See Clark, *Putting Asunder,* pp. 142, 287.

60 See Instone-Brewer, *Divorce and Remarriage in the Bible,* pp. 198-9; Adams, *Marriage, Divorce and Remarriage in the Bible,* pp. 34-5; Guy Duty, *Divorce and Remarriage* (Bloomington, Minnesota: Bethany Fellowship, 1967, 1983), p. 92; William E. Heth & Gordon J. Wenham, *Jesus and Divorce* (Carlisle, Cumbria: Paternoster, 1997), pp. 138-40.

61 See Susan Treggiari, "Marriage and Family in Roman Society", in *Marriage and Family in the Biblical World,* ed. Ken M. Campbell (Downers Grove: InterVarsity Press, 2003) pp. 155-7;

David Atkinson, *To Have and to Hold* (London: William Collins, 1979), p. 109; Instone-Brewer, *Divorce and Remarriage in the Bible,* pp. 73-4, 190; Clark, *Putting Asunder,* p. 143.

62 See Jones, *Biblical Christian Ethics,* p. 200.

63 Since God's Word calls this woman "unmarried" she cannot be "still married in the eyes of God". See Adams, *Marriage, Divorce and Remarriage in the Bible,* pp. 42-3.

64 *Agamos* occurs in 1 Corinthians 7:8, 11, 32 & 34. See Clark, *Putting Asunder,* pp. 279-85; Adams, *Marriage, Divorce and Remarriage in the Bible,* pp. 42-3; MacArthur, *1 Corinthians,* pp. 85-7; B. Ward Powers, *Marriage and Divorce: The New Testament Teaching* (Concord, NSW: Family Life Movt. of Australia/Petersham, NSW: Jordan Books, 1987), pp. 181-8.

65 Philo (*Special Laws* III.30) said: "If a woman after parting from her husband for any cause whatever marries another and then again becomes a widow (*chera*), whether this second husband is alive or dead, she must not return to her first husband...". The Constitutions of the Holy Apostles was written (in Greek) by unknown authors some time no later than the fourth century. It says (III.1), "But if any younger woman, who has lived but a while with her husband, and has lost him by death or some other occasion, and remains by herself, having the gift of widowhood, she will be found to be blessed..." (Roberts & Donaldson, eds., *The Ante-Nicene Fathers,* vol. VII [Grand Rapids: Eerdmans, 1994], p. 426).

Similarly, the Hebrew word for "widow" (*almanah*) "refers to a woman who has been divested of her male protector, usually though not always through death" (Bob Burns, *Recovery from Divorce,* [Nashville: Thomas Nelson, 1989, 1992] p. 162). See 2 Sam. 20:3.

66 In Deuteronomy 24 a divorced man was not permitted to marry his former wife, but that was only when the wife had married a different husband in the intervening period.

67 Jones, *Biblical Christian Ethics,* p. 200.

A useful article is "The SBJT Forum: Perspectives on Church Discipline", *Southern Baptist Journal of Theology* 4/4 (2002). http://www.sbts.edu/resources/sbjt/2000/Forum.pdf

68 See Clark, *Putting Asunder,* pp. 174-5.

69 See Instone-Brewer, *Divorce and Remarriage in the Bible,* p. 211; David W. Chapman, "Marriage and Family in Second Temple Judaism", in *Marriage and Family in the Biblical World,* ed. Ken M. Campbell (Downers Grove: InterVarsity Press, 2003), p. 231. The concept of "free from bed and board, but not free from the marriage bond" would never have occurred to the Corinthians.

70 *The Mishnah: Translated from the Hebrew with Introduction and Brief Explanatory Notes,* ed. Herbert Danby (London: Oxford University Press, 1933), Gittin 9:3.

71 See Treggiari, "Marriage and Family in Roman Society", p. 150; Grubbs, *Women and the Law in the Roman Empire* (London & New York: Routledge, 2002), p. 84.

72 See Instone-Brewer, *Divorce and Remarriage in the Bible*, p. 289.

73 See Keener, *Matthew*, p. 191. Also William Heth, "Jesus and Divorce: How my mind has changed", *Southern Baptist Theological Journal* 6/1 (2002) http://www.sbts.edu/resources/sbjt/2002/Divorce.pdf, p. 14.

74 See Jones, *Biblical Christian Ethics,* pp. 200-1. In addition, Paul made no distinction between whether the state of being not married occurred before or after conversion.

75 Owen, "On Marrying after Divorce in Case of Adultery", in *The Works of John Owen,* vol. 16 (Edinburgh: Banner of Truth, 1968), p. 256.

76 See Treggiari, "Marriage and Family in Roman Society", pp. 136-9.

77 See Instone-Brewer, *Divorce and Remarriage in the Bible,* pp. 101, 121, 289.

78 Acts 18:8; 1 Cor. 12:13.

79 See Thomas Edgar, essay in *Divorce and Remarriage: Four Christian Views,* ed. H. Wayne House (Downers Grove: InterVarsity Press, 1990), p. 189.

80 See Instone-Brewer, "1 Corinthians 7 in the Light of the Jewish Greek and Aramaic Marriage and Divorce Papyri", *Tyndale Bulletin* 52 (2001): 225-43.

81 See Instone-Brewer *Divorce and Remarriage in the Bible*, pp. 202-3. For guidelines where both spouses are unbelievers, see appendix 4.

82 *Westminster Confession of Faith for the 21st Century,* ed. Douglas Milne (Strawberry Hills, NSW: Christian Education Committee of the General Assembly of the Presbyterian Church of Australia, 2001), ch. 24 clause 6.

Notes to chapter 5
Fighting the Giants

83 See Duty, *Divorce and Remarriage,* pp. 85-7.

84 See Instone-Brewer, *Divorce and Remarriage in the Bible,* p. 210-11; Duty, *Divorce and Remarriage,* p. 91; Atkinson, *To Have and to Hold,* p. 122.

85 See Instone-Brewer, *Divorce and Remarriage in the Bible,* pp. 127-30; Clark, *Putting Asunder,* p. 201.

86 The priest-divorcee marriage may have been forbidden because the extra "baggage" the divorcee might be carrying could affect the priest's home life, a thing especially undesirable for a priest whose role as law keeper and religious leader (and therefore a type of Christ) was a heavy responsibility.

87 *The Interlinear Bible, Hebrew-Greek-English,* 2nd edition, ed. & trans. Jay P. Green (Lafayette, Indiana: Sovereign Grace Publishers, 1986).

88 Contemporary English Version, Holman Christian Standard Bible, New Revised Standard Version respectively.

89 See Gordon D. Fee, *The First Epistle to the Corinthians* (Grand Rapids: Eerdmans, 1987), pp. 355-6; Instone-Brewer, *Divorce and Remarriage in the Bible,* pp. 208-9; ibid. *Divorce and Remarriage in the Church,* p. 100; ibid. "1 Cor. 7 in the light of Jewish Greek and Aramaic Divorce Papyri", p. 238.

90 Clark, *Putting Asunder,* pp. 160-72. Depending on the context, the words *gyne* and *aner* may be translated "wife" and "husband", "woman" and "man", or "betrothed wife" and "betrothed husband". If a betrothed Israelite male died, his betrothed wife was regarded as his widow; see m. Ketub. 1:2, m. Yebam. 4:10, 6:4, in Craig Evans & Stanley Porter, eds., *Dictionary of New Testament Background* (Downers Grove: InterVarsity Press, 2000), p. 685; Chapman, *Marriage and Family in Second Temple Judaism,* p. 187.

91 See Luck, *Divorce and Remarriage,* p. 24.

92 Jones, *Biblical Christian Ethics,* p. 204.

93 See Edgar, *Divorce and Remarriage; Four Christian Views,* pp. 63, 155; Luck, *Divorce and Remarriage,* pp. 8-14, 25, 187; Blomberg, "Marriage, Divorce, Remarriage and Celibacy", pp. 168-9.

94 Thanks to Michael Hill for assistance in the wording of this paragraph.

95 See Gary Collier, "Rethinking Jesus on Divorce", *Restoration Quarterly* 37/2, www.restorationquarterly.org/Volume_037/rq03702collier.htm p. 4 of web version; Jones, *Biblical Christian Ethics,* p. 193.

96 See Luck, *Divorce and Remarriage,* pp. 20-23, 224.

97 Ibid., pp. 29-30, 202-7.

98 See Edgar, *Divorce and Remarriage: Four Christian Views,* pp. 137, 154; Luck, *Divorce and Remarriage,* pp. 19-20.

99 I have modeled this imaginary example on a genuine case given by Paul Steele & Charles Ryrie in *Meant to Last* (pp. 119-121) which is cited in David Phypers, *Christian Marriage in Crisis* (Bromley, Kent, UK: MARC Europe, a ministry of World Vision, 1985), pp. 116-7.

100 See Adams, *Marriage, Divorce and Remarriage in the Bible,* pp. 42-3.

101 See Powers, *Marriage and Divorce,* p. 211.

102 See Instone-Brewer, *Divorce and Remarriage in the Bible*, p. 309.

103 See Clark, *Putting Asunder,* pp. 199-200.

104 See Powers, *Marriage and Divorce,* p. 198; Edgar, *Divorce and Remarriage: Four Christian Views,* p. 63.

105 See Instone-Brewer, *Divorce and Remarriage in the Bible,* pp. 227-8; Luck, *Divorce and Remarriage,* pp. 208-18; Keener, *...And Marries Another,* chapter 7; Heth "How my mind has changed", p. 22; Andreas Köstenberger, "Marriage and Family in the New Testament", in *Marriage and Family in the Biblical World,* ed. Ken M. Campbell (Downers Grove: InterVarsity Press, 2003), p. 276; Page, "Marital Expectations of Church Leaders in the Pastoral Epistles", *Journal for the Study of the New Testament* 50 (1993): 113-19; www.christiananswers.net/q-eden/eden-f008.html

106 See Treggiari, "Marriage and Family in Roman Society", pp. 133-4, 166-9; Baugh, "Marriage and Family in Ancient Greek Society", pp. 116-7, 121.

107 See Page, "Marital Expectations", p. 110.

108 See Luck, *Divorce and Remarriage,* p. 217; Adams, *Marriage, Divorce and Remarriage in the Bible,* p. 93.

109 See Keener, *...And Marries Another,* pp. 88, 90; Page, "Marital Expectations", p. 108; Treggiari, "Marriage and Family in Roman Society", p. 169; S. M. Baugh, "Marriage and Family in Ancient Greek Society", in *Marriage and Family in the Biblical World,* p. 116.

Notes to chapter 6

Is there any Hope from the Old Testament?

110 The following authors are welcome exceptions to this generalization: Clark, Instone-Brewer, Luck, Daniel I. Block, "Marriage and Family in Ancient Israel" in *Marriage and Family in the Biblical World;* Joe Sprinkle, "Sexuality, Sexual Ethics", in *The Dictionary of the Old Testament: Pentateuch,* eds. T. D. Alexander & D. W. Baker (Downers Grove: InterVarsity Press, 2003); ibid., "Old Testament Perspectives on Divorce and Remarriage", *Journal of the Evangelical Theological Society* 40/4 (1997): 529-50. There may be other exceptions the author is unaware of.

111 There is some dispute about whether this term means "sexual relations" or "oil".

112 See Block, "Marriage and Family in Ancient Israel", p. 48; Brewer, *Divorce and Remarriage in the Bible,* pp. 9, 26; Luck, *Divorce and Remarriage,* p. 32; Clark, *Putting Asunder,* pp. 33, 232-4.

113 See Block, "Marriage and Family in Ancient Israel", pp. 50, 60, n.124.

114 See Instone-Brewer, *Divorce and Remarriage in the Bible,* p. 30; Allan Harman, *Deuteronomy: The Commands of a Covenant God* (Ross-shire, Great Britain: Christian Focus, 2001), p. 198;

Josephus, *Judean Antiquities,* 4.259.

115 The RSV, ARV, ASV (1901 & 1929), KJV, and Tyndale's Pentateuch all wrongly gave the idea that "If a man becomes displeased with his wife then let him divorce her…" Adams (*Marriage, Divorce and Remarriage in the Bible,* p. 62) notes that modern commentators all agree on the change in translation.

116 See Luck, *Divorce and Remarriage,* pp. 51-2; Mishnah Gittin 8.5; Instone-Brewer, *Divorce and Remarriage in the Bible,* pp. 127-8.

117 Josephus saw the divorce certificate as the man's written promise that he would never have sex with the woman again (Judean Antiquities 4.253).

118 The following passages are examples of some of these meanings: Gen. 9:22-23; 42:9,12; Lev. 18; 20:11; Isa. 20:4; Ezra 4:14; Hos. 2:9.

119 See Clark, *Putting Asunder,* pp. 92-3, 238, n.16; Adams, *Marriage, Divorce and Remarriage in the Bible,* p. 64.

120 See Clark, *Putting Asunder,* pp. 36, 38-9; Instone-Brewer, *Divorce and Remarriage in the Bible,* p. 78.

121 Mishnah Sotah 4.2 states that such women were to be divorced; see Clark p. 124.

122 See Clark, *Putting Asunder,* pp. 42-46, 124. The Ordeal of Bitter Water was performed right up until A.D. 70 and the rabbis saw the marriage contract as "in the balance" while the ordeal was being carried out. See Instone-Brewer, *Divorce and Remarriage in the Bible* pp. 95-99, 143; Josephus, *Judean Antiquities,* note by Feldman on p. 311.

123 Joseph Blenkinsopp, "The Family in First Temple Israel", in *Families in Ancient Israel* (Louisville, Kentucky: Westminster John Knox Press, 1979), p. 65. Also Adams, *Marriage, Divorce and Remarriage in the Bible,* pp. 63-4.

124 See David Clyde Jones, *Biblical Christian Ethics,* p. 190; Clark, *Putting Asunder,* pp. 129-31, 253, n. 86.

125 See Westminster Confession ch. 5, para. 4.

126 The KJV aptly says *Moses because of the hardness of your heart* underline{suffered} *you to put away your wives* (emphasis added).

127 The woman is not said to have two husbands at the same time. She is forbidden to become the wife of the first husband again, which means she must have not been his wife in the interim period. See Adams, *Marriage, Divorce and Remarriage in the Bible,* p. 44; Luck, *Divorce and Remarriage,* p. 284; Sprinkle, "Old Testament Perspectives on Divorce and Remarriage", p. 532.

128 Hosea's story was possibly an exception to the rule prohibiting renewal of the first marriage. If so, the exception occurred providentially as a figure for God's marriage with Israel; God acted mercifully rather than according to law.

129 See Westbrook, "The Prohibition on Restoration of Marriage in Deuteronomy 24:1-4", in *Studies in Bible XXXI,* ed. Sara Japhet (Jerusalem: Magnes Press, The Hebrew University, 1986), p. 404.

130 J. G. McConville, *Deuteronomy,* Apollos Old Testament Commentary Series 5 (Leicester, UK: InterVarsity Press, 2002), pp. 355-60.

131 "…it is better to regulate sin than to relinquish control over it altogether." Keener, *The IVP Bible Background Commentary N. T.,* p. 96.

132 Philo saw the husband's offense as allied to pimping; see appendix 6.

133 If the woman received money upon the termination of the second marriage, the first husband could have profited by remarrying her, bringing the resemblance to pimping even closer. See Westbrook ("Prohibition", pp. 393-405) though his differentiation between the first divorce (as justified) and the second divorce (as unjustified) is not convincing. See Sprinkle, "OT Perspectives", p. 532; Edgar, *Divorce and Remarriage: Four Christian views,* p. 139.

134 Unfortunately quite a few commentators have seen the likeness to adultery but not the likeness to pimping, thus tending to emphasize the woman's sin and underplay the man's.

135 Sprinkle, "Old Testament Perspectives on Divorce and Remarriage", p. 532.

Notes to chapter 7
But I want to be Faithful to my Marriage Vows!

136 See Instone-Brewer, *Divorce and Remarriage in the Bible,* pp. 16-19, who suggests that because of the current distinction between "covenant" and "contract", it is preferable to use the term "marriage contract" when discussing marriages in the ancient Near East.

137 John Murray, *The Covenant of Grace* (Tyndale, 1954), p.10, reprinted in *The Collected Writings of John Murray,* vol. 4 (Banner of Truth, 1982); cited by D.C. Jones in "The Westminster Confession on Divorce and Remarriage", *Presbyterion* 16 (1990): 28.

138 If this seems somewhat unfair to husbands, it should be remembered that the Bible teaches male headship, and that male headship entails the responsibility of the husband to lead his wife in a God-glorifying direction (see the Council of Biblical Manhood and Womanhood's website).

139 See Rousas John Rushdoony, *Law and Society* (Valecito: Ross House Books, 1986), p. 121.

Notes to chapter 8
"God Hates Divorce" - Slogan or Scripture?

140 See Jones, *Biblical Christian Ethics,* p. 190.

141 Verse 16 in the NASB reads: *"For I hate divorce," says the LORD, the God of Israel, "and him who covers his garment with wrong," says the LORD of hosts.* Many other versions also have "I hate divorce" with the "I" referring to God.

142 Muriel Canfield, *Broken and Battered: A Way Out for the Abused Woman* (West Monroe: Howard Publishing Company, 2000), p. 27.

143 For other OT usages, see Gen. 49:11; Job 29:14; Ps. 35:26; 109:29; 132:9; Prov. 31:25; Isa. 14:19; 59:17; 61:10; 63:1-2; Lam. 4:14; Zech. 3:3-5. Kruger ("The Hem of the Garment in Marriage", *Journal of Northwest Semitic Languages* 12 [1984]: 79) notes that the cultures of the Ancient Near East saw the garment as an extension of a person's personality; see also Leland Ryken, et al., (eds), *Dictionary of Biblical Imagery* (Downers Grove: InterVarsity Press, 1998).

144 See Thomas V. Moore, *A Commentary on Haggai and Malachi* (Edinburgh: Banner of Truth, 1960; first published in *Prophets of the Restoration* [New York: Robert Carter, 1856]), pp. 138-9; Douglas Stuart, "Malachi", in *The Minor Prophets: An Exegetical and Expository Commentary,* vol. 3 *Zephaniah, Haggai, Zechariah and Malachi,* ed. Thomas Edward McComiskey (Grand Rapids: Baker Books, 1998), p. 1343.

145 See Jones, *Biblical Christian Ethics,* p. 192; also Stuart, "Malachi", p. 1344; C. John Collins, "The Intelligible Masoretic Text of Malachi 2:16 or, How does God Feel about Divorce?", *Presbyterion,* 20/1 (1994): 38.

146 See Carl F. Kiel, *Biblical Commentary on the Old Testament: The Twelve Minor Prophets,* vol. 2., trans. J. Martin (Grand Rapids: Eerdmans, 1954), p. 454; C. John Collins, "The Intelligible Masoretic Text of Malachi 2:16", pp. 38-9; Gordon P. Hugenberger, *Marriage as Covenant: Biblical Law and Ethics as Developed from Malachi* (Grand Rapids: Baker, 1994), p. 75; Instone-Brewer, *Divorce and Remarriage in the Bible,* p. 57; Andrew E. Hill, *Malachi: A New Translation with Introduction and Commentary,* The Anchor Bible (New York: Doubleday, 1998), p. 253; Markus Zehnder, "A Fresh Look at Malachi 2:13-16", *Vetus Testamentum* 53/ 2, (2003): 256.

147 Stuart, "Malachi", p. 1343.

148 Gen. 29:31; Deut. 21:15-17; 22:13, 16; 24:3; Judg. 15:2; Prov. 30:23; Isa. 60:15. See Hugenberger, *Marriage as Covenant,* p. 70.

149 Akkadian, Neo-Assyrian, and Elephantine (Egyptian Jewish of the 5th century BC).

150 Westbrook, "The Prohibition on Restoration of Marriage", pp. 400, 403.

151 See Westbrook, "The Prohibition on Restoration of Marriage", p. 403; Hugenberger, *Marriage as Covenant,* pp. 70-2; Sprinkle, "Old Testament Perspectives on Divorce and Remarriage", p. 539.

152 See Zehnder, "A Fresh Look at Malachi 2:13-16", p. 254.

153 The half-brackets indicate words supplied for clarity by the translators of the HCSV.

154 English Standard Version, 2001.

155 See Hugenberger, *Marriage as Covenant,* p. 51.

156 Stuart, "Malachi", p. 1344.

157 And to a degree the New English Bible.

Notes to chapter 9
Isn't Adultery the Only Ground for Divorce?

158 Rushdoony (*Law and Society,* pp. 698-9) speaks critically of these two pastoral decisions against victims of abuse.

159 Mishnah Git. 9.10 (trans. Danby; translator's emphasis). The proto-rabbis Hillel and Shammai were Jesus' predecessors by at least 20 years.

160 See Instone-Brewer, *Divorce and Remarriage in the Bible*, p.111.

161 Ibid., pp. 114-7.

162 For where Jesus agreed, and disagreed, with both Shammai and Hillel, see appendix 8.

163 See Instone-Brewer, *Divorce and Remarriage in the Church,* p. 45; ibid., *Divorce and Remarriage in the Bible,* pp. 113-5.

164 See Instone-Brewer, *Divorce and Remarriage in the Bible,* pp. 97, 115; Raymond E. Brown, *The Birth of the Messiah* (New York: Doubleday, 1979), pp. 127-8; Keener, *Commentary on the Gospel of Matthew* (Grand Rapids: Eerdmans, 1999), p. 93; ibid., *Dictionary of New Testament Background,* p. 685.

165 Instone-Brewer, *Divorce and Remarriage in the Bible*, pp. 113-7; Keener, *IVP Bible Background Commentary N.T.,* p. 96.

166 See Instone-Brewer, *Divorce and Remarriage in the Bible*, pp. 99-110, referring to Mishnah Ketub. 5.5-8, 7.1-6; *Divorce and Remarriage in the Church,* p. 86.

167 See Instone-Brewer, *Divorce and Remarriage in the Bible*, pp. 113-7.

168 See Instone-Brewer, *Divorce and Remarriage in the Bible,* pp. 85-90, 151-2; Instone-Brewer cites evidence that the courts could order a husband to be whipped if persuasive words had failed to induce him to sign the divorce certificate.

169 The word "just" in verse 3 is italicized in the NKJ, indicating it is not in the original Greek.

170 See Jones, *Biblical Christian Ethics,* p. 193.

171 See Blomberg, "Marriage, Divorce, Remarriage and Celibacy", p. 169; also Blomberg, *Matthew,* New American Commentary Series vol. 22 (Nashville: Broadman Press, 1992), p. 290.

172 Clark, *Putting Asunder,* pp. 83, 222; Adams, *Marriage, Divorce and Remarriage in the Bible,* p. 43; Atkinson, *To Have and to Hold,* pp. 111, 148; Luck, *Divorce and Remarriage,* pp. 10, 19; Edgar, *Divorce and Remarriage: Four Christian Views,* p. 137; Instone-Brewer, *Divorce and Remarriage in the Bible,* pp. 141, 283.

173 "And whoever marries her who is divorced commits adultery" does not appear in some manuscripts, but the issue is not significant because the clause is identical with Matt. 5:32b.

174 See Edgar, *Divorce and Remarriage: Four Christian Views,* pp. 165-8; Blomberg, "Marriage, Divorce, Remarriage and Celibacy", pp. 175-6.

175 Edgar, *Divorce and Remarriage: Four Christian Views,* pp. 168-9.

176 Owen, "On Marrying after Divorce in Case of Adultery", p. 256.

177 For thorough discussions of *porneia*, see Clark, *Putting Asunder,* pp. 64-5, 110-36; and Edgar, *Divorce and Remarriage: Four Christian Views,* pp. 162-4, 169-87.

178 Westminster Shorter Catechism, q. 87.

179 John Owen, "On Marrying after Divorce in Case of Adultery", p. 3. Heth & Wenham (pp. 115-18) argued for "divorce but no remarriage". Their syntactical argument has been successfully refuted by Phillip H. Wiebe, "Jesus' Divorce Exception", *Journal of the Evangelical Theological Society* 32/3 (1989): 327-33 ; Edgar, *Divorce and Remarriage: Four Christian Views,* p. 156-62; Luck, *Divorce and Remarriage,* pp. 141-5; Blomberg, "Marriage, Divorce, Remarriage and Celibacy", p. 178-80; D. A. Carson, "Matthew", in *The Expositor's Bible Commentary,* vol. 8 (Matthew, Mark, Luke), ed. Frank E. Gaebelein (Grand Rapids: Zondervan, 1984), pp. 416-7; Clark, *Putting Asunder,* pp. 257-62, n. 95. See also Clark, pp. 90, 100, 107, 265-268. Heth now believes remarriage is permitted after sexual immorality or desertion by an unbeliever ("Jesus and Divorce: How my mind has changed").

180 See Murray, *Divorce,* pp. 68-78.

181 See Instone-Brewer, *Divorce and Remarriage in the Bible*, pp. 134-5.

182 Instone-Brewer, *Divorce and Remarriage in the Bible,* pp. 134-6; ibid., *Divorce and Remarriage in the Church,* pp. 47-51, 85-7, 130-9.

183 See Instone-Brewer, *Divorce and Remarriage in the Church,* p. 85; Blomberg, "Marriage, Divorce, Remarriage and Celibacy", pp. 164-5.

184 See Clark, *Putting Asunder,* pp. 77-8.

185 Blomberg, *Matthew,* p. 289-90. Also see Heth, "How my mind has changed", p. 15.

186 See Clark, *Putting Asunder,* pp. 92-3, 238, n. 16; Adams, *Marriage, Divorce and Remarriage in the Bible,* p. 64.

187 See Instone-Brewer, *Divorce and Remarriage in the Church,* p. 37.

188 Whether the remarriage of an adulterous spouse constitutes adultery is discussed in appendix 9.

189 Blomberg, "Marriage, Divorce, Remarriage and Celibacy", p. 174; Collier, "Rethinking Jesus on Divorce".

190 See Collier, "Rethinking Jesus on Divorce".

191 See Keener, *Matthew,* p. 120.

Notes to chapter 10
What about where Jesus seems to Forbid all Remarriage?

192 Eusebius mentions that Mark wrote down what Peter taught and that Peter adapted his teachings as necessity required (Ecclesiastical History III.39). See also Luck, *Divorce and Remarriage,* pp. 132, 155; Instone-Brewer, *Divorce and Remarriage in the Bible,* p. 175.

193 See Keener, *A Commentary on the Gospel of Matthew,* p. 463.

194 See Owen, "On Marrying after Divorce in Case of Adultery", p. 256.

195 See The Presbyterian Church in America's 20th General Assembly "Report on Divorce and Remarriage", pp. 216-7.

196 See Blomberg, "Marriage, Divorce, Remarriage and Celibacy", p. 162.

197 See Edgar, *Divorce and Remarriage: Four Christian Views,* pp. 165-9.

198 Matt. 12:39; 16:4; cf. Mark 8:12.

199 See Instone-Brewer, *Divorce and Remarriage in the Bible,* p. 153; Blomberg, "Marriage, Divorce, Remarriage and Celibacy", p. 174; Edgar, *Divorce and Remarriage: Four Christian Views,* p. 168.

200 See Clark, *Putting Asunder,* p. 105.

201 See Keener, *Matthew,* IVP New Testament Commentary Series, p. 467; Clark, *Putting Asunder,* p. 108; Blomberg, *Matthew,* p. 292, and "Marriage, Divorce, Remarriage and Celibacy", p. 173; Treggiari, "Marriage and Family in Roman Society", p. 165.

202 See Treggiari, ibid., pp. 134, 165-9; Grubbs, *Women and the Law in the Roman Empire* (London & New York: Routledge, 2002), p. 84.

203 Keener, *The IVP Bible Background Commentary NT,* p. 161 says, "Rabbis distinguished between what Scripture commanded and what it allowed as a concession."

204 See Josephus, *Antiquities*, 15.7.10; 18.5.4.

205 This double standard could not be completely justified from the scriptures. Job made a covenant with his eyes that he would not look upon a young woman (Job 31:1). Proverbs 5 focuses on the damage adultery does to the man who indulges in it, rather than the damage to the rightful husband of the adulteress.

206 The only exception was if a divorce certificate had not been properly filled out, with the consequence that a remarried woman had two husbands at the same time. See Instone-Brewer, *Divorce and Remarriage in the Bible,* pp. 127-30; *Divorce and Remarriage in the Church,* p. 98; Clark, *Putting Asunder,* pp. 87-8.

207 See Instone-Brewer, *Divorce and Remarriage in the Bible*, p. 130.

208 See Heth & Wenham, pp. 53-68.

209 Robert H. Gundry, *Matthew: A Commentary on His Literary and Theological Art* (Grand Rapids: Eerdmans, 1982), pp. 381-2.

210 See Keener, *Matthew* IVP New Testament Commentary Series, p. 470.

211 See Keener, *...And Marries Another,* pp. 45-7.

212 See Leon Morris, *The Gospel According to Matthew* (Grand Rapids: Eerdmans 1992/ Leicester: InterVarsity Press, 1992), p. 486.

213 See Instone-Brewer, *Divorce and Remarriage in the Bible,* p. 168; ibid., *Divorce and Remarriage in the Church,* pp. 53-4; Chapman, "Marriage and Family in Second Temple Judaism", pp. 183, 211-15.

214 See Keener, *Matthew* IVP New Testament Commentary Series, p. 471.

215 See Edgar, *Divorce and Remarriage: Four Christian Views*, p. 188; Clark, *Putting Asunder*, p. 55; Atkinson, *To Have and to Hold*, p. 143.

216 In English, Luke 16:18a and Mark 10:11 seem identical, but Luke's "divorces" and "marries" are present participles, whereas Mark's "divorces" and "marries" are aorists.

217 See Keener, *...and Marries Another*, pp. 26-7.

218 See Clark, *Putting Asunder*, p. 242, n. 30.

219 See Keener, *The IVP Bible Background Commentary NT*, p. 235.

Notes to chapter 11
If I'm the Innocent Party, Why do I Still Feel Guilty?

220 The Pharisees had many absurd rules about what things one should or should not swear by; see Matt. 23:16-22.

221 See Atkinson, *To Have and to Hold*, p. 141; Adams, *Marriage, Divorce and Remarriage in the Bible*, p. 66; The Presbyterian Church in America's "Report on Divorce and Remarriage", p. 213.

222 See Clark, *Putting Asunder*, pp. 247-8, n. 52.

223 Edgar, *Divorce and Remarriage: Four Christain Views*, p. 155; Dale Noonan, http://lists. ibiblio.org/pipermail/b-greek/2002-October/023108.html; the verb is an aorist infinitive (*moicheuthenai*).

224 De-married women who remained single might return to their father's house (Lev. 22:13; Judg. 19:1-2). Others might have had sufficient dowry or other assets to remain independent (Luke 2:36).

225 We should not see this "adultery" as simply non-sexual or metaphorical. When the word "adultery" refers to human relationships, it always has something to do with sexuality; it only is metaphorical ("idolatry") when referring to relations between humans and the Divinity.

226 Contra Adams, *Marriage, Divorce and Remarriage in the Bible*, pp. 66-7. It is unkind and unrealistic to tell victims who were unjustly dismissed that they ought to renew their marriages. If the other spouse has obstinately shut the door against them, they will not be able to go back.

227 See Clark, *Putting Asunder*, p. 64; Luck, *Divorce and Remarriage*, pp. 107-8; The Presbyterian Church in America's "Report on Divorce and Remarriage", p. 213.

228 See Lenski, *The Interpretation of St Matthew's Gospel* (Minneapolis: Augsburg, 1964), pp. 230-33; and, using slightly different reasoning, Powers, *Marriage and Divorce*, pp. 166-70

229 See Murray, *Divorce*, p. 24.

230 Suggestion made by Douglas Milne in a conversation with the author.

231 See Instone-Brewer, *Divorce and Remarriage in the Bible*, p. 150.

232 Murray (*Divorce*, p. 21) suggests "suffer adultery". Donald S. Deer ("The Implied Agent in Greek Passive Verb Forms in the Gospel of Matthew", *Bible Translator* 18 [1967]: 165), noting that a passive verb implies an agent, renders the clause as "produces a situation in which someone commits adultery with her".

233 See Heth & Wenham, *Jesus and Divorce*, p. 69.

234 See Wenham, "Does the N. T. Approve Divorce After Remarriage?" *Southern Baptist Theological Journal* 6/1 (2002): 35.

235 Blomberg, "Marriage, Divorce, Remarriage and Celibacy", p. 163, notes that "Parallel 'sentences of law' (e.g., Matt. 5:22, 27, 39, 41) also contain implicit qualifiers."

236 See Instone-Brewer, *Divorce and Remarriage in the Bible*, p. 150.

237 The verb "commit adultery" (*moichatai*) in Matthew 5:32b is present indicative middle, the same as in Matthew 19:9.

238 For an example, see Caroline's story in *Broken and Battered* by Muriel Canfield.

Notes to chapter 12
Fitting it all Together

239 See Murray, *Divorce,* p. 55-58; Edgar, *Divorce and Remarriage: Four Christian Views,* pp. 188-9.

240 Adams, *Marriage, Divorce and Remarriage in the Bible,* p. 40.

241 As observed by the Catholic scholar, Erasmus, in the 16th century. The likeness between the Pauline exception and Jesus' exception has been noted by Keener, *Matthew* IVP New Testament Commentary Series, pp. 191-2; Jones, *Biblical Christian Ethics,* pp. 202-3; The Presbyterian Church in America's "Report on Divorce and Remarriage", p. 229.

Further Reading for Victims

Some of the books below are Christian, others are secular. The secular titles are marked with an asterisk. All have something to offer victims who are trying to understand their predicament and decide how best to handle it.

Titles are ranked according to how helpful the author found them in her own recovery. The most helpful books are placed at the start of the list.

*Evans, Patricia. *The Verbally Abusive Relationship: How to recognize it and how to respond.* 2nd edition. Holbrook: Adams Media Corporation, 1996.

Canfield, Muriel. *Broken and Battered: A Way Out for the Abused Woman.* West Monroe, Louisiana: Howard Publishing Company, 2000.

*Jones, Ann and Susan Schechter. *When Love Goes Wrong: What to do when you can't do anything right, strategies for women with controlling partners.* New York: HarperCollins, 1992.

Alsdurf, James and Phyllis. *Battered into Submission: The Tragedy of Wife Abuse in the Christian Home.* Downers Grove: InterVarsity Press, 1989; Guildford UK: Highland Books, 1989.

*Wileman, Robin and Bud. *How to Stop Domestic Violence: A Victim's Guide.* Main Beach, Queensland: Wileman Publications, n.d.

Blue, Ken. *Healing Spiritual Abuse: How to Break Free from Bad Church Experiences.* Downers Grove: InterVarsity Press, 1993.

Thomas (no surname given). "A Prison Epistle" in *Women, Abuse and the Bible: How Scripture Can Be Used to Hurt or Heal.* Ed. Catherine Clark Kroeger & James R. Beck. Grand Rapids: Baker, 1996

Bibliography

Adams, Jay E. Marriage, *Divorce and Remarriage in the Bible*. Grand Rapids: Zondervan, 1980.

Alsdurf, James. "Wife Abuse and the Church: The Response of Pastors." *Response* Winter (1985):9–11.

Alsdurf, James and Phyllis. *Battered into Submission: The Tragedy of Wife Abuse in the Christian Home.* Downers Grove: InterVarsity Press, 1989; Guildford UK: Highland Books, 1989.

Alsdurf, James and Phyllis. "A Pastoral Response", in *Abuse and Religion: When Praying Isn't Enough.* Ed. Anne L. Horton & Judith A. Williamson. Lexington, Massachusetts: Lexington Books, 1998.

Atkinson, David. *To Have and to Hold.* London: William Collins, 1979.

Augustine. *Confessions and Enchiridion.* Trans. and ed. Albert C. Outler. Library of Christian Classics, vol. 7. London: SCM Press, 1955.

Bagshaw, Dale, & Donna Chung. *Women, Men and Domestic Violence.* University of South Australia & Partnerships Against Domestic Violence, Canberra, Australia: Commonwealth Government, 2000.

Bagshaw, Dale, Donna Chung, Murray Couch, Sandra Lilburn & Ben Wadham. *Reshaping Responses to Domestic Violence Final Report.* Australia: Commonwealth Government Partners Against Domestic Violence and University of South Australia, 2000.

Baldwin, Joyce G. *Haggai, Zechariah, Malachi.* London: Tyndale Press, 1972.

Barr, Debbie. *Children of Divorce: Helping Kids When Their Parents are Apart.* Grand Rapids: Zondervan, 1986, 1992.

Basil. *Saint Basil: The Letters.* Trans. Roy J. Defarrari, vol. 3. London: Heinemann 1930; New York: Putnam, 1930.

Bauer, Arndt, Gingrich and Danker (BAGD). *A Greek-English Lexicon of the New Testament and Other Early Christian Literature,* 3rd edition. Chicago and London: University of Chicago Press, 2000.

Baugh, S. M. "Marriage and Family in Ancient Greek Society" in *Marriage and Family in the Biblical World.* Ed. Ken M. Campbell. Downers Grove: InterVarsity Press, 2003.

Bingham, Joseph. *Antiquities of the Christian Church, and other works,* vols 6 & 7. London: William Straker, 1834.

Blenkinsopp, Joseph. *Ezra–Nehemiah, A Commentary.* Philadelphia: Westminster Press, 1988.

——"The Family in First Temple Israel", in *Families in Ancient Israel.* Louisville, Kentucky: Westminster John Knox Press, 1979.

Block, Daniel I. "Marriage and Family in Ancient Israel" in *Marriage and Family in the Biblical World.* Ed. Ken M. Campbell. Downers Grove: InterVarsity Press, 2003.

Blomberg, Craig L. "Marriage, Divorce, Remarriage, and Celibacy: An Exegesis of Matthew 19:3–12." *Trinity Journal* 11n.s. /2 (1990): 161–96.

——*Matthew*. New American Commentary Series vol. 22. Nashville: Broadman Press, 1992.

——*1 Corinthians*. NIV Application Commentary Series. Grand Rapids: Zondervan, 1994.

Bloomfield, Peter. *Divorce, the Big Picture.* Fortitude Valley, Queensland: PCE Press, 1996.

Blue, Ken, & John White. *Healing the Wounded: The Costly Love of Church Discipline.* Downers Grove: InterVarsity Press, 1985.

Brown, Raymond E. *The Birth of the Messiah.* New York: Doubleday, 1979.

Bruce, F. F. *1 and 2 Corinthians.* New Century Bible. London: Oliphants, 1971. Reprinted Grand Rapids: Eerdmans, 1996.

Bruner, Frederick Dale. *The Christbook: A Theological/Historical Commentary — Matthew 1–12.* Waco, Texas: Word Books, 1987.

——*The Churchbook: Matthew 13–28*. Waco, Texas: Word Books, 1990.

Burns, Bob. *Recovery from Divorce: How to Become Whole Again after the Devastation of Divorce.* Nashville: Thomas Nelson, 1989, 1992.

Burtner, Robert W. & Robert E. Chiles (eds.). *A Compendium of Wesley's Theology.* New York, Nashville: Abingdon Press, 1954.

Canfield, Muriel. *Broken and Battered: A Way Out for the Abused Woman.* West Monroe, Louisiana: Howard Publishing Company, 2000.

Carson, D. A. "Matthew", in *The Expositor's Bible Commentary,* vol. 8 (Matthew, Mark, Luke). Ed. Frank E. Gaebelein. Grand Rapids: Zondervan, 1984.

Chapman, David, W. "Marriage and Family in Second Temple Judaism" in *Marriage and Family in the Biblical World.* Ed. Ken M. Campbell. Downers Grove: InterVarsity Press, 2003.

Chrysostom, John. "On Virginity, Against Remarriage," trans. Sally R. Shore. *Studies in Woman and Religion* vol. 9. New York: Edwin Mellen Press, 1983.

Clark, Stephen. *Putting Asunder: Divorce and Remarriage in Biblical and Pastoral Perspective.* Bridgend, Wales: Bryntirion Press, 1999.

Clines, D. J. A. *Ezra, Nehemiah, Esther.* New Century Bible Commentary. Grand Rapids: Eerdmans, 1984.

Collier, Gary. "Rethinking Jesus on Divorce." *Restoration Quarterly* 37/2, http://www. restorationquarterly.org/Volume_037/rq03702collier.htm viewed 5 May 2004.

——"A Note on the Translation of *poieil au)th\n moixeuqh=nai* ['causes her to commit adultery'] in Matthew 5:32", http://www.onlinebibleclass.com/garydcollier viewed 5 May 2004.

Collins, C. John. "The Intelligible Masoretic Text of Malachi 2:16 or, How does God Feel about Divorce?" *Presbyterion* 20/1 (1994): 36–40.

Collins, John J. Review of *Marriage as Covenant* by G. P. Hugenberger. *Journal of Biblical Literature* 114/2 (1995): 306–8.

——"Marriage, Divorce and Family in Second Temple Judaism", in *Families in Ancient Israel.* Louisville: Westminster John Knox Press, 1997.

Cornes, Andrew. *Divorce and Remarriage: Biblical Principles and Pastoral Practice.* Grand Rapids: Eerdmans/London: Hodder & Stoughton, 1993.

Craigie, Peter C. *The Book of Deuteronomy.* Grand Rapids: Eerdmans, 1976.

Crispin, Ken. *Divorce: The Unforgivable Sin?* Rydalmere, NSW: Hodder & Stoughton, 1988.

Crouzel, Henri, S. J. "Remarriage after Divorce in the Primitive Church: A Propos of a recent book." *Irish Theological Quarterly* 38/1 (1971): 21–41.

Dal Grande, Eleonora, Jacqueline Hickling, Anne Taylor &Tony Woolacott. "Domestic Violence in South Australia: a population survey of males and females." *Australian and New Zealand Journal of Public Health* 27/5 (2003): 543–550.

Danby, Herbert. *The Mishnah: Translated from the Hebrew with Introduction and Brief Explanatory Notes.* London: Oxford University Press, 1933.

Deer, Donald S. "The Implied Agent in Greek Passive Verb Forms in the Gospel of Matthew." *Bible Translator* 18 (1967): 164–7.

Domestic Violence and Incest Resource Centre Newsletters. Collingwood, Victoria: Domestic Violence and Incest Resource Centre, 2000–2004.

Douglas, J. D. (organizing editor). *New Bible Dictionary,* 2nd edition. Downers Grove: InterVarsity Press, 1982.

Down, M. J. "The Sayings of Jesus about Marriage and Divorce." *Expository Times* (1984): 332.

Dubin, Marc. "Men as Victims of Intimate Violence." www.xyonline.net/menasvictims.

Duty, Guy. *Divorce and Remarriage.* Bloomington, Minnesota: Bethany Fellowship, 1967, 1983.

Edgar, Thomas R. Essay and responses in *Divorce and Remarriage: Four Christian Views,* ed. H. Wayne House. Downers Grove: InterVarsity Press, 1990.

Ellisen, Stanley A. *Divorce and Remarriage in the Church.* Grand Rapids: Zondervan, 1980.

Engelsma, David J. "A History of the Church's Doctrine of Marriage, Divorce and Remarriage." Reprint from Nov. 1993 *Protestant Reformed Theological Journal.* www.rsglh.org.

——"Marriage-Divorce-Remarriage." A series of editorials appearing in the Standard Bearer. www.rsglh.org/marriage_divorce_remarriage.htm.

Evans, Craig & Stanley Porter, eds. *Dictionary of New Testament Background.* Downers Grove: InterVarsity Press, 2000.

Evans, Patricia. *The Verbally Abusive Relationship: How to recognize it and how to respond.* Holbrook, Massachusetts: Adams Media Corporation, 1996.

Fee, Gordon D. *The First Epistle to the Corinthians.* Grand Rapids: Eerdmans, 1987.

Fensham, F. Charles. *The Books of Ezra and Nehemiah.* Grand Rapids: Eerdmans, 1982.

Flood, Michael. "Claims About Husband Battering," 1999. www.xyonline.net/husbandbattering.shtml

Flood, Michael. "Domestic Violence Against Men," 2003. www.austdvclearinghouse.unsw.edu.au/RR_docs/Flood-DV_against_men.pdf viewed Oct 2006.

Floyd, Michael H. *Minor Prophets: Part 2.* The Forms of the Old Testament Literature Series, vol. 22. Grand Rapids: Eerdmans, 2000.

Fuller, Russell. "Text Critical Problems in Malachi 2:10–16." *Journal of Biblical Literature* 110/1 (1991): 47–57.

Gelles, Richard J. *Intimate Violence in Families.* Thousand Oaks, California: Sage, 1997.

Glazier-McDonald, Beth. *Malachi: The Divine Messenger.* Atlanta: Scholars Press, 1987.

Goldstein, Jonathan A. *1 Maccabees: A New Translation with Introduction and Commentary.* The Anchor Bible. New York: Doubleday, 1976.

Green, Jay P., Sr. (ed. and trans.). *The Interlinear Bible, Hebrew-Greek-English* 2nd edition. Lafayette, Indiana: Sovereign Grace Publishers, 1986.

Grubbs, Judith Evans. " 'Pagan' and 'Christian' Marriage." *Journal of Early Christian Studies* 2 (1994): 361–412.

——*Women and the Law in the Roman Empire.* London & New York: Routledge, 2002.

Gundry, Robert H. *Matthew: A Commentary on His Literary and Theological Art.* Grand Rapids: Eerdmans, 1982.

Harman, Allan. *Deuteronomy: The Commands of a Covenant God.* Ross-shire, Great Britain: Christian Focus, 2001.

Hawthorne, Gerald F., Ralph P. Martin (eds.), Daniel G. Reid (assoc. ed.). *Dictionary of Paul and his Letters.* Downers Grove: InterVarsity Press, 1993.

Hendriksen, William. *The Gospel of Matthew.* Edinburgh: Banner of Truth, 1973.

Heth, William E. & Gordon J. Wenham. *Jesus and Divorce.* First published London: Hodder & Stoughton, 1984; Biblical and Theological Classics Library edition, Carlisle, Cumbria: Paternoster, 1997.

Heth, William E. "Divorce and Remarriage: The Search for an Evangelical Hermeneutic." *Trinity Journal* 16 n.s. (1995): 63–100.

——"Divorce and Remarriage", in *Applying the Scriptures: Papers from the ICBI Summit III,* ed. Kenneth S. Kantzer. Grand Rapids: Academie Books, Zondervan, 1986.

——"Jesus and Divorce: How my Mind Has Changed." *Southern Baptist Theological Journal* 6/1 (2002): 4–29. Also at http://www.sbts.edu/pdf/sbjt_2002Spring2.pdf

Herman, Judith Lewis. *Trauma and Recovery.* New York: Basic Books, 1992.

Hill, Andrew E. *Malachi: A New Translation with Introduction and Commentary*. The Anchor Bible. New York: Doubleday, 1998.

Hines, Denise A. & Kathleen Malley-Morrison. *Family Violence in the United States: Defining, Understanding and Combating Abuse.* Thousand Oaks, California: Sage Publications, 2005.

Horst, Balz & Schneider. *Exegetical Dictionary of the New Testament.* Grand Rapids: Eerdmans, 1993.

Hugenberger, Gordon P. *Marriage as Covenant: Biblical Law and Ethics as Developed from Malachi*. Grand Rapids: Baker, 1994.

Hughes, Philip Edgcumbe, ed. and trans. *The Register of the Company of Pastors of Geneva in the Time of Calvin.* Grand Rapids: Eerdmans, 1996.

Hurley, James B. *Man and Woman in Biblical Perspective.* Downers Grove: InterVarsity Press, 1981.

Instone-Brewer, David. *Divorce and Remarriage in the Bible*: *The Social and Literary Context.* Grand Rapids: Eerdmans, 2002.

——*Divorce and Remarriage in the Church: Biblical Solutions for Pastoral Realities.* Carlisle, Cumbria: Paternoster, 2003.

——"1 Corinthians 7 in the Light of Graeco-Roman Marriage and Divorce Papyri." *Tyndale Bulletin* 52 (2001): 101–16. Also at www.instone-brewer.com

——"1 Corinthians 7 in the Light of Jewish Greek and Aramaic Marriage and Divorce Papyri." *Tyndale Bulletin* 52 (2001): 225–43. Also at www.instone-brewer.com

Jones, David Clyde. "A Note on the LXX of Malachi 2:16." *Journal of Biblical Literature* 109/4 (1990): 683–5.

——*Biblical Christian Ethics,* Grand Rapids: Baker Books, 1994.

——"The Westminster Confession on Divorce and Remarriage." *Presbyterion* 16 (1990): 17–40.

Josephus, Flavius. *Judean Antiquities* vol. 3, ed. Steve Mason with commentary by Louis H. Feldman. Leiden: Brill, 2000.

——*Life of Josephus,* ed. Steve Mason. Leiden: Brill, 2001.

Judicial Council of California. "Parenting in the Context of Domestic Violence." www.courtinfo. ca.gov/programs/cfcc/resources/publications/articles, viewed March 2003.

Keener, Craig S. *A Commentary on the Gospel of Matthew.* Grand Rapids: Eerdmans, 1999.

——*…And Marries Another: Divorce and Remarriage in the Teaching of the New Testament.* Peabody, Mass.: Hendrickson, 1991.

——*Matthew.* IVP New Testament Commentary Series, ed. G. R. Osborne. Downers Grove: InterVarsity Press, 1997.

——*IVP Bible Background Commentary N. T.* Downers Grove: InterVarsity Press, 1993.

Kiel, Carl F. *Biblical Commentary on the Old Testament: The Twelve Minor Prophets* vol. 2., trans. J. Martin. Grand Rapids: Eerdmans, 1954

Kimmel, Michael S. "Male Victims of Domestic Violence: A Substantive and Methodological Research Review." *Violence Against Women, Special Issue: Women's Use of Violence in Intimate Relationships,* Part 1. 8(11), 2001. www.xyonline.net.downloads/malevictims.pdf

Kittel, Gerhard. *Theological Dictionary of the New Testament.* Grand Rapids: Eerdmans, 1964.

Köstenberger, Andreas. "Marriage and Family in the New Testament", in *Marriage and Family in the Biblical World.* Ed. Ken M. Campbell. Downers Grove: InterVarsity Press, 2003.

Kroeger, Catherine Clark & James R. Beck (eds.). *Healing the Hurting: Giving Hope and Help to Abused Women.* Grand Rapids: Baker, 1998.

Kroeger, Catherine Clark & Nancy Nason-Clark. *No Place for Abuse: Biblical and Practical Resources to Counteract Domestic Violence.* Downers Grove: InterVarsity Press, 2001.

Kruger, Paul A. "The Hem of the Garment in Marriage: The Meaning of the Symbolic Gesture in Ruth 3:9 and Ezek. 16:8." *Journal of Northwest Semitic Languages* 12 (1984): 79–86.

Laney, J. Carl. *The Divorce Myth.* Minneapolis: Bethany House, 1981.

Lange, J. P. *Commentary on the Holy Scriptures.* Grand Rapids: Zondervan, 1960.

Lattey, Cuthbert. *The Book of Malachy.* The Westminster Version of the Sacred Scriptures Series. London, New York, Toronto: Longmans Green & Co., 1934.

Lenski, R. C. H. *The Interpretation of Luke's Gospel.* Minneapolis: Augsburg, 1961.

——*The Interpretation of Mark's Gospel.* Minneapolis: Augsburg, 1961.

——*The Interpretation of St Matthew's Gospel.* Minneapolis: Augsburg, 1964.

——*The Interpretation of St Paul's 1st and 2nd Epistles to the Corinthians.* Minneapolis: Augsburg, 1963.

——*The Interpretation of St Paul's Epistle to the Romans*. Minneapolis: Augsburg, 1961.

——*The Interpretation of the Epistles of St Peter, St John and St Jude.* Minneapolis: Augsburg, 1966.

Liaboe, G. P. "The Place of Wife Battering in Considering Divorce." *Journal of Psychology and Theology* 13 (1985): 129–138.

Liddell, Henry George, & Robert Scott. *A Greek-English Lexicon,* 9th edition. Oxford: Clarendon Press, 1940.

Luck, William F. *Divorce and Remarriage: Recovering the Biblical View.* San Francisco: Harper & Rowe, 1987.

Lundgren, Eva. "I am Endowed with All the Power in Heaven and on Earth: When men become men through 'Christian' abuse." *Studia Theologica* 48 (1994): 33–47.

MacArthur, John Jr. *On Divorce.* Chicago: Moody Press, 1983.

McConville, J. G. *Deuteronomy.* Apollos Old Testament Commentary Series 5. Leicester, UK: InterVarsity Press, 2002.

McDowell, Josh & Norm Geisler. *Love Is Always Right: A Defense Of One Moral Absolute — The Answer to Ethical Dilemmas, Challenging Situations, Difficult Decisions.* Dallas, London, Vancouver, Melbourne: Word, 1996.

Mackin, Theodore, S. J. *Divorce and Remarriage.* New York/Ramsey: Paulist Press, 1984.

Merrill, Eugene. *An Exegetical Commentary: Haggai, Zechariah, Malachi.* Chicago: Moody Press, 1994.

Miles, Al. *Domestic Violence: What Every Pastor Needs to Know.* Minneapolis: Augsburg Fortress Press, 2000.

Miller, Patrick D. *Deuteronomy.* Interpretation: A Bible Commentary for Teaching and Preaching Series. Louisville: John Knox Press, 1990.

Milne, Douglas. *1 Timothy, 2 Timothy, Titus.* Ross-shire, Great Britain: Christian Focus, 1996.

——*Westminster Confession of Faith for the 21st Century.* Centenary Study Edition. Strawberry Hills, NSW: Christian Education Committee of the General Assembly of the Presbyterian Church of Australia, 2001.

Moore, Thomas V. *A Commentary on Haggai and Malachi.* Edinburgh: Banner of Truth, 1960. (First published in *Prophets of the Restoration.* New York: Robert Carter, 1856.)

Morris, Leon. *The Gospel According to Matthew.* Grand Rapids: Eerdmans 1992; Leicester: InterVarsity Press, 1992.

Murray, John. *Divorce.* Phillipsburg: Presbyterian & Reformed, 1961.

Nason-Clark, Nancy. "When Terror Strikes at Home: The Interface Between Religion and Domestic Violence," *Journal for the Scientific Study of Religion* 43:3 (2004): 303–10.

Olsen, V. Norskov. *The New Testament Logia on Divorce: A Study of their Interpretation from Erasmus to Milton.* Tübingen: J. C. B. Mohr (Paul Siebeck), 1971.

Owen, John. "On Marrying after Divorce in Case of Adultery", in *The Works of John Owen* vol. 16, pp. 154–57. Edinburgh: Banner of Truth, 1968. A modernized version by Richard J. Vincent is available at www.theocentric.com/originalarticles/divremarry.html.

Packer, J. I. *A Quest for Godliness: The Puritan Vision of the Christian Life.* Wheaton, Ill.: Crossway, 1990.

Page, Sydney. "Marital Expectations of Church Leaders in the Pastoral Epistles." *Journal for the Study of the New Testament* 50 (1993): 105–120.

Pawson, J. David. *Leadership is Male.* Guildford UK: Highland Books, 1988.

Petersen, David L. *Zechariah 9–14 and Malachi: A Commentary.* Louisville: Westminster John Knox Press, 1995.

Phillips, Colin A. "Equipping Religious Professionals to Engage Effectively with Domestic Violence." *Journal of Religious and Theological Information* 4/1 (2001): 47–70.

Phillips, Roderick. *Putting Asunder: A History of Divorce in Western society.* Cambridge UK, Melbourne Vic, New York: Cambridge University Press, 1988.

Philo. *Philo's Works.* English trans. F. H. Colson, Loeb Classical Library, vol. 7. London: Heinemann; Cambridge, Mass: Harvard University Press, 1958.

Phypers, David. *Christian Marriage in Crisis.* Bromley, Kent, UK: MARC Europe, a ministry of World Vision, 1985.

Piper, John, & Wayne Grudem. *Recovering Biblical Manhood and Womanhood: A Response to Evangelical Feminism.* Wheaton: Crossway Books, 1991.

Powers, B. Ward. *Marriage and Divorce: The New Testament Teaching.* Concord, NSW: Family Life Movt. of Australia; Petersham, NSW: Jordan Books, 1987.

Presbyterian Church in America. "Report of the Ad-Interim Committee on Divorce and Remarriage to the 20th General Assembly." Atlanta: Georgia, 1993. http://www.pcanet.org/history viewed 24 June 2003.

Presbyterian Church of Victoria, J. Stasse ed. *Let's Get Married! — Living Together is no Substitute.* Melbourne, Vic: The Church and Nation Committee, PCV, 2001.

Pressler, Carolyn. *The View of Women Found in the Deuteronomic Family Laws.* Berlin: Walter de Gruyter, 1993.

Redditt, Paul L. *Haggai, Zechariah and Malachi.* New Century Bible Commentary Series. London: Marshall Pickering / Harper Collins; Grand Rapids: Eerdmans, 1995.

Retief, Frank. *Divorce*. Ross-Shire, Great Britain: Christian Focus, 1998.

Rinck, Margaret J. *Christian Men Who Hate Women*. Grand Rapids: Zondervan, 1990.

Roberts, Alexander & James Donaldson (eds.). *The Ante-Nicene Fathers*. American reprint of the Edinburgh edn, vol. VII. Grand Rapids: Eerdmans, 1994.

Rudolph, Wilhelm. *Haggai, Sacharja 1-8, Sacharja 9–14, Malachi*. Kommentat zum Alten Testament. Gutersloh: Gutersloher Verlagshaus Gerd Mohn, 1976.

——"Zu Mal. 2:10–16." *Zeitschrift fur die Alttestamentliche Wissenschaft* 93 (1981): 85–90.

Rushdoony, Rousas John. *Law and Society*. Valecito: Ross House Books, 1986.

Rutledge, Peter Francis. "The Role of a Local Church in Ending Marital Abuse Involving Christians." Unpublished doctoral dissertation presented to the Reformed Theological Seminary, May 2002.

Ryken, Leland, et al., (eds). *Dictionary of Biblical Imagery*. Downers Grove: InterVarsity Press, 1998.

Schaff, Philip & Henry Wace (eds). *A Select Library of Nicene and Post-Nicene Fathers of the Christian Church*, second series, vol. VI: St. Jerome letters and select works. Edinburgh: T&T Clark; Grand Rapids: Eerdmans.

Schreiner, Thomas R. "Loving Discipline." *Southern Baptist Journal of Theology* 4/4 (2002). Also at www.sbts.edu/resources/sbjt/2000

Shields, Martin A. "Syncretism and Divorce in Malachi 2:10–16." *Zeitschrift fur die Alttestamentliche Wissenschaft* 111 (1999): 68-86.

Smith, David L. "Divorce and Remarriage from the Early Church to John Wesley." *Trinity Journal*, 11 n.s. (1990): 131–142.

Smith, J. M. Powis. "Malachi", in *A Critical and Exegetical Commentary on Haggai. Zechariah, Malachi and Jonah*. Edinburgh: T & T Clark, 1912.

Smith, Ralph L. *Micah: Malachi*. Word Biblical Commentary Series vol. 32. Waco, Texas: Word Books, 1984.

Smith, William, & Samuel Cheetham. *A Dictionary of Christian Antiquities*. J. B. Burr, 1880; reprinted New York: Kraus Reprint Co., 1968.

Sprinkle, Joe M. "Sexuality, Sexual Ethics" in *The Dictionary of the Old Testament: Pentateuch*, eds. T. D. Alexander & D. W. Baker. Downers Grove: InterVarsity Press, 2003.

——"Old Testament Perspectives on Divorce and Remarriage." *Journal of the Evangelical Theological Society* 40/4 (1997): 529–550.

——*The Book of the Covenant: A Literary Approach*. Journal for the Study of the Old Testament Supplement Series 174. Sheffield, England: Sheffield Academic Press, 1994.

Strong, James. *The New Strong's Exhaustive Concordance of the Bible*. Nashville: Thomas Nelson, 1995.

Stuart, Douglas. "Malachi" in *The Minor Prophets: An Exegetical and Expository Commentary* vol. 3: *Zephaniah, Haggai, Zechariah and Malachi*, ed. Thomas Edward McComiskey. Grand Rapids: Baker Books, 1998.

Sutton, Ray. *Second Chance: Biblical Principles of Divorce and Remarriage*. Fort Worth, Texas: Dominion Press, 1988.

Thayer, Joseph H. *Greek-English Lexicon of the New Testament*, 4th edn. Massachusetts: Hendrickson, 1999.

Treggiari, Susan. "Marriage and Family in Roman Society", in *Marriage and Family in the Biblical World* ed. Ken M. Campbell. Downers Grove: InterVarsity Press, 2003.

———*Roman Marriage: Iusti Coniuges from the Time of Cicero to the Time of Ulpian*. Oxford: Clarendon, 1991.

Tyndale, William. *Tyndale's Old Testament: Being the Pentateuch of 1530, Joshua to 2 Chronicles of 1537, and Jonah*, ed. David Daniell. New Haven & London: Yale University Press, 1992.

van der Woude, A. S. "Malachi's Struggle for a Pure Community: Reflections on Malachi 2:10–16", in *Tradition and Re-Interpretation in Jewish and Early Christian Literature* ed. van Henten, de Jonge, van Rooden, Wesselius. Leiden: E. J. Brill, 1986.

VanGemeren, Willem A. (ed.). *New International Dictionary of Old Testament Theology and Exegesis*. Grand Rapids: Zondervan, 1997.

Verhoef, Pieter A. *The Books of Haggai and Malachi*. Grand Rapids: Eerdmans, 1987.

Vine, W. E., M. F. Unger & W. White. *Vine's Complete Expository Dictionary of Old and New Testament Words*. Nashville: Thomas Nelson, 1985.

Vuilleumier, Réne. "Malachi", in *Commentaire de l'Ancein Testament XIc*, eds Delachaux & Niestlé. Paris: Neuchatel, 1981.

Walker, Lenore E. *The Battered Woman*. New York: Harper & Rowe, 1979.

Weinfeld, Moshe. *Deuteronomy and the Deuteronomic School*. Winona Lake: Eisenbrauns, 1992.

Wenham, Gordon. Review of Hugenberger's *Marriage as a Covenant* in *The Evangelical Quarterly* 70/4 (1998): 356–7.

———"Does the New Testament Approve Remarriage after Divorce?" *Southern Baptist Theological Journal* 6/1 (2002): 30–45.

Westbrook, Raymond. "The Female Slave", in *Gender and Law in the Hebrew Bible and the Ancient Near East*. Journal for the Study of the Old Testament Supplement Series 262. Sheffield: Sheffield Academic Press, 1998.

———"The Prohibition on Restoration of Marriage in Deuteronomy 24:1–4." *Studies in Bible,* vol. XXXI, ed. Sara Japhet. Jerusalem: Magnes Press, The Hebrew University, 1986.

Whipple, Vicky. "Counseling Battered Women from Fundamentalist Churches." *Journal of Marital and Family Therapy* 13/3 (1987): 251–8.

World Health Organization. "World Report on Violence and Health—Summary." www.who.int/violence_injury_prevention/media/en/559.pdf. 2002.

Wiebe, Phillip H. "Jesus' Divorce Exception." *Journal of the Evangelical Theological Society* 32/3 (1989): 327–33.

Winnett, Arthur Robert. *Divorce and Remarriage in Anglicanism.* London: Macmillan, 1958.

Witte, John Jr. *From Sacrament to Contract: Marriage, Religion and Law in the Western Tradition.* Louisville: Westminster John Knox Press, 1997.

Zehnder, Markus. "A Fresh Look at Malachi 2:13-16." *Vetus Testamentum* 53/ 2, (2003): 224-259 .

Zodhiates, Spiros. *Complete Word Study Dictionary: New Testament.* Chatanooga: AMG, 1992.

——ed. *The Hebrew-Greek Key Study Bible.* Grand Rapids: Baker, 1984, and revised edition, 1991.

——*May I Divorce and Remarry? An Exegetical Commentary on First Corinthians Seven.* Chatanooga: AMG, 1994.

——*What About Divorce?* Chatanooga: AMG, 1984.

Novels

Bronte, Emily. *The Tenant of Wildfell Hall.*

Dickens, Charles. *David Copperfield.* (especially chs. 2, 4, 14).

Price, Nancy. *Sleeping with the Enemy.* London: Arrow, 1988.

Thompson, Morton. *Not As A Stranger.* London: Michael Joseph, 1955.

Videos (dramas)

Fischer, Preston (producer) & Jorge Montesi (director). *Sleeping with Danger.* Tristar Television, 1996.

Goldberg, L, (producer) & J. Ruben (director). *Sleeping with the Enemy.* Twentieth Century Fox, 1991.

Greenwald, Robert (director). *The Burning Bed.* Metro-Goldwyn-Mayer, 1984.

Scott, Michael, (director). *Escape from Terror: The Teresa Stamper Story.* Cosgrove Meurer Productions/Odyssey Video 1994.

Gimbel, Roger (producer) & Robert Iscove (director). *Shattered Dreams.* Carolco International N.V., 1990.

Jaffe, Stanley, & S. Lansing (producers) & A. Lyne (director). *Fatal Attraction.* Paramount Pictures, 1987. (male victim and *femme fatale* perpetrator)

subject index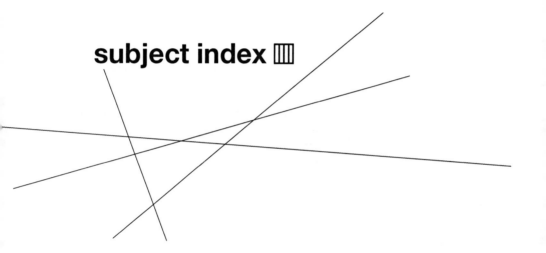

scripture index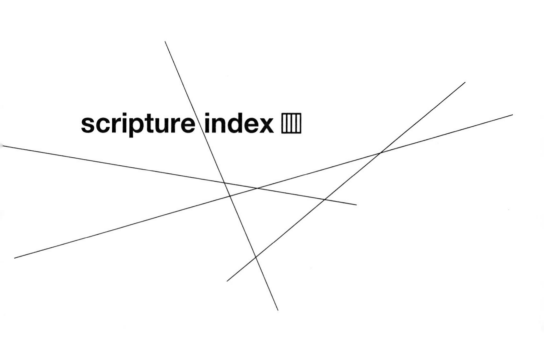

OLD TESTAMENT:

Genesis

1:28	94
2:18	99
2:24	58, 91-2, 107, 123
4:6-7	33
38:	28

Exodus

20:14	107
21:7-11	48, 61-2, 66, 71, 81-2, 87, 108
22:16-7	124
33:1-12	70

Leviticus

18:	84-5, 142
19:17	27
21:7, 13-15	56, 63

Numbers

5:11	65
13:2	28
14:	70
14:8, 23, 29-37	28
30:	64, 70-1, 100, 109

Deuteronomy

17:6	65
19:5	65
21:10-14	62-3, 66, 71, 108
22:13-19	124
22:22	107
22:23-27	24
22:28-9	124
23:12-14	64
24:1-4	58, 63, 65-6, 68, 80-3, 86, 91-2, 107, 111, 126, 131, 132-3, 137

Joshua

2:4-6	29
9:	70
10:	70

1 Samuel

2:27-36	70
19:11,12	29
19:18a	27
25:	43

2 Samuel

3:16	125
13:12-16	27, 29
15:13-15	29
21:1-9	70

1 Kings

19:2-3	29

2 Chronicles

11:13-14	29

Psalm

18:48	30
23:4	24
55:21	16
72:12-14	30
97:10a	27
141:4	30

Proverbs

14:7	29
22:10, 24-5	29
23:6-7	29
24:1-2	29
27:6a	31

Job

7:11	27

Isaiah

42:6-7	30
61:1	30

Jeremiah

2 and 3:	70, 107
7:9	49
22:3	30

To purchase this book, kindly visit our website
www.notunderbondage.com

It may also be ordered through Christian bookstores.

On our website you will also find free articles:
Why didn't you leave?
Unhelpful Comments: and how to respond to them
Walking on Eggshells — Flyer
Checklist for Repentance
Still married in the sight of God?

LaVergne, TN USA
11 March 2011
219762LV00001B/2/P